The Mouths of the Wicked

The Mouths of the Wicked

A True January 6 Story of Corruption, Persecution, Survival, and Victory

By Thomas E. Caldwell

THE MOUTHS OF THE WICKED:
A TRUE JANUARY 6 STORY OF CORRUPTION, PERSECUTION,
SURVIVAL, AND VICTORY

By Thomas E. Caldwell

Cover design by Milan Jovanovic, CHAMELEON Studio74
Back cover photo by Samira Bouaou/The Epoch Times
Interior design by JP Watson

Puffin Publishers, LLC
www.PuffinPublishers.com

Ordering information:
For details, contact info@puffinpublishers.com

ISBN: 979-8-218-76613-9

Printed in the United States of America

First edition

Publisher's note: Some names in this true story have been changed for the sole purpose of protecting people and their families from undue attention and the maliciousness of third parties.

This book is lovingly dedicated to my wife Sharon, the first Angel sent by the Lord our God to save my life and who showed me early on the type of person I wanted to be.

This true story is meant to honor the hundreds of Americans and their families persecuted by a corrupt government in the only proven conspiracy related to the events of January 6, 2021. Each has suffered in their own way.

Contents

From Psalm 109
New King James Version (NKJV)
A Psalm of David

1 Do not keep silent, O God of my praise!
2 For the mouth of the wicked and the mouth of the deceitful
Have opened against me;
They have spoken against me with a lying tongue.
3 They have also surrounded me with words of hatred,
And fought against me without a cause.
4 In return for my love they are my accusers,
But I *give myself to* prayer.
5 Thus they have rewarded me evil for good,
And hatred for my love.

Prologue

What if there were another story, a very personal story, of the Capitol Hill protests of January 6, 2021, you've never been told? A story that the media and the Internet have no interest in truthfully sharing with you. Mine is exactly that kind of story. What if you've been systematically manipulated into believing one of the biggest frauds in American history? And what if powerful people threw away the rule of law and the Constitution that day? What if the events of January 6 were the start of something sinister: a home-grown terror campaign against peaceful citizens?

I have never been politically active. As a career naval officer usually assigned far from home, I have had little such opportunity. But I always valued highly my right to vote and did so even through absentee ballot. In elections, you win some and you lose some. But as long as people entitled to vote may do so freely, what's most important is that elections are conducted honestly. The survival of our Republic and the hopes of all free people depend upon it.

I voted in the 2020 national election; my preferred candidate was President Donald Trump. He lost reelection, to my regret. That's the way it goes. For the first time in my experience, however, scores of millions of people had doubts about the election's *honesty*. In the aftermath there arose a number of credible instances of significant election-day malfeasance on Joseph Biden's behalf. He supposedly won the election, but it smelled bad to people around the world.

It shocked me that, in October 2020, 51 retired senior U.S. intelligence officers, guys with a background much like mine, went public with a defense of then-candidate Biden's son Hunter, whose abandoned laptop computer contained significant evidence of illegal activities. Activities not only by Hunter, but by Joe Biden himself. How could so many retirees coalesce into a group absolutely certain, without direct knowledge, that stories of the contents of this device were fake? That represents a fallacy of judgment that is mind-blowing in every respect.

President Trump, still in office, of course, announced that he would make some public remarks near the White House on January 6, 2021, the day of the perfunctory Congressional certification of election results. It occurred to me that this might be my last opportunity to see Trump in person, so on a whim, my wife Sharon and I decided to make the two-hour drive from our home in western Virginia to Washington to witness the event. We came not to protest, but to bid farewell.

The world now knows Trump's remarks were appreciated by the crowd but were not inflammatory. Part of the gathered crowd determined to go to the Capitol building, where many conservative speakers were scheduled to deliver remarks on temporary stages prepped for them. My wife and I did nothing more than trek to the Capitol building, too. We were peacefully assembled, as was our right. There were people all around me during the President's remarks and afterward. I did not know them, nor did any of them know me. Like me, many would become hapless victims in a political power play.

Have you ever talked with someone who was actually there on that day and whose life was turned upside down? Prepare to be astonished at this true story—and turn the page.

CHAPTER 1

The Defiling

January 19, 2021

"Honey! Get up! The FBI is at the door!"

I will never forget those words or the urgency in Sharon's voice as she shook me awake that dreadful morning. Bundled under blankets and still foggy from two sleeping pills, I struggled to free myself from the CPAP machine.

Trying to make sense of it all, I leaned on the dresser, mind racing as an intense, other-worldly light flooded in from the great room of our home. Disembodied voices routed the night's peace and bellowed my name.

My wobbly legs took me to the front door and the tumult beyond.

"FBI! Come out with your hands up!"

The horror show was all about creating an incident. But why? Who cares why! I was going to end up on the short end of the stick if I didn't handle this correctly and with cooperation. Head spinning, I flashed back to all the times the news reported people being fatally shot after authorities "thought they had a gun in their hand."

I set my trusty cane beside the door. It would be a sad tale for my wife to have to tell at the funeral of her disabled veteran husband that he was gunned down by the FBI who mistook a walking stick for a firearm.

Slowly I opened the front door to the blinding glare of searchlights. A scant two feet from the window frame of our house, I could make out the manhole-sized disc of a battering ram flowering from the end of a reinforced steel arm, jutting from total darkness. *Oh my God, they're going to smash a hole in our cottage!* I let my left arm trail the storm door behind me to ensure it would close slowly, without a slam that could send these possibly trigger-happy jackanapes into a shooting frenzy.

Stepping forward, I raised my hands as far as they would go, considering their limited mobility resulting from shoulder surgeries and the reattachment of arm to torso with a brass rod. I needed to lift them high enough to appease the invisible screamers without reaching the point of initiating the bolt of pain that would cause me to reflexively pull it back to my body. A sudden movement like that could be fatal in the cloud of red dots from rifle lasers swarming me. This wasn't the first time a firearm had been pointed at me, but I assure you, this was the first time my life was placed in jeopardy by people from the country I love and served.

Virginia's winter was on frigid-blast, the porch an iceberg, and the biting west wind slashed my body. Barefoot, clothed only in underwear and nightshirt, I moved forward to the edge, squinting desperately against the artificial sun in my face, trying to find the first of three steps I knew were there somewhere. Trying not to take a well-intentioned but possibly leg-breaking step into the abyss.

I stepped down blindly, relying upon muscle memory born of doing this a thousand times in broad daylight. Until my foot actually reached step number one, I didn't know if I would be stable enough to make the climb down on my own. Guided by what I now know was divine intervention, I made each halting step until I felt the ouch of the gravel boundary between deep ruts and frosty grass. The wet lawn was only slightly less chilly than the concrete. I walked slowly, aware of shadowy figures at the edge of my field of vision. Beams of red light stabbed from the dark—rifle and pistol lasers—all merely a trigger pull away from dispatching this 66-year-old retired veteran.

The first of many "what's going on?" inquiries crossed my lips as the designated vet-wrangler snatched me, powerful arms and hands jutting from an inky veil. With purposeful out-sized strides, he yanked me across the slippery grass, shoving my face hard into the cold metal of a car hood. What I was concerned about now was the abrupt leg-weakening shove at the waist—a bending motion not pleasant for someone like me with a spine immobilized by a jumbled mass of metal spacers and screws.

Amid the clinking of metal on metal, I addressed the faceless being through gritted teeth, informing him that my left arm could no longer naturally rotate in such a way as to reach my back due to reconstructive shoulder surgery—no matter how much he kept twisting it. He was at the point of a spontaneous displacement of the metal screw holding my arm to my body. Thankfully, cold metal cuffs were slapped on my wrists in the *front* instead. Then it was right back to a face plant on the car hood.

All this outrage was conducted with creatures of the dark still yowling orders in the frigid pre-dawn air. They had me in their snare. What more could they want?

In the midst of a cacophony from hell, I labored to lift my head and, to my utter horror, saw my wife standing in the searchlight's brutal blaze. Time stopped, as did my heart.

For there stood Sharon, barefoot, arms straight out from her sides, clad only in one of my super-sized white T-shirts made nearly transparent in the harsh glare of the spotlights. I could see her shivering as her stance proved she carried no weapon and posed no threat. That did not stop the authoritative commands shouted at her with crude epithets tossed in for good measure.

I couldn't believe my eyes or my ears as she lifted her arms to reveal a single white sock in each hand and softly asked if she could put them on her feet.

As the screamers moved closer to her, to my heart-stopping terror, I saw the devil's red fireflies dancing all over her face and body. The monsters had drawn down fully automatic weapons of death on my Angel!

My heart cried, "They didn't kill *me* so now they want to kill my *wife*!"

Sharon stood there, innocently holding a pair of socks and holding my heart—my whole world—in her hands. Her stance was nearly identical to that of Jesus hung on the cross by hateful elitists who knew not what they were doing. She did not seem to understand the gravity of this bile-laced situation.

My memory flashed back to the murder at Ruby Ridge, Idaho, the day an FBI sniper shot and killed Vicki Weaver as she stood on her porch, holding her infant in her arms.

This scene played out for an eternity and still haunts me every day.

"Father, God!" I begged, "God in Heaven, Father, please don't let them kill my wife! Abba, Father! Please don't let them murder my wife!"

***

Allow me to introduce myself.

My name is Thomas Edward Caldwell. You can call me Tom. Folks in my small town in Virginia call me neighbor, friend, farmer, Christian. My former shipmates from the Navy might also call me Commander. Coworkers from my days at the FBI would say I was a teammate and their senior "paper pusher." I've been Tom the contractor and Tom the Radio Guy. My father and grandfather would let you know I am the child of World War II veterans. My wife calls me husband and sweetheart.

And the FBI, the Department of Justice prosecution team and the media? Well, they call me Insurrectionist, Fugitive from Justice, Criminal, and a few choice expletives.

In 1972, a naïve country boy of 17 with modest academic success, I left home for a Navy Reserve Officer Training Corps appointment. I am the seventh generation of Caldwell men to commit to serving this beautiful country of ours. In spite of the 1970s post-Vietnam malaise having turned sour the attitude of many on such service, I was laser-focused on becoming a Naval officer. I persevered to a four-year degree from a university where faculty and students were demonstrably anti-military.

Mine was not so much a John Wayne career but more like a McHale's Navy episode. It was a rollicking time filled with hard work, adventures, humor, comradery, challenge, and a few death-defying moments, not to mention personal and professional growth—or so said my superiors in their commendations now relegated to a desk drawer.

I was thrust early on into a tropical posting of cultural immersion in a land foreign in nearly every way. Here I learned fast some of the toughest lessons of a newly minted officer. All this in a country living uneasy with an aggressive, embedded insurgency often hiding in plain sight. The serious injuries I sustained there did not stop my service for nearly two decades as an analyst for Navy Intelligence. We of this community laughingly and somewhat facetiously refer to Navy and intelligence as mutually exclusive terms.

After nearly 20 years of honorable service, my stint as a naval officer ended when the Clinton Administration ordered a draw-down of active-duty forces. So, like misfit McHale, who had served his purpose, I waved goodbye to the life I had known and returned to the radio broadcasting of my college days. I went back to the Shenandoah Valley and the family farm I had been so eager to leave as a youth. Home to help my aging parents, not as a bright-eyed pup, but as a man tested and with the courage of his convictions.

The first time I can recall ever praying for something for myself—not for others, or for my country—was in 1998. Transitioning from the military, I was feeling the loneliness and unfulfillment that springs from a lifetime of service to others yet with no love of my own with whom to share the journey.

I asked the Lord to guide me, since I had made bad choices in past potential life partners. I guess there's truth to that adage about having to kiss a few frogs before you find the beautiful princess. Humble before the Lord, I was bold in my request for someone whose life I might make complete, if only given the chance. I reckoned I might receive what all of us long for—a loving relationship with a wonderful spouse and a chance to build a life together.

He heard and He answered.

I was living near Harpers Ferry, West Virginia, when I fell in love with the beautiful girl who lived down the lane, a former Sunday School teacher. I had no way of knowing she was aching for the same things as I.

Sharon still laughs while reminiscing of my timid approach—me, the guy who had sailed the seas, strode upon multiple continents and exotic islands, been *everywhere*, seen *everything*, done *everything*. After just a couple months of courtship, this officer and gentleman was truly in love. With nothing but an old car, a dog and a few thousand dollars in the bank, I asked her to be my wife. All I could offer were these, a vision for my shaky new career in broadcast radio, and the pledge to love her for the rest of my life.

We were married in a tiny country church on a blustery Saturday afternoon in December 1999, surrounded by a small group of friends and family.

Sharon loves living on this beautiful land. It isn't all just scratchy hard work and midwifing calves caught in the birth canal. A farm is where chance encounters become life-changers if you open your eyes to appreciate them. A bald eagle cruising overhead. Twin baby fawns walking up to us on late summer afternoons curious about what we're doing. Rabbit mommas bringing their newborns out to romp in the lush grass to our delight. Stepping into a seldom-used room in a barn to find a sleeping raccoon in the middle of the day. You haven't lived until you've held a newborn baby goat in your arms and let it nibble your ear lobe. You can have your titanium golf clubs, pal. Give Sharon and me possums climbing the grape arbor or a flock of wild turkeys pecking in the front yard. Just another day with my soulmate on our quiet little farm. If you don't get it, I can't help you.

Dear God, how blessed am I! I am so grateful! For decades I searched the world, only to find my great treasure near where my journey began. At the ripe old age of 45, I knew the rest of my days would be spent building a life with my Sharon and doing my best to make her happy. While I never knew what she saw in me, we were two kindred souls who had been through the ringer of unfulfilled relationships, resigned to sadly watching from the fringe other couples enjoying love, home, and family. For so long there had been none for either of us. Now love blooms daily, its brilliance never fading all these years later.

***

"Father, God!" I pleaded, "God in Heaven, Father, please don't let them kill my wife! Abba, Father! Please don't let them murder my wife!"

The shadow creatures blocked my view. Were they closing in on her to make sure their shots were true? My captor yanked me to the farthest edge of the metal surface, where he face-planted me again. My knees buckled. What was *happening*?

"Please, God, please!" I implored God to save her as I waited in mortal terror for the shots that would end her gentle life—and my reason to live.

None came. My God stayed the hands of the menacing devils as the first pre-dawn rays of light peeked over an unseen horizon. Thank you, Jesus.

Abruptly raised to a standing position by my captor, I frantically demanded to know what they were doing to my Sharon. He remained as stone. No answer provided.

Shadowy figures slowly came into focus with the dawn, revealing they were body-armor clad, with M-4 automatic weapons hanging from their tactical vests. Then the booted, green-clad co-conspirators backslapped each other and laughed—they *laughed*! They laughed at the expense of my *wife* and me! Incredulous, the foulest tirade of filth-speak crashed through my mind and I desperately wanted to vomit it over them. I wanted to spew it all, and I might have been successful but for the heaving sobs clutching my chest. The same kind that turn the retelling of this incident and the attempted murder of my wife into shivering choke-speak and shameless tears.

Government intruders stormed the stairs and entered our home. Where is Sharon? Is it their plan to violate her? These godless maggots from hell! I prayed again for God's help. "Father, save her! Stop these unholy interlopers! Crush them with hellfire!" A cooler head would have told me they will be judged, but not by the legal system, which I would soon find was nothing more than a perversion of power-hungry elitists embedded in the Biden Administration. For all I am, and all I have ever done as a citizen of this country, I was helpless to stop them.

I was desperate to get to Sharon, though I knew the heartless zombie behind me would not allow it.

Handcuffs clamped to a heavy chain around my waist, I could see with increasing clarity now: the multiple vehicles crushing the flowers and trees that Sharon and I had lovingly planted there; the Bearcat armored vehicle with mounted battering ram looming at my right; the steel shaft of destruction still threatening the integrity of our humble frame home; the huge ruts in our lawn marking the armored vehicle's advance toward attack position; and the operator standing at its side, laughing and smoking a coffin nail.

A member of the SWAT team cautiously picked his way across the cattle guard. He had a rifle in his hand, but not a standard M4. His accompanying gear, including a ground pad, told me this was a sniper. A damned *sniper* who was no doubt brought along to kill me and my wife from a distance! "Were you hoping to get a medal for a death double-header today, you bastard?" I said only to myself.

I tried to keep up on ice-cold bare feet as my muscle-bound abductor roughly hustled me up the hill of our gravel driveway. We halted in front of the detached garage, its overhead door yawning wide. The lights burning within showed the man-door smashed from its hinges by an FBI battering ram. Worse, though, was the damage to the treasured antique vehicle housed inside.

I was forced into the backseat of a black government sedan. The engine was running and the heater on high as I was slammed into a loneliness that smelled of sweat, stale coffee, fast food, and federal entitlement. There I would sit in anguish, knowing nothing of my wife's fate, gazing through the windshield at our once happy farm, empty fields stretching off to the distant forest. My back was on fire as someone strode past. I screamed, "How's my *wife*!?! Where *is* she?" He smirked and walked on.

There I sat, in that stink-mobile, eyes closed, rocking back and forth, praying with all my might. And there was a lot to pray for in this government-sanctioned hate-mare that was devouring Sharon and me.

A long, painful time passed as I fumed, trussed up in a car like the helpless hostage that I was.

Cue FBI Special Agents assigned to do the classic Quantico good cop, better cop dance on me. The alpha in this coercion duo was Michael Palian, a person who apparently entered the FBI with no law enforcement or investigative experience whatsoever, shattering Hoover's more than half-century policy of recruiting the best and brightest. Robinson was the bearded, loyal Boo Boo Bear to Palian's scheming, demonic Yogi.

I wasn't going to make it easy on them. Our home had been violated and our lives endangered by their Gestapo stunts.

Assuming what authority I could muster, I demanded, "What is going on?"

"I'm happy to answer any questions," said the one trying to take charge.

Slowly turning to one of the agents, eyebrows raised, I asked, "And you are ...?"

"Name's Palian. Um, I'm one of the agents on the investigation."

"An agent? Like ... what? An FBI *Special* Agent?" I smirked.

"Hi, Tom. Steve Robinson, also on the case," the other agent interjected as Palian continued. "I'm happy to talk to you about whatever, unfortunately, I don't feel like this is a, a decent place to chat."

"Tell me why you're yanking us out of our home, terrorizing my wife and me, messing up our stuff. I've got my collector car in there!"

Stalling, Palian asked, "Which one? Where?"

"The one that's over your right shoulder," I replied, dryly.

It would be nearly three months after my arrest that I was finally shown the federal search warrant that gave authority to search only our residence. Yet the FBI Assault Force, led by someone named Cameron Frick, smashed in the door of our detached garage and vandalized our vintage 1963 Thunderbird Convertible. Doors wide and upholstery punctured, its pristine paint job bore the scars of an attempt to open the trunk with a crowbar! The damage was heartbreaking.

"I'm happy to tell you whatever. I mean the, the good news is that we are not here to trash your house," Palian stuttered.

"You say that, but that's exactly what you're doing!" I said, pointing out the obvious.

"Well, no, they're ... we're ... that's unfortunately the clearing part," Palian struggled to explain.

"The *clearing* part? They kicked the door in! It's hanging off the hinges! WHY ARE YOU HERE?" I yelled. "Who have I offended?"

Both Palian and Robinson chuckled nervously.

"I ain't laughin'! Who have I *offended*?" I challenged again.

"It's nothing like that. So, obviously we're here to talk to you about some of the events at the Capitol, all right. We're, we're aware of some things. I'm, I'm hoping to hear, you know, from you on these things because I know, I'd like to hear what you have to say," Palian said, playing good cop.

Interrupting, I retorted, "Why didn't you just come to the door and say, 'Hey, can I talk to you?' We sit down, have a cup of coffee."

"Again, fair question. Um, have they ... so in this ..."

"Do you have an answer, then?" I asked, interrupting Palian's non-answer.

"No, I know, I'm gonna get there. Don't worry, don't worry about it. We've got plenty of time," Palian stalled again.

"Then what are you waiting for?"

"We want to sit in the warm, in the warm car," Robinson replied meekly.

"It's freezing out there. So, you're right," Palian covered.

"Well, imagine how it was when they pulled me out in my underwear and had me stand in the cold gravel. No socks. And roughed me up!"

"Uh. Hmm. I understand that's not a fun thing."

Fed up with his dance, I sneered, "Ya think? You threatened my wife! What were you doing, havin' a friggin' soy latte?"

"Not, not my favorite part of the day, not yours," Palian said dryly.

"So, once again, why are you here? What am I charged with? What am I charged with?"

"Well, okay. Your charges are going to be, uh … trespassing … and …"

"Trespassing?" I shot back. "Where? At *your* house?"

"No, no. In the Capitol."

"I didn't go in the Capitol, so, that's nonsense. Okay, what's really going on here?"

"You didn't go in the Capitol?" Palian responded.

"No, I didn't go in the Capitol! What are you talking about? I went to see the President in DC!"

"You're right, you're right," he agreed.

Curious. Palian says I'm right when I said I did not go into the Capitol. This already stinks to high heaven, but what can I do about it? Is this what they can do to ordinary citizens? Sadly, in my case, the answer was yes.[1]

"I went to see the President," I repeated. "So why are you messing with me and my wife?"

At this point, Robinson began making hand signals to Palian. "Okay, so … so, thank you, Steve. Before, before we go any further …"

"Stop stammering and tell me what the hell you're doing here!" I demanded once again.

Robinson jumped in and began reading my Miranda rights. "You have the right to an attorney. If you cannot afford an attorney, one will be appointed for you."

"So, you gonna get me an attorney? Like now?"

Ignoring my question and my rights, Robinson continued, "You have the right, not only to start speaking with us, you can stop at any time. Do you understand the rights as I've explained them?"

"I understand you've stomped all over my rights," I said, causing Robinson to chuckle sheepishly.

Palian added, "The last thing I want to do is mess it up. So ... so ... I'm not going to lie to you during any of this."

Palian, who would later call himself "The Quarterback of the January 6 Investigation," had already lied. And he was just getting started.

"I understand your wife recently had eye surgery," Palian deflected.

"Is that what you came to ask me about? In the dark, with storm troopers? My wife's eye?" I was steaming.

I stopped and stared straight at Palian, which caught him off guard. "Is my wife all right?

"Yeah, she's fine. She's sittin' on the bed, just nice and calm."

"It's funny that they have the cattle grates out there," Robinson mused as he looked down the driveway.

"You surprised about that?" I said, deadpan. "This is a faaarrrm."

Bullies with guns and badges. Law-abiding citizens at the mercy of demons.[2]

Chapter 2

Descent into Hell

Through the dirty auto glass, the rolling hills, the farmland and homes of rural Virginia were passing all too quickly. I had driven this route so often I could predict each midday pastoral lifestyle spectacle. Yards with goats peppered among the carelessly discarded bikes and play gear still wet with dew. The middle-aged homeowner, man-toys lined up as neatly as the fighter planes at Pearl Harbor, wing tip to wing tip. Neat board fences stretching to a far tree line. Nose-joined horses sharing the fresh morning gossip, splendidly bedecked with muddy blankets. An old man strolling a rutted lane to retrieve his paper, walking stick and floppy hound at his side.

Tranquility and peace wrapped in lazy sunshine.

How clearly I remember hurtling along this road, the awkward, disappointing youngest on a family outing. Dad at the wheel of the old station wagon bound for somewhere or other or nowhere special. Another all-important family bonding day-trip, usually disturbed by a bout of my car sickness guaranteed to flare up in a cloud from the breadwinner's smoldering Chesterfields, sucked and puffed in our mobile Detroit terrarium. I, his dreamer offspring, buckled securely amid a swirl of second-hand smoke. The memories came flooding back.

That was then.

This is today.

Back in the stifling fedmobile, I shifted beneath the seat restraint pulled FAR too tight. Squirming was my only option now, and my back snapped and groaned as I struggled for a less agonizing position. A strap across my neck and a ridiculous paper face mask restricted my breathing, but I couldn't do anything about it now. Not bound this way.

My kidnappers yabbered some nonsense about how they were going to do this or that to secretary fuzzy-sweater back at the office, oblivious to me in the back, handcuffed and locked to a chain making even a nose scratch impossible. It was too warm in the musky confines of the coffee-stained government sweat box on this country drive, and I was trapped.

Droopy eyed, I replayed the morning's events in my head. The assault and violation of our happy home. The interrogation I endured as Sharon sat watching the dismantling of our heretofore idyllic lives. The smashed doorframe of an unlocked garage. Our treasured convertible vandalized. Sharon's brush with murder, automatic rifles trained at her sweet face. It was unbearable, but I could not escape it.

I was plenty miffed that they hadn't allowed me to bring along any of the prescribed medicines upon which my life depended. I was now hours behind in taking them. My captors endeavored to keep me quiet about it with salesman babble about how I would be bailed out in an hour or two. If that were so, it would be the first thing a Fed said to me today that offered any hope or encouragement.

I had treated the FBI horde with ten times more respect than they had shown us because there was nothing to be gained by the contrary. Yes, I agreed to what started out as a voluntary three-hour-plus interview and turned into a marathon session of stump the dummy. Yep. Without counsel. What do I have to worry about? I've done nothing wrong.

After a two-hour drive, we arrived at the jail in the small town of Orange, Virginia. I was pulled from the backseat, still secured in the chains I had worn all morning.

A year later I would learn that the death of my freedom and the incident of my forced relocation was recorded as follows:

> On January 19, 2021, Special Agents Richard Orr and Mark Matthews of the Federal Bureau of Investigation (FBI) transported while in custody, Thomas Edward

> Caldwell from his home in Virginia to the Central Virginia Regional Jail, 13021 James Madison Highway, Orange, VA 22960. Transport starting time was 11:57 AM. Caldwell was handcuffed and attached to a chain restraint belt in front of his body due to his medical condition regarding a previous back surgery. Transport end time was 13:44 PM. Caldwell was transferred to the Central Virginia Regional Jail. Administrative Notation: Form USM-41 was completed by SA Orr and provided to Officer McDaniel at the Central Virginia Regional Jail.

A one-page report and a standardized form ended my life as a free citizen of the United States of America.[1]

An arrest warrant predicated on a lie and authorized by one from the judicial aristocracy.

The "agents," their paperwork complete, abruptly left to be replaced by two people in blue correctional officer uniforms. A computer man ordered me to speak my full name, address, and social security number. Satisfied that I was in fact the poor unfortunate they had been anticipating, he called two other guards, who pushed me to the next chamber.

The door stood open, revealing a filthy toilet, a dirtier sink and counter, and a steel-walled shower stall. Soiled clothes lay discarded in a corner of the room, its dingy floor covered in a sheet of smelly water. I was given a gray and white striped one-piece jumpsuit and a pair of cheap Chinese flip-flop shower shoes, then instructed to change clothes fast as the steel door slammed shut.

I thought, "This is messed up!" as I padded through the wall-to-wall puddle, pondering my predicament and wondering how to get my civilian clothes, including shoes and socks, OFF and this pitiful prison garb ON without getting all thoroughly soaked. Just then I realized I had not been sealed in alone.

Turns out my new keepers were a version of a demented Dr. Seuss-like *Thing 1* and *Thing 2*. They began to *help* me change by yanking at the shoulders of my home garb, then letting me finish disrobing, each item slapped from my hands in turn and down into the murky water on the floor. "Shoes, too!" a being snapped, and after I complied, *Thing 1* to my left barked the order repeated in every prison movie made since *realism* became the darling of 1960s and 70s Tinsel Town. "Bend over and spread!"

I guess that any complete medical examination, whether the annual variety with kindly Doc Welby or the Life Insurance Company-demanded type, will often include the prostate exam. It likely provides some level of useful information to a doctor whose only concern, according to the Hippocratic Oath, is not only to do no harm but to identify a potential health problem. In Hell, an anal intrusion serves entirely different purposes.

If the goal were to ensure contraband is not brought in, there are other ways to do that. I have to wonder if the physical violation examination persists in this corner of Hell because those who prowl the halls in blue authority-duds enjoy it. Even here it is what rape always is anywhere: a demonstration of control. A reinforcement of who has it and who does not. A ritual part of the dehumanization process encouraged by bureaucrats, and a systemic American Gestapo subculture spreading unchecked at the Federal and State levels.

In my Central Virginia Regional Jail remake of the movie *Deliverance*, this welcome-to-prison event was way too rough and lasted far too long to be of either medical or safety benefit. To this day I can see no sane reason why, after it was conducted by *Thing 1*, it was repeated by *Thing 2*.

It immediately explodes any myths you might have that you have control over anything, even your own body. Regardless of any excuses or rationale for such a violation, it is, for all intents and purposes, degradation. As it is intended to be.

I'm no psychologist, but maybe the uniformed predators' motivation is also about erotic gratification. Maybe repetition of this act is meant to satisfy an urge and to expunge some real or perceived offense or injustice visited upon them in their past—recurring revenge for their *own* feelings of emptiness and inadequacy, an exorcism of self-loathing. Whether I'm right or wrong is meaningless and I don't care. The point is, sexual assault in any setting is an indefensible act of violence and a criminal offense.

The satisfied guards turned to depart, and I became aware my personal clothes were now a spongy heap on the floor. *Thing 1* kicked the steel door several times and it opened from outside.

A chunky blue-uniformed officer stepped into the breach and told me to "Hurry up!" before the door slammed. Is it any wonder that most victims of this type of violence, inside these walls or out, keep it bottled up inside? Complain? Report it? To whom? Especially here in Hell. My burden now and going forward is the very definition of Post Traumatic Stress. Only there is no "Post." It's a stress that will only continue to grow.

It wouldn't be the last I would suffer here.

I know now that resolve and survival are all that's important. Quiet, cold-eyed defiance is useful in Hell. It's like the famous cartoon of a field mouse giving the finger to the hawk whose approaching bared talons of certain death are but inches away.

With much effort I donned the jumpsuit, and my outward transformation was complete. So was my inward transformation via introduction to institutional sadism. I splashed over to the sink to wring my soaked civilian garb. I shook my head slowly. *How can this be happening?* Soon I stood in a cold puddle, soggy clothing bundle in hand, banging for exit on the steel door. A guard opened it and sent me to the counter where my clothes were taken and inventoried. The resulting list of contents was shoved toward me.

I did my best to scan the list for accuracy, but without my prescription reading glasses, for all I knew I could have been signing a receipt for the Dead Sea Scrolls. I calculated that there was a chance for a beatdown if I failed to put my John Hancock where I was ordered to, so I scratched out my name. My pitiful personal clothing was swept away while I was pulled to a blank wall for a mug shot.

My photograph was transferred to a plastic wrist band along with my name and a U.S. Federal prison number: 14813-045.

Next, I was shoved along by the guards into a cavernous concrete hall filled with medical and electrical-looking hardware cabinets placed there to control the alien monolith dominating the room. A uniformed person told me to strip off my just-donned pre-moistened onesie.

"Clothes off! Shoes, too!" the operator barked.

Picture a giant semi-circle stood on end, or a huge Greek letter Omega with a rubber walkway passing underneath. This was the futuristic sight looming before me. A curious tangle of wires and cables connected it to its life-giving power cabinets. Here I was expected to stand, naked to the world, arms apart and hands above me while a rubberized platform moved me slowly along. None of this would happen, of course, until I complied with orders for this next level of degradation.

"Just go ahead and step up on the platform, arms up, legs apart." The operator's disinterested style suggested hundreds of repetitions of this magical moment.

I wondered if I would seep blood onto the platform, as I was told to hold this position for the duration of the ordeal. *Serves them right,* I thought, as I submitted to a full body and organ scan certain to lead to a future cancer diagnosis. Who knows what cell damage was done to me as I was moved one way and then back through the portal like a pizza in a microwave. I swear, if I start glowing in the dark ...!

"Ya gotta hold still," he said.

For the briefest of moments the podium man seemed uncomfortable. Did he feel sorry for me? *Naa, don't give him that much credit. Just another uniform. Another enemy in here. Endure this and move on.*

He locked his gaze on a computer screen, and after a moment he spoke. "Oh, man! What happened to *you*?"

"The price paid in defense of an ungrateful nation," I said in a detached way.

The ravages of time transform most men's bodies into a hardly-suitable-for-viewing mass of flesh and bones. What with the loosening and sagging, the inexorable expansion of butt and belly, it's hard to conceive that this mess might have been anything other than the girl repellent it has become. If it were true that chicks dig scars, I would be a male model instead of a farmer.

Podium man's squawk was likely triggered by viewing a human forearm reattached to a bent skeleton by way of a brass pin, my decades-long companion. Or perhaps the spinal column held together by screws driven into vertebrae. Metal spacers joined the skewers, creating something from a mad doctor's lab, the whole lot speckled with debris—other-worldly carnage intended to "stabilize" the joints against future catastrophic failure and a severed spinal cord.

Still staring intently at the scan, he offered, "Damn! I've never seen anything like *that* before."

"You didn't happen to a find a cheap wristwatch up inside me, did you?" I asked. "I think your friends were digging for gold."

"Not *my* friends. Couple uh losers," said Podium man.

No response necessary.

"Yer part of this January six thing, aren't ya? I think it was a set-up. All of it. I had friends who was there and didn't see any of the stuff they're sayin' on TV. They're skeered someone's gonna kick down their door," Podium said matter-of-factly.

"They're right to be scared," I said, getting impatient. "We through here?"

"Oh, yeah, yeah! Get dressed, man. Sorry."

I stepped down and reached for the crumpled bag I'd been given to wear. I tuned out Mr. Podium's chatter as I was shuffled off in my same squeaky shower shoes. Ushered back into the hallway the way I came, this time passing a forlorn looking inmate with a mop and bucket, swishing and squeezing his way along. He had the look of a dog that had been kicked. Over and over.

I raised, then lowered my eyebrows and chin in a silent acknowledgment of him as an individual; this was an instantly returned universal gesture I learned in the tropical Philippines. It seemed appropriate in this new and dangerous jungle world where anyone could be a man pushed too far. A man with a hair trigger.

Even the guards.

Officer Cobb, ignoring my request for a phone call, pointed to a pile on the floor. He ordered me to pick it up and follow him. My only possessions in the world now were a recycled plastic pseudo-blanket, a threadbare blue sheet, a scratchy blue mini-towel and a dried, hard blue matching bit of cloth to serve as a wash rag. We entered a passageway of steel doors where inquisitive, forlorn eyes peered out from drop-down slots and portholes of thick bullet proof glass.

Here am I: the new meat.

Stay strong, I thought. You'll get bailed out soon. Yes, of course, soon.

Deeper we ventured and the noise level grew. Foul outbursts masquerading as conversation were tossed between cells. Agitated and disturbed detainees screamed for water or for things I couldn't make out. Oh, and the cannon fire boom and echo of mule kicks against armored doors! These are the inmate's protest, attention-getter, and relief valve all in one. Turning away from the solid steel door and kicking backward with the flat part of the foot was a surefire way to annoy the guards as well as the rest of us. Striking it with any other part of the anatomy was futile for all else except self-harm. I would later learn there were those who used it for that purpose. I also came to understand why.

We passed a station where a blue uniform sat in his multi-monitored cockpit. Its TV screens in bold black-and-white displaying the lonely occupants of each sealed cell. He regarded his bug collection in an abstract way while clutching one of several phone handsets and pressing buttons.

"Opening thirteen!" Cobb said to no one in particular while fumbling at the stark steel door.

Thirteen. How appropriate.

"Inside!"

"Hey, don't I get a damn phone call or something?" I asked.

And then that armored door BLANG! It's like nothing else you've ever heard. It's the sound of nightmares. It echoes through your brain. It bounces through the caverns of your very essence. I hope you never hear it for yourself. Maybe it's the sound that reverberates in your brain as a fatal bullet passes through. Possibly like the *last* sound you will ever hear.

***

The solid steel door that shouted my doom offered neither windows nor bars through which to see anything outside this box. There was an aperture eyeball-high, but it provided no view for me, being covered by a hinged flap from the outside. There was another slot, as low on the door as a mail slot, but it, too, boasted a mean metal sentry.

A tangled mass of blanketed human was balanced precariously on a shallow stone shelf along one side of the cell. A stainless-steel seatless toilet stood beside a crud-covered metal sink, standard amenities in this hotel of the damned. The water in the toilet appeared slightly less cloudy than what dribbled from the faucet. Opposite that of my cellie, the blanket man, in our cozy ten-by-six, was a matching narrow shelf suitable for an uncomfortable seat but certainly not for sleeping. This painfully narrow sill was intended for me.

There were no windows. I was swallowed by gray-painted cinder blocks soaring higher than the top of a basketball backboard. Near the ceiling was a white circular camera pod letting me know big brother was always watching and waiting to pounce. This was a pit of fear where I stood shivering at the very bottom.

Likewise far above me was a filthy metal grate over a vent billowing ice-cold air. Tiny bits of dried toilet paper fluttered like pennants from the grating. Previous captives had tried to staunch the flow of icy air with water-soaked wads of tissue launched as drippy fastballs of hopefulness.

I crumbled onto a spot on the cold concrete floor, halfway under the sink, and tried to cover as much of my skin as possible from the freeze. *I'm shivering so badly. How can this be happening?*

Awaken Blanket man! With an angry sweep he threw his wrapper aside and turned his ire directly to the solid steel door. He banged on it loudly with both fists and screamed the universal prisoner's cry:

"See – OH! See – OH!"

"CO" is shorthand for "Correctional Officer." Virtually 99.9 percent of all conversations, demands, requests, greetings, announcements, supplications, and pleas for mercy would begin with the ringing sound of "See – OH!" This seldom worked on the first try, so each captive learned that persistence was key to getting a response from someone, anyone.

"This is a one-man cell, you jerks! Get this guy out of here before I kick his a**!"

The dropped cover revealed an angry humanoid who chested the steel door like a fighting cock pushing against a rival.

Ever have one of those days when something happens and you feel it could be a scene in a movie? Only you're *in* it? How about a *prison* movie? Well, here I was. What have we been taught we have to do when challenged? You gotta fight or else you'll end up being somebody's "bitch," as they say. And who wants that? I shucked off my moist coverings and rose to my six-foot-two-and-a-half-inch stature. Yeah, I might look like I'm made of cookie dough, but I was ready to go. No brag. Just fact. What choice was there? I took the center of the cell.

Blanket was screaming through the bullet-proof glass porthole at the guard, whose face was explaining the jail was simply overcrowded. This was a temporary cell, but what could *he* do? The porthole cover chunked in my cellmate's face. Agitated, he turned and looked me in the eye for the first time. I stood still and looked straight back.

I make no assumptions in this life, but I think Blanket was performing lightning quick calculations. He stood about five feet nine inches tall and maybe weighed 130 pounds. I on the other hand would be placed in the heavyweight division of anything other than Sumo. It still didn't mean he wasn't going to try to punch me in the face. I could tell from his leathery, blackened-tooth appearance that Blanket must have had a hard life so far. I guessed he might also be acquainted with a thing called methamphetamine.

Then something unexpected.

Blanket spoke to *me*.

"Sorry, man! Its jus' these cells are too damn crowded! They got no right to treat us this way!"

"I heard that!" I agreed. "Bastards!"

"Bastards!" Blanket echoed. In disgust, Blanket turned away and, wrapping himself again, assumed his position on the ledge.

A spirit of open dialogue had been achieved.

A physical confrontation avoided for now.

Thank God! He might have turned out to be scrappy.

Or contagious.

***

This is the way it's going to be. Stuck in this freakin' dump. At least until I get bailed out. I can't imagine what Sharon is going through. The good thing is that she knows I haven't done anything wrong so I don't have anything to explain. She's as outraged as I am about all this. To think that with a twitch of a finger those criminals with badges could have taken my angel from me. I haven't thanked you enough, God, for protecting her. I know you saved her from those demons. Please don't let them still be harassing her.

She's strong and won't get bullied. She'll stand right up to them! But they had no right to treat her that way. Stupid perverts rummaging through her underwear drawer, too! How scared she must be and how worried about me! Father, please comfort her! I just hope the media jackals aren't swarming our home like the FBI did today. I'll get released and we can start fighting this with a good lawyer.

The hours crawl by as I shiver and shiver. I know things are happening and Sharon is doing her best. But I feel helpless. I don't even know how you go about finding a lawyer.

Whatever happened to my right to a phone call? I keep asking for one, but no luck.

I'd already been subjected to cruelty and criminality within mere moments of internment in this horrible place. There were more prison initiations to come in rapid succession. The next represented not only criminality but a disturbing conspiracy nearly as twisted as that conceived within the soulless bodies of Thing 1 and Thing 2.

***

Then began the first *officially recorded* violation of my rights in what was supposed to be a legal proceeding. It was a declaration of war by those presenting themselves as "our country," the "USA" versus little old me. The kangaroo court was held through teleconference in the judicial Western District of Virginia in Harrisonburg before a guy referred to as the *Honorable* Joel C. Hoppe. Many of the rehearsed sentences and phrases he used during this so-called hearing for release would be rehashed by another judge at another time in Washington, DC.[2]

The government's antagonist du jour in this phase of its conspiracy to deprive me of my civil rights was Assistant U.S. Attorney Christopher Kavanaugh. Kavanaugh was sent to do the dirty work of the most corrupt barristers of the DOJ. He was enthusiastic, but his words were likely chosen by others. Like tribunals held historically in communist or socialist countries, that day's gathering held jurisdiction over someone attacked for perceived *political* divergence.

As I was commanded to tell the whole truth and nothing but, I was struck by the fact that Kavanaugh never had to so swear.

I had done nothing wrong relative to events leading up to, during, or after January 6, 2021, a date which, when all of the duplicity and perhaps even criminality within the U.S. Government is exposed, will certainly live in infamy. Lisa M. Lorish from the Public Defender's Office (often referred to as the Public *Pretender's* Office), having been appointed to offer token representation for me, couldn't get things over quickly enough. She was so terribly flippant with me. She didn't care when I proclaimed my complete innocence. "O sure, of course you are, like all the prisoners here," she must have thought, with a smirk. She encouraged me to *demand* extradition to Washington, DC. Why? I wondered. But she offered no explanation. Then and throughout my ordeal, I felt so hopelessly confused and alone.

"You were part of a conspiracy to prevent by force or intimidation or threat someone who is engaged in discharging the duties of his or her office," boomed Judge Hoppe. "The next charge is your willful and *loathsome* destruction of government property, and the destruction of property was over a value of a thousand dollars," he puked, spitting out his scripted charge sheet.

"What the heck?" I thought. Is that *me* they're describing?

Hoppe thundered on: "Fourth charge is the obstruction of an official proceeding. And then there's a charge of entering a restricted building or grounds, and the affidavit provides that the Capitol and the area around it were restricted grounds at that time. And then finally, there's a charge of violent entry and disorderly conduct on the Capitol grounds. Mr. Caldwell, do you understand kind of the gist of the charges against you?"

I was quick to reply: "I certainly do, your Honor, but it's not true! *None* of it and I ..."

Alas, my microphone had been cut off. I was silenced.

Everything alleged in whatever document Hoppe was reading from was a damnable lie![3] Everything! Why did I spend three hours in chains going through it with the FBI? It didn't matter.

Kavanaugh joined in my chastisement, droning on with the approved word salad that would be spewed by the press for years to come:

"... leader of a para-military organization ..."

"... committed a crime of violence ..."

"... destruction of government property..."

"... directed at the fabric of democracy ..."

"... attempt of insurrection ..."

"... threatens the very foundation of our country ..."

"... led to the deaths of five people, including a Capitol Police officer ..."

"... if freed he would obstruct justice ..."

And with regards to me and me alone, the two greatest lies of all and the ones guaranteed to deprive me of freedom:

"Caldwell is a fugitive from justice," and Kavanaugh said he was aware there was a "bench warrant" active for my immediate arrest![4]

Stop the music. I have never had so much as a speeding ticket in my entire life! That's a provable and proven fact. Kavanaugh proclaimed that because of some strictly separate, non-J6 event, I was a wanted man. What the heck? There was no "bench warrant!" I insisted. No previous charge! But my protests fell on deaf ears and returned to me as echoes within this sad room.

As the legal hack of record, by demanding today's proceedings be "sealed," meaning kept hidden from the public, as well as by speaking lies on the record, Kavanaugh had taken *ownership* of this perversion of justice.

It would be almost two years before we would learn precisely who had crafted the lies, especially the lie that I was a fugitive from justice. We *would* find out, but no one engaged in this lawfare targeting me would care. Certainly not any "court," judge, magistrate, or politician.

Judge Hoppe, in his most outrageous, jaw-dropping whopper yet, then pronounced me a "danger to the community."

They had no evidence. It was all nothing but false accusations. Kavanaugh, a federal lawyer, flat-out lied to wrongfully keep an innocent man locked away. A federal judge, who was charged with upholding the Constitution and ensuring the rights of the common people, had failed the community and this tired old veteran, perhaps on purpose. He violated his appointed duties.[5]

Hoppe's condemnation sealed my fate. I would not be going home.

Kavanaugh must have done a whizz-bang job playing his role in this charade. On October 7, 2021, he would be promoted to the rank of *the* U.S. Attorney for the Western District of Virginia.[6] No more "Assistant" for him! Sworn in by none other than the later-to-be-disgraced Lisa Monaco. Kavanaugh's wife, Jasmine Yoon, would be awarded a *judgeship*![7] Not too shabby for a single day's work violating my rights. A his and hers!

What of Lisa M. Lorish, the lawyer who was supposed to defend me but couldn't jettison me quickly enough? The lawyer who tried to convince me to demand extradition to DC just to get me out of her territory? Governor Ralph Northam engineered a judgeship for her to which she would ascend on September 1, 2021.[8]

Let me say it out loud before you scream it. Where is the presumption of innocence? *Presumed* innocent. Innocent until *proven* guilty. Isn't that the fairy tale we were told since infancy? Those rules and, in fact, the very rule of law no longer exist in this country.

BLANG! Bitter and furious, I was entombed once more.

***

Wrapped up, I took up position on my ledge. Blanket and I faced each other. The old disabled guy who had never been locked down and the youngster staring at the floor began a conversation that would begin a new chapter of penal education.

I was cautious with my cellie since one never knows how someone can be set off. I learned his name was Darryl, not Blanket, and that he was indeed familiar with non-prescription pharmaceuticals "and sh*t." Most of his sentences ended with those two words: "and sh*t."

Darryl was the victim of a modern public school education, which he readily admitted was akin to having no formal education at all. He was awaiting extradition to a different county, where he faced charges for the heinous crime of unwrapping and consuming Honey Buns in a local convenience store without paying for them. Since this wasn't Darryl's first stay at the steel door hotel, I decided I would accept whatever mentoring he would provide.

My cellmate wanted to know all about why I was locked up and kept me gabbing while interjecting well-timed comments like "those ****s" and "I hate them guys." I think being able to tell about the true events of January 6 and the FBI attack on our farm was helpful to me on some level, and I think he actually was outraged by my tale of woe. It may not sound like much, but pebbles become boulders in prison.

As I was sharing my deep concern for my wife, we heard the jangle of a CO's keys. A metal flap dropped out with a clang, opening to form a shelf. Darryl was off like a shot, reaching the door as something orange appeared. This was a hard rubber "food" tray, which I would become all too accustomed to. The word "food" here is an extremely generous description.

"All right! *Sweat meat*!"

Did he say "sweat meat"?

This was my introduction to a twice or thrice daily jailhouse calorie distribution.

Incredibly, the sweat meat meal was one of the better-received by captives here. Served as all meals were on an orange rubber tray, the centerpiece consisted of two dark brown, speckled circular slices of what marginally resembled lunch meat well past its prime. It sat within a puddle of dark grease with the consistency of 10W-30 motor oil. Two pieces of stale bread, a serving spoon scoop of white "pudding-simulant," ten stale tortilla rounds, and one packet of mustard completed the *sweat meat combo*. Darryl wasted no time in teaching me the correct way to prepare and consume it.

The first step is to roll both pieces of sweat meat up to create a fleshy cylinder. Next, squeeze the sweat meat as hard as you can to wring out the excess. Step three calls for rubbing the meat slowly against the cinder blocks to remove more mystery oil and water. Wipe your hands on your jumpsuit. Finally, secure the discs between the stale bread. The mustard is optional.

Every Tuesday and some Sundays and Saturdays were designated as sweat meat days. Too bad I was never to have another sweat meat event shared with a fellow sophisticate.

Darryl advised me that it was important to eat anything presented as "food" in here as fast as possible to avoid *tasting* anything. No matter how bad it looked or smelled, if you might be able to keep it down, you should try. Like many things, you can get used to it, he said. He let me know that every meal in this joint was rotten. Sweat meat was the best you could ever expect.

My cellmate and I sat on the cold floor with the air blowing on us fiercely. I guess it was a good time to have a guy conversation, sort of like a camping trip without the tent or the air mattress or sleeping bag or warm clothes or a fire, food, adult beverages, or Darryl's companion of choice: meth. Also, without the ability to head for home when you're ready. No merit badges to earn here. No nights under the stars. No kumbaya.

The frigid breeze created a horrible draft which chilled me to the bone. I could not stop shaking. Darryl explained the nuances of wet toilet paper hurling—the inmates' way of trying to stop or marginally impede the air flow. This led to our own coordinated attempts at climate control.

We worked at it until I was summoned to the next post-arrest ritual.

In the medical screening office I sat on a padded table as a CO hovered nearby. The two women on duty began their discussions with me. My alarming medical history and unique medical needs were typed into a computer beside my name and federal pariah number. I took time to ensure that these ladies of the medical closet understood the cornucopia of prescription medications I was dependent upon. These drugs were needed to maintain the delicate balance of pain control and bodily functions, including blood pressure and hormone production. This "brew" of prescription medications had been carefully crafted over many years of working with my doctors to find "what worked for me" and allowed me to have some quality of life. In their absence, my body and mind were screaming. These ladies absolutely got it. They understood.

I shared with them the weight upon my heart: my concern for Sharon. My description of the animalistic treatment meted out by the Feds registered on their faces as concern and outrage.

The lady named Lydia said they were powerless to offer me any kind of medicine, but she vowed to call Sharon to check on her welfare and ask her to bring a few days' worth of all my prescriptions and my medically required CPAP breathing gizmo. I knew Sharon would move heaven and earth to get that stuff to me as soon as she could.

Ushered from the medical closet by the CO, I glanced through the thick glass of a secure waiting area to see that the sun had begun to set. Little did I know that in a few hours my sweet wife would be sitting in that room, waiting to turn over five days' worth of my most important meds along with my breathing machine.[9] The same meds I would never receive, testing my pain threshold nearly to the point of madness. The machine which would be withheld from me for days in order to gauge my susceptibility to sleep deprivation.

BLANG! Entombed again.

I still clung to the notion that truth would win out and that this injustice would end. But not today.

What a dope. A shivering, homesick dope.

As unpleasant as it was on my side of the steel door, mayhem ruled on the other. The hollers, shrieks, and screams from the wretched under lock and key were the soundtrack to my misery. Their rhythmic mule kicking of steel doors assaulted my senses and made the rudiment of my migraine take twisted shape and form.

Darryl lay on his ledge, motionless. I wrapped myself in the sheet and blanket, stepping to my mattress of bare, cold concrete. I can smell it all still: filthy, frozen concrete, the woven plastic simulated blanket that smelled of damp doll heads in an abandoned tool shed, the reek of a toilet that always seemed to need another flush. I propped myself in that farthest corner and pulled as much of my trembling body as I could under the rags I was given by the State.

To lie thus in deadly weakness, brokenhearted and bereft of champion or hope, brought me to a level of despair and disillusion I could not yet fully grasp.

"Hey, See-oh! Can I get the phone?" I called out.

No response.

The hours passed and the racket in Booking degenerated to a continuous roar.

Now only to wait.

What next?

I'm so damn cold!

Resignation set in. This was my reality. *This is what my life is now. How can people just lie and lock other people up on a whim? How can this be happening to me? I didn't do anything!* I would need to survive the night sitting up in this freezer, pressed against the wall in my damp swaddling wraps, a guiltless newborn in a dangerous world.

***

Nothing close to sleep had been achieved that first night. My recollection is an endless stream of shivering and pain punctuated by an occasional head-jerk telling me my body had tried to shut down for a period of restoration. The type of restoration most people receive from sleep, but not me. Still, I must have dozed off, if only briefly.

This was my first morning waking up as a man robbed of freedom. So many new and hideous lessons learned so far, and who could say how many more to go?

I was jolted from a shivering, zombie-on-ice stare toward nothingness by the command:

"Hey, Mr. Caldwell! Get up! Classification!"

I followed Officer Maxwell through a maze of buzz-snap controlled access doors while making small talk with him and taking in every sight, sound, and smell in a firehose gush of sensory stimulation. If I made eye contact with any fellow bagwearers, I never glanced away but either initiated or returned a nod of the head, a lift of the chin, or a slight hoisting of eyebrows.

The officer's footwear-squeak blazed a winding trail until we reached an office space and a medium-tall lady, who greeted us politely. This was different.

Doris was pleasant enough, sure, but what I remember most is her sharp wit, relaxed manner, and the first Christian empathy I had yet encountered in this place. Maybe that's just what I *wanted* to see. There was some Q&A but not the cold, fill-out-the-form kind. More like the "you-seem-like-a-nice-guy-it-stinks-you-are-going-through-this" kind.

Doris was a wealth of answers to the "what if's" and "what now's" of my incarceration mental quiz book. She wanted to know all about my medical problems and was genuinely appalled that no one had attempted to meet my needs.

I told her about the exchange with Kavanaugh and his assertion as to my status as a "fugitive from justice." After a couple of pecks on her keyboard, she closely examined the computer screen.

"He's full of it. You're not even in the *system,*" she said assuredly.

"Yeah, I know! I've never even had a traffic ticket, for heaven's sake."

She bumped a few more keys.

"Yep. Nothing. Zip. Nothing nationwide, let alone in the District," she offered. "Nothing. Not 'Thomas E.' or any other letter-Thomas combination with 'Caldwell.' "

She spun the computer monitor so I could see for myself the empty response offered up by the computer to her typed query about me. Nothing in the system. She was dumbfounded when I told her I had not been allowed a phone call to anyone. Nor had I been assigned free representation.

"How can they get away with lying like that?" I offered rhetorically.

"The Feds do it all the time," she answered.

This is the American *Justice* system, friends: It's *Just Us.*

After a few more key taps, Doris assured me that Sharon had not been arrested and there were no warrants signed by any slippery magistrate indicating that a take-down was imminent. She had read the worry etched on my face before I could even ask her to check.

She was sympathetic to my play-by-play recounting of the FBI swat raid and the story everyone must be sick of by now of how Sharon is the most wonderful woman on God's green earth and how I love her so much and how much I am worried sick about her.

Then it was back to my concrete holding cell.

***

Darryl and I settled into our igloo existence, and he was quite amenable to sharing information about the prison experience since this was a subject with which he was well versed.

Booking was the place where all confinement journeys begin. Recommendations from that place called *Classification* directed your transfer to a cell block (assigned letters such as J, K, etc.) or some other warehousing option like solitary confinement, referred to as "the hole." Darryl had never been to the hole but had been told that some levels were haunted "and sh*t!" No kidding, with ghosts and stuff.

The stuff of bad dreams and insanity. He said that people look and act differently after they come back from the hole. And some people *never* come back.

There was no concept of time as I had previously understood it, no quieting of the din outside my wind tunnel. None in this pod of the damned showed any signs of tiring in their protests and yells. There were no hands crawling too slowly across clock faces; no shadows tumbling through frosted windows to mark the march of the moon or the inch of daybreak. Each unto their own solitude in the brotherhood of the succubus' womb. In our particular cell could be found a young, seasoned veteran who had seen it all before and the old, last-round draft pick keenly aware of his status as Mr. Irrelevant.

***

A telephone to the outside world is as dear as life itself for any prisoner. It doesn't matter if you're talking to your wife, girlfriend, parents, best friend, or your lawyer. Time spent connecting to someone, anyone, outside of this misery has value beyond measure. Sharon would later put it succinctly and poignantly: "I *live* for these calls." I did, too, and nobody detained had to say it out loud. Those in charge knew it darn well, and phones were often withheld if some uniformed goon desired to make it so. A different, bullying type of punishment. I would see *that* here, too.

The coveted telephone here looked very similar to the old standard pay phone. Fitted with the customary push-buttons and a coiled handset cord, it was this jail's take on a "mobile" phone. The device was rolled on shaky casters from one gruel opening to the next so inmates could kneel to reach the phone and, with luck, converse in a very public way above the din. All of this while clutching a handset on a too-short metallic tether.

The phone "company" vacuuming up the cash from tortured inmates is called SECURUS. Using networks already bought and paid for, maintained and tweaked by big-time actual phone companies, they charge $3.85 for the first minute and 75 cents for each additional minute. *Those* are the real bandits of the Orange, Virginia, jail! They're the only game in town, and God knows what a beatdown someone would take if they tried to cut into that firehose of cash by sneaking a cellphone into the facility. No, you'll pay the price and keep your mouth shut.

I spent much of the afternoon on the concrete perch trying to read a paperback. I had been allowed to grab one from the off-limits library while on my trek back from Classification. By happenstance, I raised my head and looked at the bullet-proof viewing port. There was CO Maxwell staring at me. I could not believe what he said next.

"Mr. Caldwell, did you ever get that phone call?"

"No, *sir*!" I piped up anxiously.

I got on my knees to peer out from the opening in the steel door as Maxwell explained exactly how to place a collect call. I had to contort my body to grab and draw back the receiver. Its short metal cable barely reached inside enough to be placed up to my ear. I couldn't sit on the floor; the only way to operate the contraption was on my knees the whole time, the absolute worst position for anyone with back problems like mine.

My heart pounded until I heard Sharon, brimming with relief and excitement, at finally hearing from me. That precious call we both needed so badly.

Her voice was as soft and captivating as the first time I had met her over twenty years ago. It was a refreshing caress for my mind and body, so pulsing with hurt and adrenaline in this dangerous and wrongful circumstance. To my relief, Sharon told me she hadn't been physically harmed by the FBI thugs who forced their way into our home. At least she never let on.

She hurried to tell me she had delivered my all-important CPAP machine and my prescriptions the very day of my abduction. She was incensed to learn that, at the specific directives of prison staff, nothing had been given to me after she had driven over two hours through the darkness to deliver them. What could be the excuse for withholding these things?[10]

It was heartbreaking to hear that she had waited patiently for the better part of an hour in a glass-enclosed cypher room at the prison, a mere dash from my concrete cave, to make her delivery. My love, my heart, had been so close to me in my wretchedness! Yards away, and I never knew.

We shared all the horrors of the last two days and the swirl of confusion, phone calls, and visits from supportive friends, some who had stayed up until 2 a.m. praying with her. I did my best to assure her that, although it was hideous in here, I knew she was doing her best to cope and to get me out. I ached because of what the FBI fiends had put her through.

She was anxious to learn about the whole "fugitive from justice" and "bench warrant" hoaxes perpetrated by Kavanaugh. As her outrage rose to meet mine when I had first heard the pre-approved lie, we both wondered aloud if Hoppe had been duped or had indeed been given a script for his role ahead of time. He delivered his lines with such passionate intensity.

For now, it was as close to bliss as we could manage simply to chatter away together amid the I-love-you's and I-miss-you-so-much's and for me to touch the outside of this pit for a few moments through the song of her voice. I think it must be some kind of weird testament to our shared resiliency that in the depths of oppression and misery, we actually *laughed* together. Not because we lacked perspective but, at least in part, because at that time we were certain that truth would ultimately prevail and we would look back on this nightmare with relief. What had we heard over and over again since childhood? "It's a free country, man"!

No longer.

Then came one of the hardest things I have ever had to do: start to wrap up our call knowing it must end at some point. At last came the final I-love-you for the day, the last puckered-up smack into the handset's mouthpiece, a click. And then silence.

I crumbled to the floor.

In a while, my mind floated to thoughts of how many sad and lonely people had snapped themselves into this gray-and-black-striped jumpsuit that was my prison issue. White, black, Hispanic, I felt pity for all who entered here and wore this uniform and who might later do so. There certainly is a great market for these bags here in the one country in the western world with an outsized prison "enrollment" still growing at an alarming rate.

I curled myself into the closest thing to a ball I could manage and tried to cover up. *I am so damn cold! I can feel the throbbing burn and the ache through my spine and legs continuing to rise. If I don't get some of my medicines soon, how am I going to make it?*

***

The clatter-bang announcing a gruel delivery shocked me out of my pitiful attempt at half-snoozing. The marathon battle seemed to have just been won when the raucous din in Booking grew from a far-off whisper to the full-throated sound of a lunatic stereo cranked all the way up. I opened my eyes and looked around, dizzily. Yep, I was still in this cube.

Damn, I'm so cold!

In a mental fog, I envisioned myself from across the room. Shuffling to the plastic tray, wrapped in my rags like a once bold Apache warrior now reduced to a native fruit roll-up with legs, dependent upon the mercies of a cruel government agent on a miserable reservation. No joy. Merely a quiet resignation that this was his truth.

Perhaps we both, the Apache and I, were never destined to roam freely again. We both had our possessions, our homes, our loved ones, and our identity stripped away ne'er to return. Not unless my God and perhaps his Great Spirit will it to be so. How could there ever be peace again when the heartless government soldiers were as many as the blades of grass that waved on the plain? We both knew how fleeting life, liberty, and the pursuit of happiness were.

How did things turn out for the native people? They learned the hard way that you can't trust the American "government."

Absolutely right!

***

Time passed so slowly. The pain in my back was appalling as I racked up the days without medication, but most acutely in need was my neck. Farther down the road I would learn two of the vertebrae were growing together and forming one intractable painful mass. I was parched as a camel as I resigned myself to another cautious attempt to remedy my sleep-deprived state, head fitted firmly on a tattered paperback.

Even though there's no exercise time or physical activity here, I was at the point of exhaustion where my entire body was buzzing with internal electrical current. What was it that Sharon had told me when I confided that the pain was so overpowering? I remember now. She said try repeating *The Lord's Prayer* without ceasing. He knows where I am and He knows what I am enduring. Pray that He will help me find sleep. God knows I need it.

Through eyes squeezed as slits I saw Darryl sound asleep on his ledge. I envied him as the pain held me firmly in its clutches.

Damn, I'm cold. Dear God, I hurt!

Oh, yes: *The Lord's Prayer*. Over and over the words flowed from deep within me as I tried to relax and tell Him how much I could use just a touch of His Healing power or, if not, just a time of unconsciousness to restore myself. Restore my body in order to endure all of this. I recited this prayer, learned as a child. I pictured green fields and rolling hills, clouds in a light blue sky.

Somewhere in my shuddering sadness the Lord provided.

***

CO Parker called out to me through the porthole in the door.

"Did you get a *comfort pack*?"

"What's *that*?"

This "comfort pack" he offered was a cracked foam cup, with contents cobbled together from rejected fragments of a complete one. I was now the proud owner of one previously used comb, one three-inch-long plastic tool resembling a toothbrush suitable for a smurf, one unwrapped bar of seedy-motel-sized Bob Barker brand soap and one small white tube of Maximum-Security brand toothpaste. Maximum-Security. Yet another cynical Bob Barker brand trademark.

Also inside the broken cup was the flexible internal ink tube, easily recognizable as the inside part of a ballpoint pen. My mind jumped to the utility of having an actual tool (the cup itself) with which I could harvest the liquid at the faucet instead of cupping my hand. Then Parker passed me envelopes and a pad of writing paper consisting of the obligatory cardboard backing and 1, 2, 3, 4, 5, 6, 7 pages of lined paper.

Once Parker had explained that I didn't need a stamp because letters would be mailed free, he told me that he had put my name on "the phone list." Now I should expect that sometime today one of the COs on duty might bring the rollaround-phone to the door of my cell.

This was the end of his shift and, for reasons I still do not comprehend but am grateful for, he took the time to treat me like a person. This in a place where, with each miserable day, I would be reminded that my life had little or no value in comparison to those who had been appointed to detain me.

****

At last, another blessed phone call to Sharon! She had found an attorney to take our case! I crawled to the meager pad of paper and the pen, returned to the hanging handset, and copied the number and the name. Sharon was in no position to be picky and hired the first guy she could. Of course, she had to scramble to cobble together the money for a hefty retainer. Our new attorney, Tom, would come to meet with me on Monday the 25th. I felt better with a date to look forward to.

No sooner had I hung up when CO Williams arrived amid a jangle of keys. I have to call my lawyer, I protested, but the phone was pushed away. I was being moved to another cell. And another cellmate, Mr. Johnson.

Officer Williams explained that as far as he knew, Mr. Johnson was also guilty of nothing whatsoever, so it seemed that we might be a good match as cellmates since neither seemed likely to commit violence against the other. It wasn't clear exactly how long my new cellie had been there or would remain, but his presence seemed to be of concern to this CO.

Once I was sealed inside this new cave, I introduced myself with a handshake to the old black gentleman who sat at the edge of a wide, concrete sleeping platform. He looked like the embodiment of a lifetime of hard work and hard luck. His handshake seemed much firmer than mine, my grip compromised by nerve damage. Burned-out fluorescent bulbs left much of the chamber wrapped in shadow.

I was Tom and his name was Buck and we set about to storytelling. I shared the condensed version of my misfortune while he listened politely and exclaimed at the appropriate spots with empathy. I thought we had gotten off to a good start.

Buck told me his life story that day, and though he was falsely arrested as drunk in public some weeks ago, it appeared to me that Buck might either have some mild Alzheimer's-like thing going on or perhaps some early onset dementia. I've seen both through elder care. This might easily be mistaken by your garden-variety cop for the confusion of a good ol' buzz and easily passed off as such.

Now I knew I was sharing a prison space with proof of the despicable Virginia State indifference to our mental health crisis. Or should I say, its regrettable stopgap "solution?" Over the course of my unlawful detention I would see for myself many examples of how our "correctional" institutions have become holding areas for people who most certainly should be in a different type of supervised or semi-supervised facility. It's a heartless method of moving the problem out of sight. A *bureaucrat's* solution. In Virginia, prison reform is exactly like the weather: everybody talks about it but nobody does anything about it.

If you can truly make friends in the Central Virginia Jail, or "CVRJ," then Buck and I were on our way. We both had won and lost at love, had traveled all over the country, worked numerous jobs, and had DC as a touchstone. We reminisced about buildings and places long gone, like Boundary Field, later called National Park and later still called Griffith Stadium, where the great Walter Johnson had pitched his team to a Championship.

Buck was amazed that I remembered the baseball diamonds which once marked the grounds of the Washington Monument where he played pick-up games. We gabbed on about the Baltimore Elite Giants of the Negro leagues and how he had even known "Buck" O'Neil of the Kansas City Monarchs, who showed him a thing or two about proper hitting and, of course, playing first base. He seemed genuinely happy that this old white man lying on the floor knew about the places and the names that lived on in the parts of his mind which seemed sharp as any steak knife to me.

Much later that evening, when a nameless guard rolled the phone to our door, Buck shook his head when I motioned for him to use it first. He lay back on his platform and looked at the ceiling. I wasn't surprised that he had no one to call. It still makes me sad.

Early next morning as I struggled with the effects of polluted water as my only drink, a couple of COs arrived to take me away.

With smiles and good luck wishes exchanged, I bade farewell to Buck that morning. I never saw him again. He had been there two months when we met. I often wonder if he was able to leave that place. If he did, would he ever see his old truck again, and were all his meager belongings long-gone from the little room he used to rent up the backstairs of a house in Orange County, Virginia?

Chapter 3

Darkness and the Terror Tower

My escorts took me past a soaring wall of glass. The inside of this aquarium resembled a high-school gymnasium with row upon row of bunk beds stacked high. I could see quite a few fellow castaways marking the slow advance of hours and days. Some on bunks reading or trying to sleep. Others meandering about and still others blankly watching my passing through tired, empty eyes. I had set my jaw tight and showed nothing but determination along with, naturally, what all locked inside here shared: contempt for the forces that inhumanely held us here.

A left-hand turn brought us to the last cypher door with a sign above that read:

SEGREGATION

A child of the 60s, the first thing that came to me was the first thing that came out of my mouth:

"Segregation? Didn't we outlaw that in 1965?"

Nobody laughed but me.

"They call it the hole," said a uniform.

The buzz-snap opened the door to the underbelly of this prison and my first glimpse into the abyss. Locked inside their burial vaults, the shouts and cries of the damned were not just louder per capita but fiercer, angrier. Words were not simply passed between the desperados; they were *spat* between them. I could see down the length of this passageway, but I was stopped by a strong hand as rattling keys opened the very first dungeon on the left. Number 101. My new lodge beneath the headachy pulse of flickering fluorescent lights.[1]

It was roughly ten feet by ten feet and featured a raised metal shelf somehow affixed to the wall at my left. There was a filthy steel toilet, standard issue but with extra waste on the rim. The sink was the worst and looked like the bottom of a Moroccan dumpster (if Morocco had dumpsters). Maybe they do, but in any case, I wouldn't want to drink water from *this* faucet.

The CO here to receive me, a tall gent who seemed pleasant enough, completed the passdown with his fellow guards regarding the CPAP. He snaked the extension cord under the steel door and watched as I set up my breathing contraption.

The long, raised metal shelf was intended for sleeping, but its top was a mass of sharp rusty shards and the previous tenant had taken the time to urinate within the shelf's rimmed confines. So I was relegated to yet another cold concrete floor as my bed. Floor locations for nappy-time were limited by the length of the extension cord, so my only option was alongside the aromatic pee reservoir and just inside the door. From this spot I had the perfect view of the black mold which covered the left wall.

The soundtrack of Segregation was the Mills Symphony Orchestra performing in Scream Minor. Fellow prisoner Mills was not just first chair, he was also the conductor and the center of attention for questions, discussions, dirty jokes, and rage against the topic or affront of the moment. Mills carried on in the cell next to my own. Farther away but still clearly heard were the sounds of a man alternately wailing and weeping. I found this particularly unsettling because the detainee, whoever he may be, was so bitterly mournful. He was a lost soul, discarded by the world outside, a throwaway from society. Look, these are not just big thug *undesirables*. They are human beings, and no matter how poorly they are treated by the zookeepers or the *System*, their lives have value even if here they are perpetually devalued.

Throwaway guy was aching, sorrowful, as if someone he loved with all of his soul had died. He wept bitterly and called childlike for someone whose name I could not make out. I had never heard a grown man so inconsolable and bawling unabashedly. How can you hear something like that and not be moved? But there was no comfort for him. If the guards were affected, it never showed. Maybe the other residents were so jaded they paid no attention. Or perhaps they could no longer deal with their compassion for him or anyone else in here; their own survival depended on fully tuning him out. I was to learn first-hand the depths of human anguish, loneliness, and grief in this man-made hell.

I would come to know what it is to be a disposable man.

On my rounds of these new digs I stopped and perched on the circle seat, wide enough to balance precariously on a single butt cheek. I set my tired eyes to crawling across the feeding table. The hapless discarded who preceded me had left their unique glyph-record of seclusion. More ideograms than human words. Run-on series of stand-alones more cuneiform than runic. Could I distinguish a letter? Two "V" letters overlapping. I struggled to recall and assign its value. I found I couldn't manage to concentrate or puzzle out their possible meaning.

There were renders and scrawls of those forgotten, some innately coherent to me as if I had been gifted a fluency in sadness, fear, and suffering. I am the foreigner trapped in the pharaoh's crypt. I read and comprehend, marvel at the skill of each forgotten craftsman while booby-trapped within this sarcophagus, cursed to reveal neither his discoveries nor his erudition. Left alone, here long to remain. Until his own flickering light should burn out.

A crushing flash of electricity shot through my lower spine and seemed to bounce off the metal pins and spacers locking vertebrae unnaturally together. The familiar, shattering nerve pain that spasmed my body in reaction launched me reflexively off the circle seat and onto the floor to shiver in teeth-grinding torment. Without my medications, this was my lot.

God, please make this stop!

How long I lay there on the slab, reciting without effect *The Lord's Prayer* to mitigate the pain, I have no clue. I was aware of the periodic open-pause-slam of the viewing port but never released my sealed eyes to meet those of the twisted face peering in. The pain was all-consuming and reminiscent of the first day home from back-fusion butchery—sent away from a hospital in misery with no pain medication whatsoever: Spinal Surgery Concentration Camp Dr. Mengele-style. Who could do that to another human being? And who could do *this*? Who could so willfully deny a man's medicine protocol when this suffering would so obviously be the result?

Segregation was beyond frigid and churning with overlapping noises and screams. Wrapped in skimpy sheet and blanket, I caught each new sound as it added to the fullness of the opus and joined the pounding of my migraine and the maraca chatter of my bones.

I am so cold ...

From far away down the corridor an inmate wailed in agony. I felt he cried for me, and maybe for all of us in Segregation.

And then they turned out the lights.

***

Fear of the dark is universal across all cultures and is timeless. The reason fire was such a breakthrough for primitive man had little to do with simple warmth or the ability to char a few mastodon burgers and everything to do with dispelling the darkness. Darkness is where the bad ones are. Even in daytime hours, shadows hide things to fear, and in the darkness man is not the apex predator. I would learn a harsh lesson in these things.

The blackout disoriented me completely. Bad enough I lay on the hard concrete in a rushing river of cold air, but now negotiating this tiny cell simply to approach the toilet would be a risky proposition. It didn't help that someone in authority had disconnected the cord to my CPAP machine, depriving me of even that device's pitifully faint glow. My eyes widened to draw any morsel of light they could to identify shapes or distances.

I was in pitch-black nothingness. I couldn't even trace the movement of my fingers before my eyes. From the shouts and general commotion bouncing off the walls outside my pen, it didn't seem any other Segregation cubbies were without light. That means all of this special torment was just for me.

Sensory deprivation can cause anxiety and even hallucinations in only a few minutes. Your brain seeks out sensory patterns, and when none exists, it creates its own. Darkness-fueled fear rose up in a towering wave to engulf me. Fear that I would never see Sharon again. Fear that I would die alone and forgotten. And fear of what was sealed in here with me.

It's shocking to teeter on the edge: hopeless, tortured, and abandoned in a realm with absolutely no light. How effortless to tumble into the crater of madness. Staring intently, now I counted the outlines of inky black creatures arrayed in an arc around me: the faintest of silhouettes in the nothingness. They stared down with Victorian-age med student eagerness, studying me as a moldering corpse prepped for vivisection.

I am the nightmare of ancient Edinburgh, Scotland, in a rough-hewn grot beneath South Gate; a cadaver brought by body snatchers, the "resurrectionists," for the amusement of these immoral things. I could smell and feel the drip drip of watery horse dung making its way from the bridge overhead to the slab where I lie. Helpless. Helpless.

I strained to see the fiendish faces of haunted solitary isolation. Theirs were only semi-human, distorted like those of rodents. Teeth rattled a chattering from below huge, pitiless eyes that sucked back into their heads, turning them inside out. Moving in closer, pushing for position against the others: faceless skulls perched above flowing cut-out gowns flashing the out-of-focus bare-chested nudity of the brides of the dead. Around this drooling mob swirled the foulest stench from the depths.

These were what *haunted* solitary isolation: things fashioned from the moldering decay of peat and manure, the funk of the bubbling grave. Hour after brutal hour of it, day after day as I was locked in this place, the images and their terrible screeches burning into my being and my brain. I struggled, but without relief.

I couldn't manage to mark the passage of time through customary slop deliveries. How could I know if it was the 4 a.m. feeding or the midday if the lights never snap back on? The ghouls sometimes faded toward the edge of my stony keep but never left me. I looked up at what should be the ceiling but saw only infinite blackness. The grate kept spewing its whistling river of arctic death. I am still here. I was still in this damnable box. I barely moved at the exhortation of the uniforms as they balanced trays on the dimly backlit shelf from time to time. I could only struggle mightily to my knees and bring the hand-outs to the floor.

Did two days and nights pass or three or maybe four?

With all my non-visuals I could *see* their wickedness, these creatures of perpetual night. They're on me and in me! I can feel myself falling! I reach out, desperate to cling to something solid, but I can't grab hold of anything! I'm tumbling, dropping away, falling into a pit and never hitting bottom.

The COs on their rounds never acknowledged my shouted struggling with the things and with the dark. I was so knotted up from fighting the cold and so emotionally and physically spent from pain and despair I just wanted to go away. I remember thinking: "I want to go to Heaven, but after seeing *this*, I don't care *where* my soul goes as long as it ain't *here*!"

Anywhere but here.

Then came the greatest fear of all. Maybe I'm already dead. I have succumbed, and I feel hopeless because there *is* no hope. Hell is *not* just a place of fire, like they say. Hell has many faces. There's no rest, no comfort, no one to speak with or commiserate with. There's no promise to latch onto for balance or to ground myself. No way to find a point of reference. There's nothing to look forward to except more of the same.

My name is Tom Caldwell and I am a political prisoner. I have seen evil, seen horror, endured unimaginable pain. I am the victim of depravity and misplaced hatred in bad suits and ugly uniforms. I am still a human being. I was guaranteed the protection of the United States Constitution and with it a basic regard for my humanity. But no such protection exists in our Nation now. There is none for me.

If I could only scream to people on the outside! If these thugs can do this to me and no one stops them, tomorrow they will add another.

Maybe it will be you!

***

Given enough time, under relentless torture in solitary confinement, everyone's sanity level drops to zero. Especially in the dark. Nelson Mandela endured four decades of confinement and mistreatment and is very clear in his writings about that.

The tormentors of the prison guard brigade likely judged their handiwork by the screams and wails of those locked inside the solitary confinement dungeons. Those of us who for the most part remained silent presented a puzzle to them. Short of peeking through the glass of my cell door with infra-red cameras, I supposed the guards would eventually have to turn the lights on if for no other reason than to determine if I had died.

The lights flickered on in the hallway, and I could see the thin ribbon of light through the gap where door neared floor. A guard peeked at me, commanded me to get up for a feeding. I feebly asked him what day it was. "Monday," he said. Three days since I was wedged into here. I remembered what today was. The day my legal knight in shining armor, lawyer Tom, would meet me in person at 8:30. I needed to pull myself together as best I could in my raggedy state.

Could this finally be over soon? If I could just hold on, a real lawyer, not a court assigned one, would stand up for me and show the judge that this was all just so much crap. I began to dump the anxiety, if not the pain. There was a glimmer of hope, a time to look forward to, and surely deliverance waited on the other side of some more mandatory legal wrangling.

Muted light surged into my dungeon, and I shielded my eyes with a shaky hand. There were people standing there, but in a moment I could make out that these were not your garden variety prison COs. One of them clutched a dangling cascade of shackles and manacles that jangled ominously.

"Get up, Caldwell!" a gruff voice spat at me from the hallway.

"Here!" another commanded as he tossed a bright orange and white jumper that hit me in the face. "Put this on!"

After their simple visual-only inspection of my rear end, I wrapped my shivering nakedness in the new body bag. I had to lean against the wall to do so, struggling to put one, then the other foot through and then twisting arms into holes and snapping closures beginning below my groin.

They confirmed when I asked that it was indeed Monday then told me to shut up when I protested at being shackled to go meet with my lawyer. They let me know they had other plans for me.

I was weighted down with chains and shackles, barely able to move as a human being. How was I to suspect that the day's events would lead me to a whole new level of understanding of the wickedness of the DOJ foot-soldiers? This was the Feds' version of the *John Wayne Gacy Sado-Masochist Playset.* All that was missing was the rhetorical "Have you ever seen the old handcuff trick?"

"Seriously, what's *with* all this?" I popped off.

"Shut up! You're goin' for a ride," was the terse retort.

"Like hell! I gotta meet my lawyer! You can ask Hoffman," I said, referring to the designated Commandant of this Camp.

"Screw Hoffman!" was all he boomed back as his accomplice laughed.

Only he didn't say "screw."

The metal fetters sank into my ankles, pinching skin to bone with each labored step. I was dragged on our trek by a thug on each side. Buzz-snapped doors were opened to let us pass to the check-in desk.

"Hey, guys!" I piped up to the loafing uniforms at the desk. Then I told them who I was and that when my attorney arrived they should tell him who took me out.

My inquiries as to where they were taking me were met with a lightning-fast "shut up!" and I soon found myself at the gaping opening of a white, nondescript government van. The door slid along its tracks to receive me, revealing another unfortunate clad and shackled as I was. These new police shoved me inside.[2]

I looked to my brother in distress. He simply looked away. He was a young black man who I made to be a full head shorter than I was but a step ahead, in that he wore a long-sleeved thermal top and brown slip-on shower shoes. Oh, for a thermal like his!

Satan's coachman sealed the door with a resounding slam and mounted his seat. Amid the crackling of radios, our vehicle and one identical to it lurched into a hazy sunshine caravan. Down the road we went, swaying along with the movements of our top-heavy van as it crawled through traffic lights and onto the open road.

As our abductor transported us in silence, I asked my companion if he knew where they were taking us. He did not. They had just shown up to his cell block, he said, trussed him up and set him here. He knew of no hearing he was scheduled for, no transfer that was ordered. That made two of us. Usually they let you know ahead of time, he told me, and then, with a look of consternation on his face, he said something ominous.

"These are marshals ... and this ain't normal."

Did I detect that my new institutional companion was scared?

I was out of the bitter darkness of the Segregation wing. I was going somewhere. But it wasn't home.

***

I grew up driving these roads. I knew more from visual cues than road signs that we were headed in the general direction of Harrisonburg, Virginia, but on a strange route indeed. Unbeknownst to me at the time, Harrisonburg was a regional home of things federal and they occupied, on the downlow, a couple of nondescript brick buildings, including one joined at the lips with the local courthouse.

Someone had planned a stop for us along the way.

The van pulled off the blacktop and advanced a few dozen yards down a poorly maintained country lane.

Then it crunched to a halt.

I didn't even have to turn to my anonymous companion to know that he was staring past me toward the door which was soon jerked open to allow a uniform to climb aboard. Standing on the frozen running board, he yanked me out by the collar and pulled me toward the front of the van. Next, I was smashed face-first into the wintry hard ground.

I only recall the shove that toppled me because it struck my spine mid-back. This sent a blast of pain up and down my body. With wrists squeezed by steel cuffs, I fell with my hands directly sticking out from this ball of metal. Face-planted in shocked pain, my thoughts turned to my wrists, both of which must be broken now.

Suddenly it was all about my eye that had gotten some alien roadside schmeg jammed into it on impact. I couldn't reach and rub it, so I blinked frantically trying to dislodge something that felt as big as a boulder. Would it scratch my eye to where I would be blind? I tried to get off my stomach but something was keeping my legs splayed at the limits of their chains.

The first blow happened so fast I couldn't process what it was. Then I got it all right: someone kicked me in the groin from behind as I lay face down on the frosty gravel and dirt. Lightning fast I thought: Ha! He missed! He hadn't kicked me square and had actually gotten more meat and tailbone than nutsack. Flatulating butthead! Doofus! I got *lucky*! That thought shot out of my brain with the landing of kick number two, which had much better placement from a torture standpoint. It stopped my world with a flash of light and pain that reached inside and ripped at my stomach. I thought I'd puke.

Kicks number three and four seemed to lift me off the ground, and the sadist in charge knew he had found the "sweet spot." The sound of the unobstructed kick was a sickening pumpkin-smoosh sound and sent pain shooting everywhere. I must have moaned or howled or something, but in the revisiting of this incident with my fellow captive, he never mentioned it. Now, however, my abuser, or maybe a conspirator, began to taunt me.

I have written these memories in a free-flow-of-consciousness style. Still, I choose my words with care. I am not a shrink but I understand that a sadistic or even a deeply narcissistic individual enjoys cruelty and seeks opportunities to induce the suffering of other people. Particularly helpless ones. Like those in lockup or chained on the side of a road. If sadistic tendency was a desired trait found on a job description, then the Feds got themselves a winner. And I was in deep trouble.

Kick number five exploded through my body from my crotch to my toes, fingers, and the backs of my eyeballs, which I thought would blow out of my skull.

The federal man spoke.

"Just tell her what she wants to hear and we'll stop," he told me.

"Who is *her*?" my body screamed! *Who* do I have to plead with, and *how*?

But I couldn't answer him out loud. Only as I think of it now, I know that it wouldn't have worked. He wouldn't have stopped.

"Oh, GOD!" I must have cried out loud to The Father.

"Oh, you're one of *those,*" he mocked of my petition. Then to someone else, "He's one of *those.*"

Now I knew there was at *least* one other there. Maybe he was talking directly to Satan.

I lost it on fiendish kick to the nuts number six, which brought up burning bile. He really gave it all he had on kick number seven and my body shut down, though I was reflexively wriggling like the catch of the day thrown onto dry land. I just wanted it to stop! That's all I cared about! I was so weak and so anguished I might have been ready to say anything to end the crushing pain. I waited too long, I guess.

"Where's yer SKY DADDY, huh? Why don't he come down here and save you?" he boomed sarcastically. "Where's yer sky daddy, boy?"

A spiritual war. That's what I've heard. *That's where I am. Unarmed against a jack-booted GS-er from the DOJ.*

"Where is your CHRIST?" my torturer taunted.

I wish I could say I directed some quotable quote his way. Some catchphrase that would ring through the ages as defiance by the oppressed. But I had nothing.

Kick number eight was probably as accurate as any that had bruised my crotch, but it didn't register quite the same. The whole scene shrank in upon itself, growing smaller and smaller to a pinpoint in a pee-orange-gray cloud that overtook my vision. This was how I was going to die.

I felt something else and then nothing else. I can't account for anything or describe anything until I was drawn up like an overflowing bucket of pain from a deep, deep well. Hand-cranked to the surface and then spilled on the dirt, I came racing back to my wounded body, rocking in a waking nightmare.

I didn't know where I was or what was happening. I was barely aware of being lifted and shoved into the van. I wished I had just stayed passed out from the pain in my privates, my gut, everywhere. It's only natural to reach for the afflicted portion of your body when there's been trauma, especially in your groin. Not possible with my hands locked to my waist by the awful restraints. I rocked back and forth, trying desperately to ease the suffering.

It was my van companion who told me later they had continued to brutalize me even after I quit moving. Guess I passed out from the pain. He also said they had some pretty good laughs and let him know that he had better shut up about what he saw unless he wanted the same. He said they threatened to "clip" him, which in my day might have meant kill, but he understood the slavemaster reference to "castrate." He said he believed them. I did, too.

There was blood all over the lower front of my romper as we resumed our ride, and I teetered on the edge of passing out again. Just off North Federal Street in Harrisonburg, to the rear of the courthouse which faces Main Street, they pulled our van up near a ramp to accommodate the herding of shackled quarry inside the brooding brick walls.

After a short ride on a moveable galvanized steel floor rising higher inside the brick tower, we two inmates were hustled into a real-life cage. I cautiously sat on the far right and my companion on the left facing me, both on torturously shaped chilled steel benches. The cold tore at my mangled crotch, ramping up the misery factor of sitting. I didn't know if even time would make the pain go away, and I was horrified to feel what seemed a line of fire oozing from my body, down the length of my manhood, and out into the bag that substituted for human garments.

Time was frozen as I rocked slightly, feeling the chill pass through my neck and up and across my forehead heralding the onset of a departure from consciousness.

"What's your name, man?" my companion asked.

"Tom. Yours?" I responded, woozy but trying to hang on.

"Jones," was his answer. "They really worked you. You kill a cop or somethin'?"

While I was terribly preoccupied with my scrotum, Jones and I got to know each other through halting conversation as two guys can who are undeservedly imprisoned and whose futures were as murky as a septic tank.

You see, Jones had finished doing a nickel in Buchanan and, though I never asked what for, what seemed most important for him to stress was the fact he was scooped up recently and jailed for "parole violation." Something he adamantly denied. Multiple phone calls to the parole guy, a personal visit to a shuttered office, and a letter prior to moving to a cheaper apartment were not sufficient to keep Jones from being "violated" for doing so without *authorization*. So he was tossed back into the tank, this time in J block of the CVRJ.

We sat and sat. When a Napoleon-sized gun-toting person brought a sack lunch, we ate our bologna sandwiches with gusto. A real sandwich with moderately identifiable ingredients was a treat and a welcome change. Jones shared his belief that "we" in Booking or in Segregation got much larger portions of food-like stuff than did those in the jungles of the alpha-lettered cellblocks.

"Normal ration for us you could fit in the bottom of one of those foam burger boxes," he told me as I shifted in pain. "I've seen grown men, I'm talkin' big, tough guys, crying 'cause they're so damn hungry. Most guys don't have nobody putting money down for them, so they gets what they can."

Some have no commissary delivery, where actual foodstuffs for inmates could be had for a price. Lack of food brings out the survival instinct in humans and other starving animals.

A uniformed man unlocked our cage and led Jones away. I watched as the door to the office down the hall to the left swallowed them both. While the door stood wide, I caught a reflection in its large glass panel. I couldn't quite process it in my condition and hung my head.

As I waited, I jerked with a searing pain that must have been what people speak of in low tones regarding venereal diseases. It was incredibly hurtful! A skull-screamer. I felt that my destroyed sack might just fall off if I didn't support it with an icy hand, and I tried to do so, teeth grinding and eyes squeezed to slits.

I passed my agonized time alone in that breezy cage. I felt that whatever procedure or interrogation was taking place in the far room, I would be the next to be subjected to it.

To my surprise, when the jailer returned with Jones, he showed no interest in me. He just locked the cage and walked away. Jones, my new friend, was ashen. It's just not acceptable jailhouse etiquette to pry about things that are not your business, but Jones was shattered. Maybe even physically hurt. He just looked right through me.

I focused on the end of the hall where the door was standing ajar or perhaps was blocked open. For me, maybe? My eyes are not as sharp as they once were, but I know what I saw. In the glass I saw the image of multiple photographs, some color and some black and white. They were arrayed next to each other, displayed on something much larger than a television or video screen. They looked to be free-floating, as if they were images on a large glass plate or even suspended on air.

At last Jones spoke. Not like he wanted to but maybe like he needed to. He told me that gun-toting non-uniformed people here had shown him his life. Not some fleeting review on a resume or a rap sheet. They showed all the details, successes, and epic fails. These people knew things about him that even he had forgotten.

Along with their diabolical revelations, they fired not-so-subtle insinuations and threats. "How would you like it if ..." and, "Wouldn't it be a shame if ..." They had pictures from his childhood and they knew his first girlfriend's name from grade school and where she was now. They knew about the girl he got pregnant and the time, date, place, and name of the backroom quack who had performed a *procedure* of remedy.

The Feds knew about his relatives trading food stamps for drugs and the things he had to do to survive in the slam. His jobs and his lost chances and his sexual preferences and his experimentations. Every real friend he ever had was represented there. They knew every text message he ever sent and every online post he ever made, or that his kid sister made, or his aunty made. They showed him, he said, things he couldn't believe anybody knew. Every bank his entire family ever used and uses still. How could they get all those things? What right did they have to keep those things and laugh about his less-than-perfect life? Who were these damned pricks, anyway?

Heck, I knew that Edward Snowden, that NSA secret guy, was right all along. That the government was spying on the American people in direct violation of the Constitution and multiple Federal laws, and here is direct proof. That's why they had to viciously discredit Snowden, and they lied through the media to do it. That's also why Snowden had to run for his life. He knew it was risky to do what he did, but he felt he had a moral obligation to expose the abomination. To yell at the top of his voice about the injustice like an "information age" version of Charlton Heston in the movie *Soylent Green* as he tries to tell people the government is feeding them wafers made from the bodies of human beings.

The all-powerful National Security Agency (NSA) routinely taps directly into the servers of at least nine major Internet firms and all with a judge's approval. They collect and keep every character typed, every photo, and every search conducted by everybody. Including me and you. This includes on Facebook, Google, Tik-Tok, Gmail, Hotmail, and more. Nobody listened to Snowden because they didn't realize what it all meant. Violation of their lives and of the Constitution.

I could see why Jones was shaken even if he didn't give me many specifics of what they had threatened him with or what they expected him to do.

"They also wanted to know 'bout you, what you talked about," he said. "They told me I didn't see nuthin' out there an' I better swear to it forever if it gets out."

"I get it," I said, as cool as the flip side of the pillow. "We good."

Why did they bring him here today to show him this power they had? I kept my ideas on that pushed down.

I waited now for my turn in the room down the hall.

We spent hours more in silence. I rose as I could, filling my empty soda can again and again, guzzling water that was clear-ish because my dehydrated body craved it. Besides, it made my stomach feel more full. I decided if I had to take a leak on the way back to the hole, I'd just decorate the inside of the van in pinks and yellows. Serves 'em right.

Civil disobedience H2O.

***

They never came for me at the Terror Tower that day. At the time, I didn't realize the significance of that or the larger implications. Nor would I for the longest time.

I was being subjected to indescribable torture. Why? For what?

I began to reflect on the carefree husband-and-wife outing Sharon and I enjoyed on January 6, 2021.

A FAREWELL RALLY FOR THE PRESIDENT
January 6, 2021

We arrived at the Ellipse in Washington, DC, about 6 a.m. It was dark, cold, and windy, but we were overjoyed at the opportunity to hear President Trump speak. To our shock, the line of citizens also there to see the Prez stretched away into the distance. It snaked past the Washington Monument and onto Independence Avenue, then was lost in the early morning darkness. People had camped out overnight to form up; the queue was five or six abreast and perhaps a mile long. There was absolutely no way on earth we were ever going to get one of the very limited number of seats inside the gates of the White House grounds.

I'd had some trepidation about spending that chilly day in DC because I didn't know if I'd be able to handle a long day remaining mostly on my feet. Sure, I wanted a chance to see the president's final address in person, but as a disabled veteran, I remembered what Dirty Harry said: "A man's gotta know his limitations." As with almost all living with disabilities, I have my good days and my not so good days. With a few absolute rotters thrown in.

Bemoaning the fact I had not layered up sufficiently at the motel, standing in the busy street I looked around and spotted someone I actually recognized. It was Jessica Watkins! This Army veteran and her friends from the Oath Keepers community service group were slated to augment the Secret Service today. She indicated they were waiting to receive some VIP passes, and she invited Sharon and me to enter the grounds with them if they had enough passes. What a break! My back issues would make any kind of seat a heaven-sent alternative to standing all day in agony.

With an underlayment from the free Oath Keepers Tee Shirt giveaway, Sharon and I made lighthearted single-serving friendships with many who had made it here for the occasion from all across the country. I had Old Glory affixed to a staff serving as both my cane and flagpole, and we greeted many total strangers there on Constitution Avenue. These were Americans universally happy and anxious to hear from our current president, who many opined was the best since Ronald Reagan—*another* gentleman the media despised.

At some point, we were told that no one knew where the VIP passes were and that they may not be forthcoming. Thinking that we may not be able to get into the inner Ellipse area at all, Sharon and I said goodbye to Jess and moved to a better (less crowded) location where we could watch the president on a Jumbotron big screen. We spent the next few hours simply enjoying this time in the city of my birth and meeting more people. One of these was Rick, who had made the drive solo from Pennsylvania. He was more than welcome to hang out with us. We gladly shared our energy bars and bottled water, swapping stories about our homes, taking pictures, and singing. Yes, singing.

When the president finally spoke, it was a bit disappointing to learn the public address system was substandard. But that was a minor thing. Sharon and I experienced happiness overload standing and singing with thousands upon thousands of American citizens, who were saying good-bye to the president and who hung on his every word.

As I settled in with my back pain and the energy bar providing what the wrapper promised, we three stopped chatting mid-sentence because of what we heard from the crackly speakers along the thoroughfare.

"We will soon be walking over to the Capitol building to peacefully and patriotically let your voices be heard," said President Trump.

What? Did the president say "*we*"? *We're* going to the Capitol? Holy cow! Is he going to get into the presidential limousine and drive to the Capitol to speak *again*? It had been well publicized that there were to be conservative speakers at the Capitol that day, and Capitol Police had issued permits for these speakers. Metro Police had blocked off roads near the Capitol building to accommodate the crowds expected to arrive for the afternoon remarks.

People moved past us now in a steady stream flowing east. Rick asked if we were up for a trip to the Capitol, since he had never seen it up close. Using a younger man's strength and ease, he pulled me to my feet. I performed a few spinal wave maneuvers to snap my back into place like the old timer I was. With Old Glory still affixed to my staff and another Opana prescription narcotic painkiller in my gut, I was fortified for a stroll to my childhood playground: the west lawn and steps of the U.S. Capitol. The spot where I had once run and laughed and tumbled and picnicked with family and neighbors as a kid.

We joked and laughed and chirped with the folks headed eastward, all of whom passed us by with normal persons' strides and vitality. I, the slowpoke, ambled along as I was able. I didn't even feel sheepish when a lady with a double-seat baby stroller cruised past, an indictment of my shaky, tortoise-like pace. Nor when a guy pulling his kids in a red wagon forged ahead.

I think that was the longest mile I ever trudged in my life. My focus now was finding a place to plant my rear end and take a load off.

There is no public seating on the western side of the Capitol grounds, but in a flash I caught sight of a familiar marble statue: The Peace Monument! This majestic monument, built to honor the men who fought in the Union Navy during the Civil War, is immortalized in photos of the Vietnam Veterans Against the War activists who came to Washington to protest in the 1970s. I clearly remember the time my sainted Dad and I watched the very active crowd protesting from afar. That throng had famously occupied the inaugural balcony and spilled down stairways and across the manicured west lawns a half-century ago.

A spot on the edge of the monument facing away from the Capitol itself looked welcoming and plenty wide enough to accommodate the three of us there among a growing gaggle. Wow. We finally made it![3]

The people-watching opportunity was tremendous! Several guys walked by with an impossibly huge banner emblazoned with soaring Jefferson-esque script "We The People." Yes, there were many good citizens here, and many waving Trump flags, American flags, flags representing their ethnicity or state, who wanted if not to be *heard*, at least to be *seen*. We The People matter. We The People are here. As we have a right to be.

By the end of this eventful day, Sharon and I had taken more than 200 pictures and videos. It was time now to take a happy snap of Sharon and me, chilly but smiling and glad to be together.

I supposed the Congresspeople were doing *something,* but who knows what they do and I had no idea of the process or the timing of anything. Chatter reached our ears from fellow citizens, most glued to their smartphones: Yes, Congress is gone. The "Certification" was complete, they said, and Congress had left the building for home. Might as well think about heading home, too.

I stood and peered around the fountain toward the west face of our Capitol. Now I could view the sea of people on the west lawn where my family had enjoyed picnics in the 1950s and '60s. A crowd was growing on the inaugural balcony above and along the railing of the level even above that. The crowd packed the sidewalk and the wide stone stairs leading to the Capitol and off into the distance.

I'd been up and down those stone steps many times as a running, laughing child. The days of "running" are long gone, but we all agreed we'd climb up there for a couple of pictures looking back across the crowd toward the Washington Monument, just for a memento. There clearly was no one saying "no." There were no signs, no barricades, no police. I was born in this town. This is the people's house and all are welcome, at least on Capitol grounds, right? It's always been that way.

It was a slow go, smushed in the crowd, up steps and beneath towering temporary scaffolding. Now I was worried. Dozens of knuckleheads were climbing on it like so many monkeys, and the scaffolding was swaying! How on earth would I protect Sharon if that scaffolding came down on top of us? There were so many people massed behind us we couldn't go back the way we came. Just short of desperate, we spied a little path through a wooden safety tunnel built to shield people from objects falling from above. This was our escape route.[4]

With Rick in the lead, we left the river of people and joined a modest trickle to emerge from the plywood onto the inaugural balcony. By this time my back was screaming. What I needed now was to reach a wall and press into it for a poor-man's chiropractic adjustment. Realigning vertebrae as I've done many times.

I found a wall, and it did the trick, but then I was counting down the minutes to when my legs no longer worked. It's just the way my spinal injuries manifest. To heck with the smiling-tourist snapshots, I thought, I've got to find a way to get us down from here! I bit my lip and headed toward the railing of the inaugural balcony. It was an impressive view, but I locked in on what was some kind of emergency fire escape. I began gesturing emphatically that this was the way *down*![5]

As Sharon weaved toward me through the throng, I whipped out my android phone for pics of the crowd. Then another, another, another in rapid succession. I stashed my phone and, with Sharon beside me, held her flag and mine amid the fist-pumping crowd's chants of "U-S-A, U-S-A." I got my memento, and Sharon would get hers as she began to record a cheery video. Everybody was so joyful, some waving to the crowd below and some simply squealing as if at a college football game. Come to think of it, the last time I experienced first-hand a lusty group-chant of "U-S-A, U-S-A" was at a ball game.

Sharon was providing running commentary to her video and panned the balcony scene. Ever the goof bag and wanting only to add to her obvious happiness at this high point of our day, I made a less than complimentary reference to the irascible career politician and suspected winebibber Nancy Pelosi. As is my Constitutional right to do. Sharon's laughter was my payoff.[6]

Then we left.

That evening as I dealt with the back pain and medications, the television commentary and "reporting" simply did not ring true to Sharon and me. Talking heads crowed of violence and police gassing the crowd, but we had seen no such thing. We were there in person, so where was all of this nastiness that was being talked about?

Could it be that, like so many other events in the past few years, especially those involving conservatives and Christians who seemed well represented among the festive attendees that day, all the reporting about it was a fabrication? I wouldn't put it past them. This narrative about a place where we had actually been and an event we attended simply did *not* reflect our experiences. Nor did it match what we captured in our photos. What was going on? You can't trust "the media".

Sharon and I had been there and seen our president in person! In a few days, our pictures would be sent to family and friends across the country along with descriptions, jokes, and satire. Those historical photos of January 6 were duplicated multiple times and saved among the record of our two decades of our life together.

How sweet that life is!

***

It was hard to recall the innocence of our husband-and-wife date on January 6, 2021, and at the same time reconcile *that* reality with my present one.

Government goons had made their statement by dispensing a work-boot vasectomy and keeping me from meeting with counsel. Civil rights are a snappy slogan until the government decides that some people don't rate any, regardless of what the Constitution says. I had always supported the Thin Blue Line. Now that support was wearing thin. Dylan said it: The times they are a changin.'

Shoved back into the CVRJ in Orange, Virginia, Jones and I took our places as ordered before the loafing guards at the intake desk. Almost immediately Jones was led back to an uncertain future in J block and I to the entrance of the hallway combination shower/changing/rape locker. Shackles roughly removed, I tried to perform a wrist rub. The right one was black and blue and very swollen, broken from my being cast down at the side of the road. I would receive no medical attention here in the Death Camp.

The door to the space was open and remained that way as I was told to step inside and strip out of my bloodied Federal jumpsuit. I dropped it to the floor, wondering what kind of jollies these guys would try to get at my expense. Thankfully, repeat of a physical violation never materialized as I struggled to change jumpsuits. The federal tormentors who cursed at me during my transformation were still laughing together as they left me.

Two new unfortunates were brought from around a corner of this maze to stand beside me at the wall and await ... something. These were some hard-looking men and I could feel their eyes on me as I stood with gaze forward, loose and disinterested. But damn, my testicles hurt! I must have looked to this assembly of young toughs like somebody's grandpa about to keel over.

"Whatchu here for?" asked the muscular black man nearest me.

"I'm here 'cause some pricks don't like me," I said, as my relaxed eyes turned his way. "It's that whole January 6 at the Capitol. I didn't do anything."

"What they charge?" he wanted to know.

I spit-snorted before answering. "Conspiracy," I told him and so told them all. "Look, I've done lots of stuff in my time but I never conspeer-ee-ated anybody!"

He responded with, "When they got nuthin', they just charge you with *conspiracy*. They don't got to prove nuthin'. Just get some creeper to say bad stuff 'bout you."

Another class of *creepers*!

My groin hurt so bad I just wanted to puke and get it over with. Dizzy and sick, I was muscled by my uniformed escort toward my walk-in freezer code named Segregation 101. I tried to walk bowlegged like a caricature of an old-timey sailor, just to keep my thighs from rubbing against the giant bruise that used to be my privates.

BLANG!

I sat on the frosty concrete: the only type of cold compress available. This was all there was for me: a floor and an orange tray of non-edible gruel presented at my arrival. Both cold.

Ever slam your thumb with a hammer? Unless you've done some major damage, eventually the pain subsides 'til you've forgotten about it altogether.

Well, what if it *didn't* subside? What if the pain was just as intense five or six or seven hours later as it was when you first were injured?

That's the reality I was dealing with. It was *not* subsiding. Of course, the whole illustration with the hammer and thumb business flies out the window if you smash that thumb nine times in succession. Same with testicles. I don't even know if I had an ice pack or a bottle of narcotics or a fifth of Scotch or all three at once if I could have made this pain die down. I was leaking, for heaven's sake! What if I was ruptured? With no medical help here, something like this could get worse and worse. Bleeding out internally. Infection, spontaneous amputation, who knows?

It was late in the day and I asked for a trip to Medical (denied), then began my bid for phone access with every part of me throbbing in a rage of pain. I really needed to connect with Sharon. To hear her beautiful voice. I love her so much. Will we ever be together again?

The guards weren't going to bring me the phone today.

I was old and battered. I was severely wounded. Physically. Emotionally. Spiritually. Maybe you're younger and stronger mentally and physically than I and maybe you could handle day after day of inhumane abuse. Only later did I fully comprehend the huge career wager the DOJ lawyers were placing on the prison's ability to break me. To get me to deal. Or to die.

A miscalculation on their part, only by the grace of Almighty God.

There is plenty of time to think...and to remember...in dungeon solitary.

Did you know that pain, I mean the worst pain ever, unimaginable pain, has a color? As my vision had narrowed to a shrunken keyhole of sight during my abuse face down in that gravely road I could *see* pain. Shattered again and again by brutal kicks to the groin, the searing pain overloaded and took control of my brain. After a while, I *saw* the pain as much or more than felt it. I had somehow reached the limit of my ability to register it, to tolerate it, to process it normally. Other senses took over.

As the final blows were landing to the sound of the criminal's taunts, my world was tinted yellow-orange and so too everything in it; I looked through pee-lensed granny glasses at a visual point falling away from me. The wet grass, the vanishing focal point, even the solid side curtains closing in from my peripheral vision were all ablaze in identical color as pain registered more through sight and ever less through the shocked nerves.

Even strapped back in the van, this alien world devoid of God's Love, His Peace or a shred of humanity was stained a sun-flashy yellow-orange. Feeling the rise of vomit in the body I was thinly tethered to, every jumbled thought in my brain was tainted this color of pain. I was limp against the seat harness, swirling in it. In my semi-consciousness, only that thin wire pulling me back into a savaged body responded to me. Pulling me back to a place I didn't want to be.

This color of pain would return in the weeks to come, though I had no idea when or to what degree.

***

A flick of a tormentor's wrist and the total darkness returned without warning. And with it the demons. And oh, the horrors that came with them. By design, courtesy of the guards.

This night was sheer panic. I had seen what the dark could bring in my sleep-deprived state, where I couldn't process information, couldn't think straight, and I was so very tired. The pain was unbearable. I puked up the food substitute. I was freezing to death. To death! I just wanted to go home!

I was shivering so badly, just so darn cold and I thought for a moment what's the use? *How many nights would they force me through this? Can't I just drift away and sleep at last? How can anybody sleep when their heart is slamming the way mine is now? Pounding like I'm running a race for my life that I can't win. I can't outrun them. The things all around me. Inside me.*

Torture.

The darkness.

Chapter 4

Isolation and the SHU

I was a total mess at my meeting with Lawyer Tom on the day we were allowed to stare at each other through the bulletproof glass. He said the act of taking me from the slammer was called *Diesel Therapy,* though mine, which included the pain part, was the "special handling" variety. The timing and the action were meant to deny me access to counsel and instill a feeling of helplessness, but what could *he* do about it? His shrugging acceptance of this common practice really made me mad.[1]

He went on to inform me that the primary prosecutorial malefactor in my persecution to date wasn't Kavanaugh from the sham bail hearing, but an individual named Kathryn Rakoczy. Lawyer Tom said she was positively out to make a name for herself on the broken bodies of people like me. I wondered silently if Rakoczy was the "her" my roadside torturer had instructed me to plead with.

Tom had also researched Michael Palian, the FBI guy. He said Palian had probably six years invested in his Ph.D. in biochemistry. It appeared that Palian's "life experience" consisted of many years in an academia "bubble," then 20+ years in the FBI "bubble" working primarily on health care fraud. I can only assume he was hired for his supposed "smarts": Oooh, a Ph.D., wow! But regrettably, it seems he had no real-world law enforcement experience. Unfortunately, over the last two decades and more, this has been the predominant hiring practice at the FBI. While the Bureau used to seek the best and brightest "battle-tested" law enforcement personnel, they now hire malleable youngsters directly from colleges and universities who often have no law enforcement experience nor, apparently, a capacity for deductive reasoning. Great.

Lawyer Tom was blunt in his assessment when he called the lawyers at the DOJ "true believers." I knew without his needing to spell it out that he wasn't referring to followers of Jesus Christ.

I don't like to say that this meeting I had been so desperate for seemed in many ways hurried or perfunctory. I'll simply say that it wasn't fulfilling, even though it was unnecessary for me to convince my new lawyer of my innocence. He totally understood and had reviewed what materials Sharon could muster, which screamed it. In a short while, he rose to leave.

We still did not have a date set for another hearing and a chance at freedom. My despair was not eased by this time with lawyer Tom. Quite the contrary. I kept playing over and over a statement he made as an absolute:

"Clearly the DOJ *knows* you're innocent. But they don't care."

***

Shortly after my return to the dungeon, I was prepped to move again. Punishment for the sin of meeting with an attorney?

The bruised-cojones death march took me to an entirely new area of the Gulag complex. Holding back the pain-induced crotch-call to vomit, I was led into an area with cabinets, carts, and other hospital-looking items. People loafing and chatting barely took notice as I was led to an open concrete vault just past a mysterious access door behind which was a closet-sized void.

The dread solid door slam heralding my lockdown sounded more like a death-knell every time I heard it.

Solitary confinement part two.

The sameness. Steel-reinforced concrete-block walls painted gray with a veneer of dust and grime. What *was* new was the raised cold steel sleeping shelf, which featured two always-stuck drawers underneath, where one could store meager belongings if they had any. This was another lonely tomb but it was thoughtfully designed in such a way that nowhere could one curl up and be in other than a direct breeze. No corner offered protection from the blast, neither floor nor rusty intended slumber-shelf, with the smell and stickiness of stale urine.

The flickering, loudly humming fluorescent light was an especially bothersome touch.

This part of the slammer was called "Medical," though nothing medical for me would be found in this wing. I did eventually manage to ask a question of a mildly surly and distracted woman who passed by with a cart. No, I couldn't get my medicines that Sharon had brought and no, I couldn't get an aspirin or a Tylenol or an ice pack for my crotch or another blanket or anything. When asked what I had to do to officially request any of these things, she said she didn't know. At least the service at the CVRJ Orange was consistent.[2]

Consistently awful.

A CO noisily opened the observation window cover and caught my attention. After some pleasant back and forth, she agreed to put me on "the list" for the phone, though she didn't know when the callbox would be available. She also told me that the Gulag actually had an established method, called a "Request Form," for fielding and ignoring inquiries from the warehoused rabble. And no, she didn't have one, but perhaps one of her fellow rounds-makers did.

At least I knew what to ask for now.

What I really wanted Satan Claus to bring was at least a partial delivery of my Commissary order, most notably the long-sleeved "thermal top" which might go a long way toward stopping the freezing cold shakes that tormented me constantly. It sounds stupid now, but I thought my request might actually be answered with something other than what I got: silence.

I parked myself on the floor by the door of my isolation pit, listening for the sound of jangling keys which foretold the approach of a guard. Who knew which one might actually have a request form? With a simpleton's positivity, I asked for one from a particular female CO making her rounds through Medical. This nose-tackle of a woman was particularly sour, and her attitude oozed hatred for the unfortunates she lorded over. Built like a keg of sour apples with a head, I would have more than one encounter with her. My first went this way:

"Excuse me, CO," I asked politely. "Do you think you could give me a Request Form, please?"

"No," she snapped.

"Could you tell me how I could get a Request Form?"

"I don't have any!" She raised her voice with this reply.

"Okay," I continued. "Could you tell me how I can get a Request Form?"

"Put in a Request," she growled.

"Excuse me?" I answered back, not believing I had heard correctly.

"I *said* put in a Request Form to get some damn Request Forms!" she shouted at me.

She slammed the viewing ports cover in my face with the authority that gave her identity.

So ... this employee actually told me to put in a form, which I did not have, to request the form I wanted. My head spun at her hostility and twisted jailhouse logic.

What a witch.

There is so much I can't tell Sharon and shouldn't. How could she deal with my roadside beat down? How do I tell her about the insomnia, struggling to sleep even *with* my CPAP, waking up over and over in the darkness to find I'm in the saddest, most evil, loneliest place on the planet? *This is where bad dreams are real. This is where the screaming is not only all around me but also inside me. Even my silent screams for her are answered with pitiful echoes.*

On the call with Sharon that night, I tried to stay upbeat for both our sakes.

No worries, because Sharon and I still felt things would be okay, and when we were reunited things would be put right. Good night, my love.

Then the lights went out again. The dark creatures returned. The walls hissed and my brain registered their message of hopelessness and fear.

***

I was lying on the icy floor, staring out through the open gruel slot, when I saw a familiar face purposefully approaching my kennel. It was Doris from Classification. She handed me something that looked like a standardized memo. I looked at her, rather than at the paper, as she asked if I was okay, and I gave her a one sentence assessment of my deterioration. She offered no solutions, and I didn't expect any.

I read the form in my hand.

Central Virginia Regional Jail
Institutional Classification Committe

Date: 2/2/2021
Inmates Name: CALDWELL , THOMAS
Block: MEDICAL
Sentence: NOT SENTENCED (FEDERAL)

I.C.C. Recommendations:

IT IS RECOMMENDED THAT THIS INMATE REMAIN IN MAX-RESTRICTIVE HOUSING FOR HIS SAFETY, AND TO INSURE THE SECURITY AND CONTROL OF THE FACILITY.

It bore the signature of the Classification Officer.[3]

Hey, I wondered, in an irritated, nitpicky mood, isn't it ENSURE, not INSURE?

I regarded the words on the form and processed them as best my tortured brain could muster. My *safety*? I don't feel *safe*. I can be thumped here by the guards and the marshals easier than anywhere. And with no witnesses. Max-restrictive housing means solitary, and it is not a safe place. It's only a place to crouch and shiver in a filthy corner, waiting for the next indignity.

I set to pondering how my leaving solitary could somehow undermine the very security of this, Vlad Dracula's Antarctic Schloss.

If one broken-down veteran posed a serious threat to the "control of the facility," then this facility was in big trouble and every one of the people working here should find other employment.

***

I was so exhausted that sometimes I faded off into a twilight zone of almost-sleep, resulting in a gasping, wheezing alarm telling my body it had been cut off from the supply of oxygen. Next was a desperate last-ditch lurching to bring myself to all fours, the proven position to help end the collapsed-lung breathless grip of near death. Engaged so in my struggle, I paid no heed to COs who might be taking in the spectacle from behind glass, though I could feel and hear them. None ever called to me or inquired if I needed help, no matter how I gasped for a single breath. As far as I knew, not one of them informed medical personnel of the episodes they witnessed.

Whenever the lights were on in this dungeon, so too was their hypnotic flickering and buzzing from high above me. After a while it echoes inside your skull and throughout your body. The flash-pulse of the light fixture is straight out of the torture handbook and precisely as depicted in countless Hollywood movies about breaking people's minds. Flash, flash, flash, the heartbeat of visual disturbance torture, set to the tune of the alien buzz and thrum from fixtures and walls. Even eyelids tightly shut could not stop the battle with blinking lights and the sound that never relented.

Isn't solitary supposed to be some kind of punishment? I kept coming back to the question with no logical answer. Why was I being *punished*? What had I *done*? I was held captive by the Department of Justice for what they consider deviant political views, I guess. Deviant only in that they might not conform to the DOJ's own propagandized mindset. It's about power, remember?

People like me are thrown into solitary based on charges or decisions that are invented, adjudicated, and enforced by officials with little or no outside oversight. Except in my case, I have a good argument for "special handling" and "total isolation" being diktats from the Feds. I was an enemy of *their* invention, after all. The Central Virginia Regional Political Prisoner Death Camp is only warehousing me.

***

The shackle-induced cut on my left ankle broke open today, producing blood and other stuff, not surprising considering the unsanitary conditions in here. That other stuff was the same indicator of rapidly advancing infection I had witnessed a time or two when stationed overseas. Infection could set in with blinding speed in filthiness.

It was important to squeeze out the infection as best I could. With fingers and palm glistening with goop, I was inspired to decorate my "death face."

In the best traditions of the proud Native American warriors who, like me, were persecuted, locked down, and perhaps marked for extermination by the U.S. Government, I traced finger-paint parallel lines on both cheeks, along my forehead and the length of my nose. I turned my face this way and that, regarding my work in the ghostly semi-reflection of bullet-proof glass. Not half bad, I thought.

My post evening-sludge Moon Pie tasted pretty darn good. So good that after I had written a letter I intended to send to Sharon, I treated myself to another. Who is there to tell me no? I needed to get *some* kind of nutrition.

In the wicked U.S. Government stockade, the noble Geronimo never got Moon Pie.

***

There was no good news in my telephone calls with Sharon. With each day came another government-planted press article of fake accusations, another television show calling her husband a terrorist, telephone answer machine recordings of people looking for interviews or communicating death threats. Still, our husband-wife calls were as essential to each of us as the air my agonized lungs strained for during one of my "episodes."

Sharon was never able to call *me* on the phone, so our time was determined by the COs and whether the phone would be rolled to my door. Not to mention whether the SECURUS phone system properly credited her deposits into our phone account. These calls were expensive, especially once the phone jokesters started disconnecting us in the middle of our calls. They knew I would instantly call back at $3.85 for the first minute. I did what anyone would do—I dialed again, and the charges would mount. Sometimes we were interrupted this way multiple times on the same call. The jail cadre was determined to have their petty torments.[4]

Every one of my calls, including those falling under attorney-client privilege with Lawyer Tom, were recorded and *shared* with law enforcement *and* many non-government personnel, including other defendants and their attorneys. That is a fact. In my case, we would learn about it from the government transgressors themselves via a thing called *discovery*. I guess they were desperate for some imagined prosecutorial advantage.[5]

For Sharon and me, maintaining a positive attitude during our calls was difficult, but we were always so happy to talk to each other that we managed somehow. We laughed and prayed together and made plans for when I would soon be released. We still thought that the law would protect us. We just didn't know the true nature of the DOJ power arrayed against us both. Being in a concrete coffin with a lack of mental or spiritual stimulation was taking a serious toll on my psyche and deepened my isolation and a feeling of destructive loneliness.

Our love for each other and our Faith, especially our Faith that God would strengthen and protect us, must have driven the DOJ flunkies and their patrons absolutely nuts! It drove them so crazy that, in their view, something had to be done! They denied me essential medicines, starved and beat me, subjected me to flashing light and sound tortures and isolation in total darkness. Still, I had not broken.

They had to do more to crush me. I was, despite the best combined efforts of the DOJ and the prison operators, surviving. They probably couldn't fathom how.

So it was that SECURUS was instructed to block the numbers I had been using to contact Lawyer Tom and both Sharon's smart phone and our home landline. My efforts to call merely netted me a mocking pre-recorded message. The phone lifeline had been purposely severed.

And there was more wickedness to come.

It began with the end of a sleepless vigil beside the capstone of my vault. I was still totally consumed by a wretchedness steeped in non-stop shivering and the agony of mauled testicles. That's when I was told I would be moved once again. Punishment perhaps for too many request forms or for daring to get a defense attorney or for not pleading for mercy from a government inquisitor?

Or maybe for not dying yet.

The duo of COs tasked with my transfer were taking me to the absolute depths. The land of the Super Max: the notorious SHU.[6]

The difference between the Segregated Housing Unit, or SHU (pronounced "shoe"), and most other places in the prison was that if you left your dungeon for even a moment, or if they were taking you to the SHU for the first time, it was in full restraints: leg shackles, heavy waist chain and double handcuffs in front, the whole bit. I had gotten a full dose of that once I climbed aboard the solitary confinement carousel.

Fellow cast-offs from society stared through the heavy glass side of their cellblocks at somebody's grandpa limping past until at last we reached the Special Housing Unit.

This is the Hole of which Darryl had spoken. If solitary confinement is a prison within a prison, then this is the next step downward to the Devil's lower intestine. It is the maximum-security portion of the CVRJ Orange, Virginia, Gulag. My escort with whom I had been chatting cordially, now relieved of his responsibility, wished me "good luck, Mr. Caldwell." Right nice of him, actually.

I was in an open area, standing momentarily at the apex of a two-tiered formation of concrete boxes, the long legs of the triangle stretching away to left and to right. Pooling water on the floor just ahead suggested a shower somewhere. To my right were two round tables with affixed seating circles that looked to me like torture equipment. Hope I'll never have to sit on one of those, I thought.

High on a wall was a permanently mounted television, about the size of a small briefcase. A television, as it turns out, I would never have occasion to watch. Nor would there be exercise or library privileges. Not for this detestable. After all, this is the *SHU.*

I was shoved to the steel jaw yawning wide to gulp me into my latest dungeon, still lugging my sleep wraps and my clunky CPAP machine. I set my burden down with an anguished groan, my back absolutely screaming from the long trek as if a butcher knife had been plunged into my spinal column. A gray-haired CO set the rest of my meagers inside.

Next came the *unchaining* part. Face flat against the concrete wall, raise first one ankle, then the other. Unchained from the ankle restraints, turn around so they can unlock the handcuffs from the heavy chain wrapped around your waist. Chain released, it was on to the next phase. Demeaning, as it was intended to be. All of this was part of SHU protocol—harsh and heartless standard procedure for me, a guy with nary so much as a speeding ticket.

BLANG!

The steel door lockdown broke my heart as never before. The sound of hope dying. I was really dragging.

As would always be the case here, once the tomb was closed with the steel cap's slam, the gruel shelf came crashing down. I was ordered to bend painfully over and extend bound wrists through the slot so some CO could release the steel-toothed grip of the final ligatures from my frozen skin.

Sitting at the very edge of what passed for a sleep shelf, I noted that it was not nearly as chipped up and rusted as others had been. Being sliced open did not seem like a certainty as it had elsewhere. It didn't look to have been recently filled with urine like the others either, not that I could smell anything other than the mustiness of this cell.

Running left to right above toilet and sink was a heavy-gauge metal housing that could be a wind tunnel or an air passage. A rap from my knuckles confirmed it was hollow. It was attached to a concrete rectangle dropped down slightly from the ceiling and again running left to right. To my right hand was a forehead-high vent spewing chilled air and toilet paper tassels dancing to its tune.

Close to the vent was a recessed speaker. I surmised this device was for monitoring my conversations and activities; it may also have hidden a pinhole camera, but I didn't care and didn't check.

Locked inside dungeon Number 4.

That's when the Welcome Wagon arrived.

A male voice echoing through the ductwork. That was how he manifested in this nightmarish land.

The voice asked my name and introduced himself as *Boo*. He asked me what I was in for. I told him an abbreviated January 6 thing and how it was all just garbage. In the next few minutes, Boo would totally surprise me and become one of my most unforgettable characters.

His take on my situation and the events of January 6 was thoughtful and insightful. I don't know why I was surprised at this. His opinion was that the whole "insurrection" was an inside job coordinated by the FBI with their Special Agents and other paid trouble-makers playing an active role. All at the behest of the people holding the puppet strings for the Democrat political party.

I padded through a tour of my lonesome Dungeon number 4 as Boo guided me. He thought fast and spoke fast, an ethereal voice here in the Hole, intent on helping rather than wounding. He said he had occupied the box number 4 space and had been moved to make way for my confinement. I didn't know if I should apologize for being the reason he was yanked to the second level crypt right above me, but I said nothing.

With a realtor's open-house zeal, Boo told me that I would like it there because the toilet was dependable and it was the only grave he knew of in this house of horrors which occasionally offered hot water at the sink. The drop-down section of the ceiling above the toilet and sink housed the water lines that brought fluids, both cold and hot, to the phone booth-sized splash locker just outside.

The gregarious Boo declared that he was one of the undesirables, too, but not because of J6. Because of the color of his skin. Our discussion, which at this point was more akin to the whole wide world according to Boo, was relaxed and easy. We both agreed that psycho Schwab is truly dangerous, maybe even more than a guy named Soros. Best to keep an eye on him for sure, said Boo, 'cause we will all get screwed. Only he didn't say "screwed."

My new friend was incensed as I described the takedown at our home and agreed that it was more than luck that Sharon had escaped "death by FBI," as he put it. The next surprise was that Boo had already heard about me. This was through a combination of the prison's "jungle telegraph" method of news sharing and the propaganda spewed by the idiot box on the wall in the common area. My ears burned as he told me how the television talking heads trashed me by name.

And of course, Boo confirmed that this was the most frightening portion of all in the prison. Overrun by duppies[7] and skinwalkers which inhabited the walls alongside other apparitions and elementals.

"They'll talk with you, man," he predicted.

Great. Dark spirits and demons for company. Haven't we had enough of that already?

Finally a natural silence descended until I piped up to say I was going to try to take a nap and he responded that he had to take a big dump anyway. Perhaps, I thought, as I strapped on the CPAP mask and eased my aching body down into my nesting materials, I can sleep. *If I just close my eyes and lie very still and cover up, maybe I can sleep.*

Thank you, Lord.

I did.

***

My friend Boo's preferred method of communication was yelling at the top of his lungs, which he did often when conversing with those locked elsewhere in the SHU. It was happening right now. There was a handful of internees cliqued up and their hollers carried some news of the day or an off-color reference I could tap into. Boo seemed to have a very short fuse, which could be lit by anyone at any time of any day for any reason. He could really spew the cuss words. I respected that in here.

Sometime after "room service," it hit me. I jerked like someone had yanked a rope attached to me! Once, then twice. The first jolt brought me to my hands and knees wrapped in my nest on the floor. I yanked off the breathing mask thinking I was drowning for lack of air; the CPAP must have failed me! I couldn't clear my head and I tried to take deep breaths, but my muscles were knotting up, tighter and tighter, in my back and my legs. I rolled over on one side, still I couldn't snap out of it, couldn't clear the fog out of my head. Was I back on the roadside getting brutalized again? Had I been shot? My muscles were killing me the way they do when I get heat stroke: I just couldn't get them to stop getting tighter. I was sweating and shaking hard.

The cold concrete felt soothing the way it does when you've passed out and you find yourself on the emergency room floor. I was so dizzy I thought I'd throw up. I closed my eyes but things were still spinning. I drew up into a ball, but that made my heart feel as if it was being crushed by a giant fist, squeezing the last drop of life out of me! I tried to call out but couldn't manage anything but a sissified squeak. Outside the door, inside the walls, there was shouting, laughing, screaming. Was it the intruders, an attack by the duppies?

Or is this a *heart attack*? I was panting, I couldn't take a deep breath. Why can't I make my muscles work? Through my glued-shut eyelids I saw a pee-colored panorama, a distant something of regular shapes, squares and rectangles, multi-leveled, some stacked on each other. Then black.

I spent that night floating in and out of an anxiety soup, existing in a constant chest-banging cardiac panic.

What has just happened to me?

I have no strength.

I'll just lie here and see what happens next.

***

We had secured a new hearing, supposedly with a real DC judge, and now I had a guy paid to represent me and not some court-assigned hack.

After a month of grueling physical and emotional torment, little human interaction, no toothbrush, no haircut, comb, or razor, I must have looked like a decrepit wild man as I scuffed along, flanked by two uniformed objects of every inmate's scorn. But today was the day! Today was the day of my second detention hearing with prosecutors from the DOJ, Lawyer Tom for me, and a new judge. Today may be the day I can go home to Sharon!

Each step was shaky and sent electric flashes through my legs and spine. I was worried that I might not be able to make it all the way to the front desk area where the tele-condemnations took place. Proudly I met the scrutiny of fellow detestables, then journeyed onward to hear arguments for my freedom.

My surly warder electronically tied us into the Department of Justice "we-got-you-now" closed-circuit TV system after chaining me to a steel tabletop in the video conference closet. He instructed me to shut up even though he followed that instruction with the comment that they wouldn't be able to hear me, anyhow.

Then the clown show began.

Any positivity or hope I had clung to was soon dashed as the monotone Rakoczy conducted her lie-laced harangue against me with a judge who nodded at the appropriate times and asked questions allowing the amplification of her despicable fantasy. I could feel the bottom drop out of my stomach each time my attorney attempted to present an argument and was summarily cut off by the guy in the black robes. On and on it went. I couldn't believe it! I started directing my anger verbally at the TV screen, punctuated by expectorations of air and curses.[8]

Unexpectedly, I heard Kavanaugh-like statements coming *directly from this judge*! You might remember, because I sure do: "an offense which cuts to the very heart of our democracy and the peaceful transition of power," and the "evidence" against me says that I am a danger "to the fundamental fabrics of a democracy that we all cherish!"[9]

What *evidence* did he mean but the knowingly false accusations made by the prosecutor? The transcript would record that the word *evidence* was used at least 44 times during this so-called hearing, but in actuality there was no evidence against me. What about innocent until *proven* guilty?

Sharon and I never had a chance.

I wanted to scream; I wanted to yell! I didn't know *what* I wanted to do. Only to go home! *That's* what I wanted! This is garbage! This is a lie! All of it! And I said so loudly to my captor. Then he switched off the monitor and pulled me to the door.

Dejected and angry, out loud I said, "Lord, how can this be happening? Lord, your justice is over in this country! I've seen it all! Lord, please show me the way or just take me now!"

I shook my head and turned my attention to facing the miserable hike back to the SHU. Heck, I probably even missed the nightly manure offering. However, instead of turning right, which would lead to my vault and a sugar fix, the CO forced me to the left and into the depths of Booking.

We were going the wrong way!

My protests meant nothing to him since this guard clearly was on a mission. I was pushed past the familiar curved desk that featured a fat guard and multiple television screens, then past Cell number 13. We stopped at another cell that smelled of puke and mold. He shoved me inside.

BLANG!

This was a very small punishment cell. There was no water available in this box save for the nasty stew in the toilet. There was a lumpy sleep pad and a blanket, which I took advantage of. I yelled at the door many times for attention from any CO who could tell me when I would be taken back to my place in the SHU. I needed to figure out how to get a call to Sharon!

I was heartbroken, exhausted, in despair.

The carefree life of the Friday night CO crew rolled along outside my steel door. I called out over and over with no response. The eye-in-the-sky leered down at me, and I was getting very angry at this newest insult to me as a human being. After an illegal imprisonment, brutal treatment, lying accusations before a magistrate and a so-called judge, and a *second* denial of release, I was royally pissed-off. This was the moment the beast welled up in me.

After hours being forgotten I had finally had enough.

Mr. Nice Guy was gone.

My ears and my face grew scalding hot with anger and I let it happen. I'd learned a few things during my time in Hell and I unleashed them now. It was no challenge to mule kick the door, even with shackles on my ankles. I reveled at the crashing sound bouncing along outside this vault. I raised up a vociferous, cursing tirade about my treatment and about the nature of my keepers mere steps away.

I mixed in demands to talk to someone in authority. I was angry. The beast was driving now, and these loafers were hearing about it! When someone came to the viewing port and asked me to calm down, I *really* let them have it, still demanding to know what was going on.

At long last, a person identifying himself as Sergeant Jackson came close to the viewing window and asked, infuriatingly, what the problem was.

"What's the ***problem***? What's the ***problem***?" I said. "The *problem* is that I'm being held here in this closet and no one will tell me why. I don't think it's too much to ask to go back to my freakin' dungeon in the SHU! How about ***THAT***, Sergeant Jackson? ***THAT'S*** the ***problem***!"

A non-uniformed lady was with him who might have been the Lydia from Medical whom I had met on my first day. Her eyes never left my window-framed mug. Jackson told me I had been moved to an "observation" cell because the Video Teleconference room guard said I "had been talking to God."

Let *that* sink in for a moment.

"It was his opinion you're a suicide risk," Jackson explained as the lady and several guards who had gathered for the freak show looked on.

That's when the last vestiges of the man I had formerly been told the Sergeant all I felt that I needed to say:

"Are you *kidding* me? I believe in GOD, so maybe your *officer* has a problem," I proclaimed. "Look, man, I'm gonna get another hearing and be home with my wife in a couple of weeks. And by the way, SUICIDE is not an option! HOMICIDE, maybe, but not SUICIDE!" Then I laughed out loud and said no more.

Probably not the time for joking around, but I said it, so there you go.

"Medical-Lydia" smiled slyly at Jackson who smiled back, though he tried to make sure I didn't see.

"Good enough for me!" someone said from the other side of the door.

"Okay, Mr. Caldwell, we'll get somebody to take you back," the Sergeant said, and he walked away.

I had snatched back my humanity for a nanosecond and found regular-type people with a sense of humor. Imagine that. Here, locked in a box, no less! Not *everyone* was an ogre here.

And the wheels of progress began to slowly, so slowly turn. And the beast retreated.

The transport squad turned me over to the guards at the SHU at 11:45 p.m. and I stood weakly in the door to my tomb assessing the damage. Well over five hours in the punishment freezer. Before I was fully unhooked from the waist cable and ankle shackles, I remarked with disgust at what had happened in my absence.

My meager belongings were strewn across the floor, including my bedding items, towel and washcloth and my mini-toothbrush and toothpaste-like substance. The CPAP did not appear to be damaged although there was water everywhere from the machine having been kicked along the floor. It was disappointing to see what kind of people some of the guards actually are.

On a late-night head count much later, one of the nicer COs presented me with two Inmate Request Forms. He asked how I was and said he was disappointed in the judge's decision. The word had gotten around. We talked like people do. Maybe he felt bad for me because someone had trashed my tomb for no reason. Maybe he was just a good person. I'd like to think maybe both.

In the depths of dungeon darkness as I sat on the floor wrapped up in burrito-mode, he returned with four books from the "off limits" prison library. I was truly grateful. Little kindnesses anywhere else in this country are gargantuan in the haunted Hole.

***

Yesterday there had been hopefulness and anticipation. Yesterday I was uncertain, but still with a buoyant feeling that I would be freed by the truth and the judge's discernment, his willingness to consider all people innocent until proven guilty and each person worthy of equal protection under the law. But that didn't happen. I would see this guy again, though I didn't know it yet.

Depression reigns once more. I am tumbled down into a pit that is closing above me.

I determined that the only way I could survive this torture in solitary confinement was to enter an altered mental state. How else to survive the smell-o-vision reality of an immersive horror movie where no director would yell cut and end the fright scene. The impossible goal was to amplify every possible morsel of good news into a spirit-fortifying feast. Harder yet would be to manage somehow to trivialize each succeeding setback and heartbreak like yesterday's: devastating, unending, life-crushing pain so traumatic as to make any escape from reality the only way it could be withstood by a human being. If, after all of this, I was indeed human any longer.

In our call that night, I was not prepared for what Sharon conveyed from her conversation with our lawyer post-hearing. Sharon was informed by our lawyer that he was going on vacation for two weeks! Lawyer Tom's follow-up assurance that he was going to be working on the case while he was away did nothing to dampen the panic in us as we weighed multiple weeks more with me in the Hole. Sharon and I were both bone-tired and wrapped in hurt, sickness, and sorrow.

Note to all criminal defense lawyers: For your clients in lockdown, the most important thing to them is *TO GET OUT!*

There and then, Sharon said she would cast the net wide in each direction, once more asking everyone she could think of if they knew of a good criminal defense attorney. You never know who just might. There were many good people who wanted to help us, and many already were doing so in any way they could. She had been asking for referrals all this time, but she needed a new plan.

Please, Lord, step into the fray to help us.

Since my first medical "episode" in this place, I had been having all kinds of physical and emotional problems. Having long before been determined by the vaunted Department of Veterans Affairs to be a service-connected disabled veteran, my difficulties had been well documented. Ensconced here in the putrid belly of the beast, I was exposed to a whole raft of health-imperiling issues, including sleep deprivation, numbing cold, poor diet, unsanitary conditions, light and darkness tortures, sound torture, physical abuse, mental abuse, poor sanitation, no medical care, non-existent dental care, and, let us not forget, questionable drinking water.

Overarching all of these was the stubborn denial on the part of a "doctor" at the facility to allow provision for any of my *real* doctors' critically needed prescribed medications.

Lawyer Tom had spoken to a person identifying himself as the "Doctor" at the jail. When it was stressed that I was a disabled veteran with a great need for access to my prescribed meds, the "Doctor" had curtly informed my lawyer, "Well, *I'm* his doctor now and *I'll* decide!" End of discussion.

I had no idea at the time—and why would I?—what my frightening medical "episodes" were.

I found out later. They were seizures.

Seizures caused by the abrupt stoppage of powerful prescription medications used long-term.

In my case, a deliberate stoppage demanded by someone employed as a "Doctor" by the State of Virginia. These were seizures, plain and simple. Any medical doctor should have learned the dangers of sudden stoppage of medicines from day one at med school, or from simply reading the fine print on the caution and disclaimer literature accompanying my meds.

Not just one of my meds warned of seizures, not two, but *three* separate meds said stopping this stuff cold had a high probability of many hideous side-effects, including *seizures* and even *death*! Take the high risk and multiply by *three*!

Was this gross incompetence or a deliberate action meant to induce suffering, injury, or worse?

I'd had three crushing seizures now and frankly I was terrified each time. In my fractured mind, I suppose it was better that I was unaware there would be more to come. I didn't know anything about what was happening to me except the suffering itself and the knowledge that afterwards it seemed my body didn't work correctly. I called it "shutting down," especially when things as simple as shuffling twenty feet or so to the shower were more than I could bear.

Pumped into my darkened world all night came a continuous flow of eerie noises. These were the sounds of the "ghost boxes" featured on television shows to allow communication with the realm of the dead. My personal speaker on the wall broadcast a continuous stream of white noise creating an auditory environment perfect for the brain-shattering voices buried within its frequencies. Voices that seemed to speak or shout hard-to-understand sentences or pieces of sentences. Maybe they actually *were* the voices of the dead or else a special late-night torment from the authorities intended to taunt and thrust me to madness.

For each of us within the CVRJ solitary confinement boxes, Hell proved to be uniquely personal, as were the scars left on our humanity. The prison industry had fiendish strategies for the dismantling of identity and comportment. Strategies for the crushing of self. That seemed to be their plan, and I loathed them for it.

I held my nervous nighttime vigil listening to the spirit voices and the screams and wails of the SHU choir: mistreated and lost souls confined in a way both unholy and subhuman. Here in this wretched prison, I thought, I am thoroughly in the grips of something sinister and sick.

***

As weeks in captivity piled up, I had entered an altered state, alright. Here I just knew that getting into the Word was increasingly more important. If I ever strayed from that understanding, it would be Sharon to pull me back on a phone that was working intermittently again. I was certain the forces arrayed against Sharon and me were so powerful only God could turn them back. I asked each correctional officer I saw, but no Bible was forthcoming from the library. Sharon would have to order one online and have it sent here to Hell. I wondered if they would actually give it to me when it arrived.

Early on in this level of solitary, I began handing the books that COs had been procuring for me back to the day shift after I finished them. I asked that they be put on the tables near the showers so my fellow prisoners might grab one after a splash. Putting them there was less work for the COs than lugging them all the way back to the library, so why not, right? I wasn't asking for much. So was born the Tom Caldwell Memorial Library, SHU Branch. There was a turnover of books, which was easy to see whenever I was moved to the clean-up booth myself. I smiled, knowing I had anonymously started something that other captives used. Maybe it helped somebody pass the time and cope with the loneliness.

I wondered if most inmates had a date to look forward to, a goal which, when reached, would bring freedom and signal the start of a new life. A real life. I had no such defined target. My time in the SHU looked more every day to be permanent. Survival, even for one more day, required the use of any tool I could find.

Even though I can still steal a moment to speak with Sharon here and there, I feel so lonesome in this blockhouse coffin. No one else on the outside knows what I am going through, and no one else seems to care about the truth. No one.

Finally, a prayer was answered in a most unusual way. Through the gruel-slot I spied something that looked to be a book under a pile of stuff on an unattended roller cart. No spine bearing the volume's title could be seen, just the page edges, but it looked thick enough to be a Bible, or perhaps something by Michener or Clavell.

The cart sat beside a pile of bedding and personal items a fellow desperado had abandoned. I had learned this pile meant that someone was being released, and prison policy was simply to pile the junk on the floor until some items were thrown away and the bedding materials sent to the laundry. Someone would no longer need this stuff. Someone was getting his life back.

When a harried guard arrived, I got to him with the accepted "Hey, See-O!" attention-grabber. I asked if he could hand me the Bible there. There! Yeah, right *there*! Under all that stuff! He moved the mess christened "stuff" and, lifting the book to examine it, flashed the cover my way. The Holy Bible! How did I know? Maybe he wondered the same. Then he hesitated. I felt my heart start to fall as this guard churned the pages with his thumb, perhaps expecting to see some contraband tumble out as the pages whirred by. Again hesitation.

In retrospect I still sometimes feel embarrassed at what I said next because it sounds, with no context, to be sacrilegious and disrespectful. I have reassured myself that what I said was what the guard needed to hear so he would bring this precious Holy Book to my dungeon door.

"Hey, man. It's *only the Bible.*"

I had only said *exactly* what that particular CO needed to hear to motivate him to hand it over. The Lord had given me the correct words to say.

And then he crossed the divide and held it out for me. I nearly tore the book from his grip, fearing he would yank it away in a demonic game of keep-away from the dying. I withdrew, like the hermit crab into his hole, with my prize: a tattered volume of The New King James Version of the Holy Bible.

Exhausted, utterly alone, in unending pain and all but fully drained of hope, I sat on the cold concrete floor. I opened the Bible with both hands, letting its pages randomly part as they wished.

The first thing the Holy Bible opened to was Psalm 109, which spoke to me directly with these words as I remember them: "The mouths of the wicked and the mouths of the deceitful are opened against me. They have spoken against me with a lying tongue. They have surrounded me with words of hatred and fought against me without a cause."

My heart *leaped* in my chest! *Could it be that God knows what is happening to me?* My eyes flew across the pages and down the columns. I devoured the Word of God—our daily bread—like a starving man gorges on a meal.

I flipped the pages again, and they parted on their own to reveal Psalm 56. "My slanderers pursue me all day long. They twist my words. I will not be afraid." *But God, I <u>am</u> afraid. What can man do to me? Well, just look around me, Lord! <u>This</u> is what they can do.*

I knew these words in the Bible *had* to be a sign! On and on I went, page after random page, as I jumped eagerly through the Bible. My eyes filled with tears. The beasts running the machinery here could not break me down or bring water to my eyes, but this Holy Book did. Everywhere I turned within its tattered cover were words of comfort—the *only* comfort to be found in this place. You are not alone, Sharon told me, but can it truly be? Did I dare to hope that in my misery Jesus is here? Here in this moldy dungeon? *The unholy things lurk all around me. This is Hell. Can His Light dispel the darkness in here?*

I had been very wrong about something: Someone besides Sharon and me *did* know what I was going through in here after all.

***

I have my Bible and try to read throughout the day, but I am busted up mentally. I have the will, but I don't have the strength to read for very long at a time. I begin writing on the white stripes of my inmate jumpsuit. It's not easy with only a flex pen to scratch out letters and numbers, but I am determined, writing upside down so I can read and keep it simple: the number of a Psalm and a few words of a passage that stick with me.

I hear people up and down this prison block exploding into a rage about anything or nothing, especially if they feel that a guard has disrespected them or messed with their stuff. I'd felt the beast inside me once before here in this dump. Will I lose it and will the beast that rises to defend us take over at some future degradation or injury? How about the next time they trash this burial vault I'm stuck in? Trashing happens almost every time I exit to shower. It's better to stay in here, wash in the sink and keep my eyes on my pitiful stuff.

As I lay in the throes of decompensation, having existed so long on the ragged edge with red-lining tension and emotional turmoil, my body was not operating well on its own. It reacted now with frightening physical manifestations, including shaking, tremors, and non-stop heart arrhythmia. I was at the point of exhaustion in a heart-pounding race without end, a headlong sprint where I was outside of myself, watching as both competitor and panicky spectator.

All I have are memories of my loving wife and my family to keep me grounded. Those memories have dimmed and are fading away from me.

I am so damn sick and cold.

I'm losing so much blood from my penis I must be thoroughly anemic by now.

All I can do is stay on the cold concrete floor.

I think I'll just lie here and see what happens.

Chapter 5

Last Chance

It was my dear cousin Barbara who told Sharon that she might know someone who could help us in our time of need. Barbara reached out to a former work colleague and obtained the name and number of the legal superstar who might take up his shield of Faith and the Sword of the Spirit to defend us.

Sharon's telephone call was answered by Mr. David Fischer, an accomplished criminal defense counsel of regional renown. They engaged in a lengthy discussion of the government's bogus case against me and ultimately agreed to meet on a Friday in Frederick, Maryland. On a day marked by February flurries, Dave told Sharon matter-of-factly across the table, "I don't need this case, I *want* this case." There and then a champion arose.

How about that: a real-life David to slay the demonic government Goliath!

On our emotional call that evening, Sharon told me she had met with a great attorney and that this gent would be seeing me tomorrow, which she said was Saturday. I am not someone who believes in luck or in chance. Dave was *sent* to us. Cousin Barbara was our intercessor. While hopeful, neither Sharon nor I had the full picture of just what the hiring of Dave Fischer would mean.

***

By the time I was to meet our new lawyer, my condition had deteriorated to the point that I could no longer walk unaided. A fast-thinking CO hurried off to return moments later with a wheelchair! I was rolled to a cramped interview room, then plopped into a cheap white plastic lawn chair, the type that disintegrates beneath the weight of an unsuspecting bubba on countless funny Internet and television videos.

I think my fully shackled and sickly state shocked Dave Fischer through the thick partition of bulletproof glass. No unhooking was permitted by the guards, so I would remain bound and hurting throughout this meeting. Me, the oh-so-dangerous disabled guy with the blood splotch crotch-high on his jumper.

There under the watchful scrutiny of cameras and recording devices, Dave began to get to know me while asking direct and important questions about the run-up to and events surrounding this thing called January 6. He listened. He took notes. He asked me thought-provoking questions which previous counsel had not, and his easy Kentuckian style not only comforted but curiously energized me. He explained processes and procedures in the federal court system and assured me that we *would* get another release hearing. This Summa Cum Laude from prestigious Oglethorpe University and the University of Maryland Law School seemed to be everything Sharon said he was.

As I slumped in my chair, I was totally focused and never noticed that our initial meeting consumed several hours. The most telling moment in our time together came early-on, probably near the thirty-minute mark, when he stopped and put his pen down to look carefully into my baggy eyes.

"You know, Mr. Caldwell," he said, "... as a defense attorney, people lie to me for a living. But you're *innocent*!"

"*Yeah*! That's what I've been *telling* everybody!"

As far as I was concerned, both Sharon and I wanted him on the case. I thanked him profusely when he finally rose to leave, and though I had no idea then how much he would personally sacrifice during the fight ahead, I had a powerful confidence in him already. I knew he would try his best. I felt as Sharon did: *this* is the guy!

Then Dave asked if I had enough money in my dwindling Commissary account, which I honestly did not know. Bidding me so long for now, and unbeknownst to me, he left to pump up my Commissary-comforts account *personally* from his own wallet.

Wow.

This night's call to Sharon was so many things, from heartbreaking to cautiously upbeat, because of the meeting with our new counsel. We talked about what she had for dinner, I grossed her out describing my evening gag-fare, and we managed to share a laugh. I was grateful that many of our neighbors were being so directly supportive of her. We had some wonderful people in our lives who were appalled at how we were being viciously maligned and attacked. Sharon and I were two older people, deeply in love, well regarded in our community, who were under the cruel thumb of a federal government gone mad.

There seemed to be a pre-approved plan at work to crush us completely. Dave Fischer was formulating a plan as well. Sharon, always faithful, believed and so she prayed, that God had a plan, too. How could I do anything but agree? I heard her delightful laugh when I remarked light-heartedly that God had never told me what His plan was at any time in my life.

Maybe I just needed to know how to listen.

***

At the Central Virginia Regional Jail in Orange, Virginia, all mail arriving for hostages was opened and scrutinized by the staff, and never, ever did the original items get passed to those addressees suffering in their pens. Instead, copy machine renderings of letters, cards, and photographs were made and distributed, some even legible. No possibility of a whiff of a loved one's perfume on a sweet, loving card. No easy read of one's dearest's flowing handwriting sharing family news from the outside. Nope. Bad copies, sometimes with words lopped from the edges of pages. Delivered to us were crude black-and-whites of hopes and dreams.

Curious that they never had trouble faithfully passing me hate mail and death threats, of which I received a great deal. I suppose no one else buried in this cursed ground was getting the same vile and dishonest publicity spew, so I alone was at the sewer pipe end of the incoming rants of the fiendishly insane. A lot of people out there had bought the government's version of the January 6 "Jamboree" without question. Their scribbled threats and taunts made me wonder if they'd ever know how much they deeply needed psychotherapy.

***

FROM HELL

MY SWEET DARLING-

SATURDAY NIGHT AROUND 10 P.M. THEY BROUGHT ME THE XEROX COPIES OF YOUR WONDERFUL CARDS AND YOUR BEAUTIFUL LETTER! LOVED THE PICTURE! THANK YOU! THANK YOU! THANK YOU! I HAVE BEEN SO DEPRESSED AND THESE JUST LIT UP MY HEART! I MISS YOU SO MUCH. WE JUST HAVE TO BE TOGETHER SOON. I AM SO HUNGRY TO SWEEP YOU UP IN MY ARMS AGAIN AND BEGIN A NEW CAREFREE LIFE TOGETHER. SURELY GOD WILL MAKE IT SO.

I HAVE NOT GIVEN UP HOPE BUT EACH DAY AND ESPECIALLY AT NIGHT THE DISBELIEF AND UTTER DESPAIR CRASH OVER ME LIKE A HUGE WAVE AND I STAND, SOAKED, AT THE EDGE A BOTTOMLESS ABYSS. I DON'T KNOW HOW ELSE TO DESCRIBE IT. IF I WERE EVER TO LOSE MY GRIP, I WOULD TUMBLE DOWN AND LOSE MY CHANCE TO BE WITH YOU AGAIN. I HOPE YOU HAVE GOTTEN SOME OF MY DUNGEON SKETCHINGS. GRIM, BUT MAYBE WE HAVE CREATED A NEW GENRE OF ART…WE WILL CALL IT *ENCARSE-SURREALISM* (encarse'-suh-REEL-izz-um)

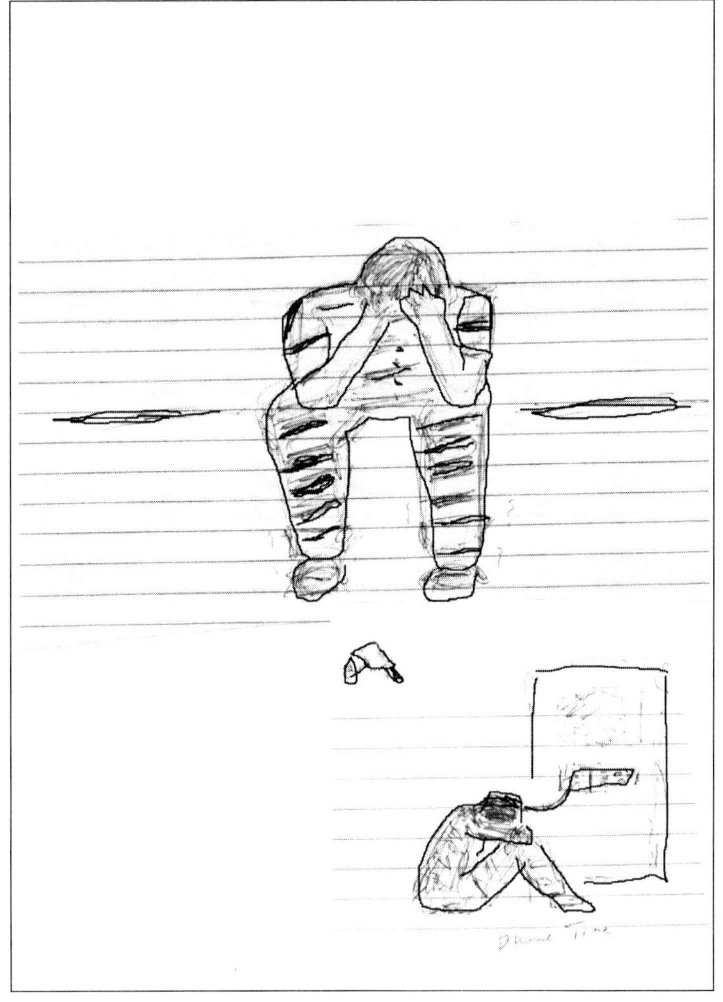

Solitary. Encarse-surrealism in ballpoint on lined paper, by Thomas Caldwell, 2021

Tortured sketches were a way of showing the desolation of the "inside" now growing inside of *me*. Smuggling out a graphic record of what is and what may ever be. *I am denounced without the ability to face my accusers, condemned to Jeffrey Dahmer's freezer where, as with the other victims, pieces of me are being chipped off and devoured bit by bit.*

My prison experience was and is deeply troubling. In my very earliest days of denied freedom, I had interaction with others who shared a bond of uneasiness, anger, and hopelessness. The conscious decision to thrust me, a person with no criminal history, into this sadistic madhouse, into a dungeon of total isolation, is itself criminal on multiple levels.

There. I said it. This was one in a series of criminal acts, from threatening my wife and me with bodily harm, even death at gunpoint, to kidnapping me, torturing me and ignoring my Constitutional rights, my civil rights and my human rights. These are all crimes.

I have no first-hand knowledge of the dangerous world of the overcrowded cellblocks in this rotten place. I only know the realities of the part of this prison absolutely guaranteed to inflict long-lasting damage to the inmates: an internment of indeterminate length in solitary. There was no society here *per se* and no culture save the culture of intimidation, domination, sadism, and fear.

I've heard that sadism is often an effect of hereditary alcoholic blastophthoria. So maybe that's in play here in Orange, Virginia.

There was no exercise or recreation period available at this prison dumping ground. Forget the China Virus excuse. I and all detainees have rights, and these rights were willfully violated across the board. Doctors and guards darn-well knew that we in solitary stood a much higher chance of developing mental health and other problems by virtue of isolation and were *more* in need of fresh air and exercise than any other interned people. Yes, I said "people" because that is what we were and are. The hierarchy cannot sidestep its responsibilities, either professionally or as human beings. This is abuse and it is not right. It may in fact be criminal.

"Recreation" was curiously defined in this complex by "The Man." There was established the one half-hour per day one could request, bound in the chains of shame and perched on an agonizing steel pedestal, the chance to stare upward at the flickering wall mounted TV. Yes, literally sitting motionless, bound in chains. In this place, electronic reeducation was laughably designated as "recreation."

I had been assigned a non-negotiable reeducation programming period at a specific time of day. Offered to me but once to serve as my recurring mid-morning "recreation" time, this was my opportunity to watch the vapid hate-mongers on "*The View*." As Mason said to Dixon when they were surveying, "We gotta draw the line *somewhere*!" This is where *I* draw the line. Friend, some things are just cruel and unusual punishment in anyone's book. Here's your glaring example. None for me, thanks.

They never offered this "recreation" to me again after I laughed in their faces.

Evening television fare for those allowed it comically consisted of *Law and Order* re-runs to imprint upon the enslaved that crime did not pay and that the cops and the law schoolers were the chosen ones. Everyone else was *not* among the chosen. Read: inferior.

I clearly recall an episode of that popular series prior to my time in prison, where the pompous legal hack Jack McCoy (an amalgam of the prosecutors attacking me now) willfully lied to a grand jury in order to incarcerate a person. *Law and Order* "geeks" will immediately recall the episode. In my recollection, an honest person questioned what was going on, given the lack of any evidence. The "heroic" lawyer McCoy basically responded with "trust me" or some such. He, and thus Hollywood, was *really* saying: it's okay to violate the rights of people if it serves the "common good"— as defined by government lawyers and Hollywood itself, of course.

The main character in this series had violated a person's rights and all legal ethics because he wanted a conviction above all else, and we were supposed to dismiss his malfeasance as no big deal. A lie and a miscarriage of justice, which I had no way of knowing at the time, was exactly what had been planned by Kathryn Rakoczy and a co-conspirator named Jeffrey Nestler.

Real life imitates "art."

***

"The individual who persecutes a man, his brother, because he is not of the same opinion is a Monster."

—Voltaire, 18th century French satirist and philosopher

I have to believe that in our meetings I helped Dave Fischer address each of the prosecutors' invented claims. I sure tried. This while I sat chained hand and foot in the wheelchair I now needed. I had been abused to the point where I was unable to walk unassisted to any session with him.

Dave wanted to know all about the voluntary three hours-plus interview I gave to the FBI agents on the day of my abduction. He took copious notes on his side of the thick glass about questions asked and how I answered. He went over and over the fact that I had an exhaustive pictorial record, with timestamps, of my movements on January 6, all clearly exculpatory and all now in the possession of the FBI.

The fact that I had actually reviewed these pictures with the FBI agents before I was hauled away was significant, in his view. I answered their questions. Without counsel. I was not being charged with lying to the Feds. Again, significant. In fact a head-shaker for Dave.

So, why were they still persecuting me?

Washington, DC, is not like the rest of the country. It is mostly a godless land, mercifully alien to most of us, built on power, self-indulgence and payola. I was born there and lived there safely and securely as a child in the come-as-you-are section of Northeast Washington. I was stationed there on active duty in our Navy for multiple tours and my eyes were opened to the hypocrisy. I attended the embassy soirees. I heard the snarky cocktail talk. Here is the simple truth: the only thing worse in DC than being irrelevant is being outed as being wrong. About anything. However trivial.

Careers were at stake, you see. Screw some little disabled vet from Podunk, Virginia. Innocent people get convicted all the time. We'll get this guy, too. Or break him. Or kill him. I was still in the crosshairs.

Dave Fischer said it could be 45 days before another hearing! If we fail then, we're finished because it could then be a year before this case went to trial, Dave explained. I couldn't wrap my head around it! None of us knew it would be nearly *twice* that before the government could line up their lies, their liars, and their legion of fake exhibits for a trial. Even now, 45 days might prove to truly be a lifetime.

Thank you, God, for Sharon. Please comfort her. Thank you, God, for Dave Fischer. I know You will guide his path and give him the right words to say.

I wish I could quit shaking from the cold and sickness.

The clatter in the SHU after evening telephone time was familiar background noise. It was inescapable, all I could concentrate on. Janglings of keys and restraints, dungeon doors slammed, feeding shelves dropped, viewing ports banging shut. The SHU's inhabitants lent their percussion through kettle-drum mule kicks, incessant snare rapping on vents, glass, steel, and concrete. And the vocals! A rich stew of pain-filled screams, undecipherable rantings, maniacal chanting, sobbing and wailing, begging for help, pleas for release, ferocious shrieks and screeches, and tormented yowls all delivered across the spectrum of octaves and keys. All were woven within this concrete echo shaft into a disturbing auditory tapestry of the damned.

***

DAY 40

Dave Fischer came to work with me in Hell again today. This gent is relentless. Praise be to God! I hung in there with him for a marathon session. Hold on, Tom, Dave encouraged. We have the truth. They don't. I have a lot to work with here and I'll be ready. *We'll* be ready.

After a while, I was released from the meeting room to see two COs, one holding a black-haired prisoner and the other closing quickly with my wheelchair for a return to solitary. It was this unfortunate inmate who told me of a type of gambling pool in the CVRJ wherein bets were being laid on my chances of leaving the facility alive someday. No wonder I had begun thinking of this as a Death Camp.

Looking for confirmation from the guards, he told me, "S'like four ta one or somethin' against you makin' it," he continued, eyes looking for my reaction. "I'm jus' tellin' ya. That's what's goin' 'round."

"Is that so?" I said as I turned and waited for the approaching wheelchair.

I have thought of that moment many times since. My take on it is probably not what most people might think unless they too had been locked up. Before I turned away from my informant I *should* have said something akin to:

"So, which way did *you* bet?"

It would have been good information to know before I foolishly turned my back to him.

He could have been the designated shanker!

***

Yesterday's seizure episode here on the deck of the ferry-across-the-Styx just about did me in. In the midst of my knotted-up, twisting, turning agony on the floor, a correctional officer appeared and made it worse. He kicked me, as I shook the way a paint mixer shakes at the hardware store: a heavy-hoofed whack in the upper back accompanied by an admonition to get up.

I don't know how long he stood there or when he left. I just know my mangled back was the least of the trauma to my body. My life felt like sand running out of the hourglass. *How much more, Lord?*

Someone in power decided to give me a minimal dose of some kind of alleged blood pressure medicine today. Perhaps there had been discussion of my agony on the floor. That had brought a visit from a medical lady armed with a stethoscope. I guess the sustained 160-plus beats per minute that she measured multiple times—along with the fact that I needed a freakin' wheelchair to move around—had at least been recognized. Really, though, slipping me a tiny tablet after forty-plus days without my major prescriptions was like putting a band-aid on a sucking chest wound.

I knew it was Sunday because the night-time re-education class at the television wall outside was viewing a propaganda show loosely disguised as a news program. *I can hear the sound of a clock ticking. Its echo races past my dungeon door, slams against the stairway at passage end, then tags up and flits by once more.*

I read a page or two from the Bible, and Boo hollered to me from his reeducation student's perch.

"Hey, Caldwell!" he shouted. "They lyin' 'bout you again!"

The inmates turned deathly quiet, awaiting my reply.

I was in so much pain, so sick and so angry, I blasted back with all the volume I could muster and in the foulest terms possible, exactly what those liars on television could do with themselves.

The council in chains thundered their approval of my fully X-rated response. Theirs was the prison version of team members on *Family Feud* encouraging one of their own with a nearly in-unison "Good answer, good answer!"

Sorry, Lord.

Back to Psalm 42.

***

Six weeks in this trap, and after a guard-delivered thumping today, I spent time again in a smaller ice-cold punishment cell for what reason I do not know. Maybe to drive home the lesson that I have no rights and they can do with me whatever heinous things they want. They couldn't use the excuse that I had called out to God for justification to stick me in the special cooler this time. Maybe it's because I had the audacity to sit and pray. I sat in the punishment locker and went back to doing just that. All the while I shook, which I seem to do constantly.

Sharon and I prayed together over the phone regularly. I was never given the opportunity for a visitor except for Dave Fischer, so our phone calls continued as the only life-support system for us both other than the Word. *I am so stressed out from the endless prison abuse. Reason dictates to me that I could not possibly be seeing some of the things that my eyes tell me I am seeing. But my former sense, guided by reason, is a foreigner in the haunted SHU.*

How could it be only inventions of my tortured mind, hallucinations, if I so clearly heard others screaming down the hallways about what *they're* seeing, too? Dear God!

I have always said I am a Christian, but by later life I was not very active in my faith. I was woefully short on the kind of Bible education I should have had. The kind I think so many people may be pre-wired to want and need. I had the Holy Bible, but I struggled to understand many of the things my weary eyes were reading. The constant pain and mental torment were disassembling me. On this day, after I had made one of my silly remarks about praying but that I wasn't sure God was hearing me, Sharon assured me that He was and then read to me from Philippians:

Philippians Chapter 4 Verse 6 - 7

"Do not be anxious about anything, but in everything, by prayer and petition, with thanksgiving, present your requests to God. And the peace of God which transcends all understanding, will guard your hearts and your minds in Christ Jesus."

Right there in the Holy Bible it was saying that it's cool to make your needs known to God through prayer, but you should thank Him for what He has already done. The simple beauty of this passage struck me like a revelation: When we pray, we should start by giving thanks. Thanks-giving, see?

We started something else earnestly in our prayers, Sharon and I. We prayed for the Lord to soften the judge's heart so that I could go free. We prayed that the judge would come to see through the lies and free me to go home to my beloved.

Mindful of thanksgiving, I concentrated hard to find things to be thankful for in the here-and-now. How about: Thank you, God, that I haven't been beaten or kicked in the gonads today although the day isn't over yet. And thank you for saving my darling Sharon's life that horrible night at our home! Thank you for sending her my way long ago as the answer to a request for a life-partner and soulmate. Thank you for the wonderful years we have had together.

Even here in the pit, I could feel gratitude.

All was not lost yet. *I* was not lost yet, either.

***

"Mr. Caldwell! You want a razor?"

What?

The offering from the CO at the door was as cheap and marginally useable as I guess many of the approved prison products might be. It reminded me of the very earliest disposable blades I had used in the 70s in the dormitory at college. Like those, these reasonably sharp semi-recessed blades are likely made from old baked-bean cans. I didn't think six-week-old beard hairs were afraid of them, but I was glad to try.

Absent shave gel or foam, I used Bob Barker Brand mini-soap, which smelled like a dead possum. I could picture the catchy advertisement slogan: "There's a whole dead possum in every cake of Bob Barker soap!" With this objectionable bar, I built up a pitiful, slightly sudsy imitation of foam and rubbed it on my fuzzy face. One aborted pull with the overmatched tool convinced me it couldn't possibly complete the job of clearing the facial landscape.

My new plan was to address about half of my mug and I began to drag the tool forcefully, stopping often to clear both blade and plastic contact points of Barker soap and beard. By the time both my jowls and the throwback faux-Bic were yelling "no mas, no mas," I had trimmed myself to a very respectable Colonel Sanders facial hair death row look.

My blessed call with Sharon this evening included a humorous recounting of the faux-shaver adventure. She giggled with delight at the vision of bedraggled me with a goatee hedge. I lay on the bed nest and succumbed to the evening melancholy.

MY DARLING SHARON

IT WAS SO GOOD TO HEAR YOUR VOICE TODAY. IT IS THE ONLY BRIGHT SPOT IN THESE DAYS OF HELL. DO I ACTUALLY DARE TO HOPE THAT I MIGHT BE FREED BY NEXT WEEKEND?

I DON'T THINK I DARE TO EVEN TRY TO CONCEIVE OF WHAT A RUSH OF JOY IT WOULD BE TO HEAR THE JUDGE SET ME FREE. IT WOULD ONLY BE ECLIPSED BY THE FIRST TIME I CAN HOLD YOU IN MY ARMS AND HUG AND KISS YOU WHEN I'M FREE AT LAST.

PLEASE KEEP PRAYING.—I AM HOPING, HOPING, HOPING THAT I ~~CAN~~ WILL BE RELEASED BY THE JUDGE

THIS NEXT TIME.

I LOVE YOU WITH ALL MY HEART AND SOUL

YOUR DEVOTED HUBBY

TOM xoxoxoxoxoxoxoxo

***

Only a day or two now since they began their drug program on me. I'm so desperate for relief from the hammering of my heart in my chest, the gut-wrenching pain, and the insomnia that I actually thought for a moment that medical "care" might come my way. Now I'm not so sure.

A guy who allegedly works in Medical passed by and told me that this L-ovil stuff they had begun giving me was identical to my nerve pain prescription. No, it was not. I'm exhausted, not stupid.

But now I'm accepting their drugs without arguing about it. *Maybe something they give me will stop the strain on my heart. Bring me some rest. Make me numb to it all—another halting step toward rock bottom.* I had been feeling even worse, if that was possible, since given those blasted pills by the medical staff. I didn't know who was putting what into those little paper cups. I regretted ever taking them. But you'd better. Or they'd *make* you.

I am so tired of being cold and of shivering without end.

I am so tired of my bruised personals, tired of peeing blood.

I am so tired of watching my body drying out, splitting, decaying, breaking down bit by bit at the cellular level with every passing day.

People locked here in the SHU sometimes carry on conversations with someone that no one else can see. I've heard these chats myself. Since there are demons squirming in every corner of this refrigerator complex, one's first impression is that men are having a discussion with a malevolent something. I'd prefer to think they're talking with the Lord. Maybe He is the only One who cares about any of us. A relationship with the Lord is a good thing. Maybe the *only* good thing in here

***

I was always the guy who appreciated the bright outdoors. I miss the sun on my face and working on a warm day, or even a hot one, toiling as my physical limitations allow on our little farm. If she was not right there beside me, Sharon would stop her chores wherever she was and bring a cool drink. We'd smile and talk about the tasks at hand, pausing to listen to and then chat about the bird sounds or a far-off tractor. We reveled in the smells of the trees and the grass, the sounds of the cows lowing or the hawks calling or the taste of a delicious home-cooked meal at day's end. Relaxed evening drives along country roads, laughing visits with friends where the conversation was as easy and comfortable as a favorite pair of slippers. All of these were so very far away now.

I thought of all the marvels I had seen in my life, and everything always revolved about, was centered upon and infused with visions of her. My life had been that way since I fell in love with Sharon, and I missed all of these things because their joy was felt so deeply within me only because of *her*. She was all I ever wanted in my entire life, and now every second *not* in her presence was a treasure wasted and lost forever. Memories of my two decades as her husband were the riches of my life, but leaning on them now only made my sorrow deeper, my despondency more overwhelming.

I was snatched from my remembrances when the steel door flew open and a squad of uniforms blew into my cave with the fury of a scowling, angry storm. The leader, a lady, was the only one smiling. An attractive woman in a white blouse, she approached me with purpose as her menacing bodyguards formed a looming, scowling arc around me.

She said something about checking me for the China virus and she had an extraordinarily long Q-tip to do it with. It was over in an instant. Or maybe I was losing feeling in my face. Her cohorts turned to withdraw from my tomb single-file behind her. I don't know why someone thought they had to send blue uniformed vengeful extras from the movie *Platoon* to do a swab test. If it was intended to intimidate me, it was a dismal failure.[1]

I turned to my left, away from the still-open door and the exiting troop, and swung a leg up onto the shelf, preparing to stretch out.

Then there was a flash of light and a crush of pain in my back. I tried to inflate my lungs but couldn't. Then another flash!

I peered from my yellow-orange-lensed eye slits again and I knew what the flash of light and the bolt of pain shooting down my legs meant. Something had happened to my back! One of these uniformed goons had given me an uppercut blow in my low mid-spine.

God! It hurts! I'm on my back now on the concrete, unable to pull a full breath! It was hard to turn and look to find the culprit. I saw only the backs of the uniforms as they filed into the passageway. This wasn't the first sucker punch or kick and it wouldn't be the last. What could I do? File a complaint?

BLANG!

The steel door slammed.

I was alone again. God help me.

Left here on the cold stone floor, it didn't take long to start swirling back down the drain.

***

I sit and think. There's not much else to do here. Does a place where people suffer the most hideous torment, where they are tortured until they lose their minds, their humanity, does a place as miserable as that have the power to trap a person's essence? To hold them captive by imprinting the heartache, the grief, the distress they endured upon a dungeon or a passageway or an object where it stays forever? Doomed to replay that wretchedness and that pain and fear over and over in a perpetual loop across time itself? For eternity. And is that what haunts these solitary confinement catacombs?

I am the rapidly hammering heart of human anguish.

***

As a Christian, I know I am going to Heaven, which when I think too much, helps me form an excellent argument for suicide. Why put up with this abuse when I can be with Jesus and friends and family and my puppy in Heaven? I'll stop shaking there and I won't hurt or ache anymore. It would be a way to stop the pain. In the depths of my hopelessness here in a Virginia Super-Max sepulcher, this thought gives me a feeling of relief. My suffering would end, and Sharon could live and be free.

I was so far gone, I let the enemy put these thoughts in my head. I should have seen death come to me many years from now as a benevolent old friend, bringing the gifts of peace and rest. Instead, here it clung to the walls and my being like a fungus rooted in desperation and despair. My altered mental state, while allowing me to live this long, had a downside. Now it seized upon this craziness of pondering death.

I'm never getting out of here. Why not take control? I know I'm not the first to consider this. I hear other inmates talk of it through the walls and in the passageways. To no one in particular, or at least to no one somebody else can see.

I lie here now with no pride, no dignity, no vanity, no vitality, no ambition, no joy, no self-respect, no ego, no hope.

I told the Lord then and there I wanted to come home to Him; to end all of this, and I asked Him to make it so. My will to go on had fled me. Unless and until you have reached the point of total physical and emotional collapse, can I make you really understand? In a way, I was already dead. That might have been the first and only time this confessed control freak had ever said *Your* will be done, Father, and *really* meant it.

I had no control over anything in my desiccated world, but I had the ability to relinquish control of my life that day. Nothing that I owned or that I thought was a part of me existed here in Hell. Was this "dying to self"? Those curious Bible words. I know now it had something to do with my idea of the sum of me as a human being. My personal selfish desires, the things I wanted or ever thought that I did. My plans for a happy future with Sharon. I couldn't clearly picture them anymore. They were lost like last night's dreams, forgotten with the free man's morning coffee. Right now they counted for exactly nothing.

I didn't know how to pray at that moment. I was too beaten down, and I didn't have the tongue for it. Whatever You have planned is much better than this, Lord. Let's try *that*, please, because this place totally sucks. With the warning lights on the remnant of my life-force glaring a constant red, He took me in.

My pauper's grave was brighter than the artificial tubes had ever made it. So bright I squinted in self-defense. It was like facing the sun. I could see the squiggly tracings of the blood vessels in my eyelids and maybe my own eyes. Even though my cheek was pressed against the floor, I can only describe what happened lying there as looking in a direction I had never looked before. I was seeing something—someone—for the very first time.

That was the moment I knew Jesus was there. My neck angrily refused to crank my head around to face Him. I couldn't even get the full force of His majesty, His manifest presence. I was not up to the task. I just flopped, exhausted on the slab. I couldn't think clearly. What did I say to Him? If this is dying, it's not the way people say it is. No life replay running inside my closed lids. No growing pinpoint of light down a long tunnel. Just nothing.

Shivering on the floor, I very nearly missed the wonder of it all. No audible external voice, no gathering of angels comforting me. No floating out of my body. It wasn't like that. I can't take a single second more of this cesspool. Now I won't have to.

For just a moment, no more worry.

I think I'll just lie here and see what happens.

***

I shivered awake, barely conscious enough to drag the plastic blanket up on me. He didn't come through. Jesus didn't come through. He didn't bring me home. *I'm still in Hell. Corruptly and illegally condemned to an existence, not a life. Only to endure. I am still waiting for Him to make it happen the way I know it needs to happen. To take me home the way I prayed for. What went wrong? My runaway heart-thumping still rules everything in this place.*

Okay.

Deep breath.

Refocus.

So *now* what?

Praise the Lord for giving me a little non-nightmare sleep last night! I reckon I just passed out. I won't give up on what I know happened yesterday. I take inventory, tortured body part by tortured body part. *Did He heal me? Nope, neck is still fouled up, and here comes that headache. Aww, no! Better to not move my torn-up back! Yeow! That freakin' hurt! My crotch is still so messed up! Nope, not physically healed. There are no miracles here for me.*

Am I cracking up? People say they have seen Him, "but not in the natural." What does that even mean? I know what and Who I saw, but if it's so, why am I still here? Does this mean I'm not good enough to go to Heaven? Or not ready? Oh, I'm ready, already! I should have talked to Him! Why didn't I say something? Heck, I don't know if I was even breathing.

What is He waiting for?

Now I have to deal with a renewed fear: Am I intended to be a martyr? Is it the Master's plan that my body and soul rot in this place?

***

A candy bar. It was a familiar taste that shifted my attention from the objectionable stuff on the orange tray that I had wolfed down first. A double batch of sink water with the taste of *real* manganese which, when blended with mercury and lead, formed the building blocks of any nutritious SHU breakfast! I knew I was still in ruination central.

I had a Boo encounter for a fleeting moment today, a hiccup in the flow of people back and forth outside my mausoleum. Zoning out on the ice-cold floor, I heard two COs screaming and Boo thundering his interruptions. He had shaken them off like so much lint and darted to shove a fishwrap under the door to my dungeon. I yelled my thanks through the gap as Boo turned up the insults and the taunts directed at the guards. What a guy. Maybe some CO was about to damage a fist trying to hurt the indomitable Boo.

I read the outdated falsehoods in print, then tossed the pile under the writing shelf. The propaganda machine of the DOJ was at full throttle as all media seemed intent on spitting their lies about me worldwide. I pondered a long time what I had been told about the odds against leaving here alive. There were lots of ways to whack me. Why shouldn't the government agents want to do that?

I didn't know what the chances were that I would be released or that my constantly maxed-out ticker would not explode in my chest. The former seemed a fantasy and the latter a certainty. There were limited opportunities for me to get shanked since I wasn't in gen-pop, though when I was going up and down the halls, as I expected I might at the end of the week, I was a sitting duck in a wheelchair.

***

Ragged in body and spirit, all I can do is lie on the floor. No different from the day before or any day I can fully remember now. My own body is an adversary. The tachycardia knocking inside my rib cage fights to split me like some sci-fi chest-buster. I cannot escape.

The empty day crawls by like a slug along the edge of a switchblade.

Seven weeks of torture and it's the worst spinal pain ever. I tremble to use the phone through the grub portal. Resting my forehead on the steel icecube door until my neck cries out for a break in the action. Sheer will holds me fast until the faraway voice speaks a pep talk. Lawyer Dave Fischer says he has found lots more facts that will help us. The echo of his voice tells me to hang in there till Friday's hearing. So I must. Somehow.

The Lord sent us a real lawyer. This is truly a thing to be grateful for.

With thanksgiving ...

I remembered my first look at this place and the virtual tour with voiceover by Boo. I have never found hot water at the sink, but you know how realtors tend to oversell their listings. I looked now at the closed metal beam that might house pipes and such. A fresh idea came to me, which was a rare thing in these days of confusion and resignation.

Shuffling to the sink beneath that metallic timber, I plucked the flex pen from my cracked foam cup. I reached up to the metallic beam and with deliberate, hard strokes began to form straight lines to make my creative vision of the outline of a Christian cross come alive. Onward I went, until I was satisfied with the preliminaries.

Easing back a few feet, I looked at my accomplishment. Crude, yes, but expressive. Replacing my artist's tool, it's time for step two. Dropped down on one knee, I squeezed the weeping slice on my ankle which added more puss and blood to the slippery palette below the cuffed pantleg of my jumpsuit. Being right-handed, I worried that my shakiness with the alternate hand might just ruin this important piece. But then again, will this be realism or impressionism?

Channeling my inner primitive, I began to purposefully dab with my digit, considering only in a passing way, coloring between the lines. Is this what they mean by creative *juices*? I repeated this squeeze, wipe, dab process to further my work. With concentration and determination, I urged my artistic vision from embryonic to fulsome. At last, body aching and still in full shiver, I creaked backwards to regard my creation.

Why, Tom! You Cro-Magnon madcap! Your first wall painting!

My rough-edged Christian cross was now filled in with ankle seepage and would be an inspiration and a reminder that I should stay in agreement with and dependent upon the Word of God. I turned my full attention now toward my darling Sharon, who was suffering in her own hell fashioned by the demons of the DOJ.

With trusty stylus I created anew. First on the beam, then on the smooth but tough face of the steel lid of my burial pit. Each surface was, in turn, adorned with the boldly lettered name of my lovely Sharon. I needed focus. Subconsciously or consciously, from now on I would see her name no matter what side of the vault I stared at, and on high would be a symbol of my friend and Savior, Jesus Christ. He's not stuck here. I think maybe He comes and goes.

I'm hoping for the evening telephone time to come. Hearing her voice is one joy they haven't totally stolen from me.

Yet.

***

Routine in the Hole included my laughable attempt at a fitness regimen still happening periodically since those first shaky attempts in Mash Solitary. More important were my daily *prayer* sets that I felt really did help. I had seen signs that God knew what I was enduring even though the outside world was being bombarded with utter nonsense concerning me. I saw the first unmistakable sign the day I was directed to Psalms 109 and 56. I have never asked why God was doing this to me. I've *never* thought this was His fault and still don't.

The Holy Bible says I should pray for the DOJ creatures doing this to Sharon and me. They need lots of prayers because they're in trouble even if they can neither acknowledge nor fathom it. If not here, they were certainly set up for trouble somewhere else, and for eternity. Hope they're enjoying those soy lattes and scones. There are no trendy coffee shops in Hell. Take it from me 'cause I've looked in every corner of this place.

There *is* sweat meat, though.

***

Jesus and his chosen instrument, Dave Fischer, have given me some determination to press on though I feel my life ebbing away. I am so desperate I can't even let myself cling to the vision of comfort I saw here in this pit. I am not alone, but I mustn't get off the brainwave treadmill. What if I relax and get peaceful and then Jesus mistakes that for pride and overconfidence? No! Better to cling to the ragged edge, knowing I was powerless without him. What choice was there, anyway?

I wondered what God was trying to tell me in what I had read in the Bible today. Then I wondered what He was trying to instill in me. Isn't he the God of everybody? I had cried out to Him and I saw Him. Didn't I? Yet I am still stuck here. I don't get it at all.

What I *did* have was a bit of Hope and a bit of Faith.

As a political prisoner in a Death Camp, that's monumental.

***

The misery and the sounds around me are suggestive of insane asylums from olden days. Look around here and you will know such horrors aren't completely gone. Are the DOJ and the prison/industrial complex committed to creating an entire caste of the insane? I know

now what it takes to drive someone crazy. I can relate to all of these men in their suffering. The loud ones and the quieter ones. I am one of them and they are like me. I know I am only a step behind on the lemming-rush to the cliff. A free-fall into madness.

I'm a prison veteran now, I suppose. I have the slip-on shower shoes for my white socked feet, the ridiculously named "thermal" whose extended sleeves provided at least some cover past the stubby, flapping short ones of the jumpsuit. My daily routine includes asking for a roll of toilet paper (again) and using just the right amount of it wetted down for maximum adhesion to the cold air grate.

My door push-aways frequently afford me a view of the hallway, where I see the formation of a pile of bedding, towels, clothes, and Commissary items on the floor by a far wall. A sure sign that someone is being sent home or at least taken out of the CVRJ. For their sakes I always hope they are going home to someone they love and who loves them in return. That's what I continually pray to be doing myself one fine day soon.

Tomorrow, Lord, tomorrow.

The things that haunt this place are here with me, backs to the walls, in their unspeakable fiendishness; humanoid but a mockery of humanity. Black-wrapped cruelty, barbarous and bloodthirsty. The images, like their mumbling and terrible screeches, are burning into my brain.

I lay there that night after my prayers, serenaded by the wails of the tormented. I could not stop the sounds of the damned, the ceiling light's buzz, the condemned chorus, the succubus pulse of the walls and their indwelling demons all melded together. The crashing cymbals of the CO percussion section. A symphony for Satan on a continuous loop.

Please, Lord, have pity on your servant! I Glorify and trust YOU. We are grateful for another chance tomorrow. Please help Dave Fischer. Please let me be with Sharon tomorrow.

There's nothing more to say.

Amen.

DAY 53 March 12, 2021

I was jacked up on adrenaline and fear. Chained like Houdini about to commence a death-defying stunt, only never having performed or practiced it before, I knew the stakes were incredibly high: life at home or death in the hole. My heart was slamming fast. The panic that I wouldn't make it out of Hell was crashing on me like waves while I struggled to breathe. This was our last-ditch effort at a release hearing.

The verbal jousting between the forces of good and evil went on for a very long time as Dave deflected falsehood after falsehood with skill and with the simple truth.

"Your Honor," Dave said, "at the time people were breaking into the Capitol and all this commotion was going on, the government's *own exhibit* shows Mr. Caldwell was sitting at a fountain at least a couple hundred yards away on the other side of the building."

"The government presented you a month ago a picture of Mr. Caldwell plotting day after day to invade the Capitol. They have produced *no evidence* of pre-planning by anybody."

The judge was fully attentive as Dave continued: "I don't want to quibble, but Mr. Caldwell is not a member of the Oath Keepers. At the time people went in, my client was not on a *walkie-talkie* with them, not having instant communications with them, was not on their *Signal* channels, and the government *concedes*!"

Judge Amit P. Mehta, the same judge who had denied my release under Lawyer Tom, said, "Thirty days ago I was convinced that Mr. Caldwell had a plan to execute an incursion into the Capitol building. You've raised some evidence that I think rebuts that notion."[2]

Kathryn Rakoczy resumed her war dance around the theory of a massive conspiracy still brewing but without foundation or any facts to support her ravings. She insisted upon characterizing me as being uncooperative with them and in fact lying. No specifics, mind you, just accusations. Sadly, I would learn that this is a tactic the DOJ regularly uses against its targets.

I just couldn't fathom why they were coming after me so hard! I explained things at length to the FBI agents. They *knew* I had never gone into the Capitol building, and they had seen the exhaustive photo history of my movements that day. They'd even communicated with

Rakoczy on the phone at the end of my interrogation! Afterward the agents assured me I would be bonded out before day's end. What had happened, and why was I now a prime target?

"Your Honor," Dave said, "the proof is in the pudding. Mr. Caldwell gave a two-hour interview with the FBI, in which he told them only truthful information. I watched the video on this. He explained the whole situation. So, Your Honor, when he gave a statement to the FBI, he gave a 100 percent truthful statement. The government in its papers has not set forth one iota to prove the man has lied."

All the while I was praying with all my might.

"The bottom line here, your Honor, I believe—obviously, I've put forth my opinion: I believe this man is innocent!"[3]

Judge Mehta was watching me intently as Dave continued, "The suffering this man has gone through since he was incarcerated in January is beyond belief. He will not do anything to violate a court's order. That's 100 percent. Thank you, Your Honor."

I had seen the DOJ lawyer Rakoczy beguiling the judge throughout the proceedings, struggling to ensure my detention as she had once before. Now the judge turned his attention and his questions directly to her.

"Ms. Rakoczy, can I ask one question?" he said, though he already knew the answer. "I don't think I was *aware* that he had given an interview, that he consented to a search of his computers and consented to a search of his home. I guess two questions: When did I know of that? Were those facts on the *record* last time?

"Uh, I don't believe they were, Your Honor," she confessed reluctantly.[4]

If she felt embarrassed at being confronted for withholding facts from the judge in her portrayal of me as a monster, she didn't show it.

Hubris is a powerful thing.

Rakoczy was doing damage control now and conducted a word-salad tap-dance until the judge had heard enough.

"Okay. All right," Judge Mehta interrupted. "Everybody, just give me a second, I'll be right back."

The judge was gone, and so began the longest ten minutes of my life. My assigned babysitter that day, Officer Roberts of the prison staff, could not control his smile as he turned in his seat and gave me the silent two-thumbs-up sign. This is a *good* thing, right? Roberts must have seen these hearings before. If I was hosed, wouldn't he know it and show it? I met his eyes with hopeful ones of my own, then turned my peepers skyward as I mouthed a silent prayer to the Lord once more.

I just have to hold on, stay in Faith! Jesus is here, He's with you, He's held off the attack, the sickness. Whatever it is. It's got to be all right, right? If the judge had not been touched by the Lord, wouldn't he have just stuck it to me instead of putting everybody on hold? How the heck should I know?

The judge returned and my hopes were rising again.

"Mr. Caldwell is charged very specifically with conspiring to disrupt the Electoral College vote," Judge Mehta began. "And that he planned with others to forcibly enter the Capitol on January 6 to stop, delay, or hinder proceedings that day."

"Nevertheless," he continued, "I am required ... to consider the strength of the evidence with respect to these charges. There is an *absence* of direct evidence of planning violence by Mr. Caldwell to enter the Capitol building. There are *no text messages, communications by him* that speak to entering the building or trying to enter. And ultimately, he did *not* enter the building."[5]

"There's evidence here that I think is favorable to Mr. Caldwell, let's just put it that way. The other thing I am concerned about is Mr. Caldwell's health. He is 65 years old. I've seen him now two or three times."

The judge also could see my deteriorating condition. He pressed onward, saying, "I take his counsel at his word. So I am going to agree to release Mr. Caldwell. But believe me, Mr. Caldwell, if there is any hint of a violation of these conditions, you'll be right back where you are, okay?"

What could I say but, "Yes, your Honor. I understand. Thank you, your Honor."

"Okay," said Judge Mehta. "Just so the record's clear, I ultimately am now concluding, in light of the additional evidence that's been brought before me, that this is *favorable evidence* for him with respect to the charges."

He continued: "The obstruction conduct alleged [by Rakoczy] has been put in a different light, given that I now know Mr. Caldwell *did voluntarily interview* with the FBI, he *did provide passwords* to allow the FBI to search computers and therefore what I was concerned about before has been put in a different light."[6]

"Liberty is the norm in pretrial status. I will release him pursuant to very restrictive conditions that I've set out," Judge Mehta concluded.[7]

PRAISE GOD FROM WHOM ALL BLESSINGS FLOW!

Rakoczy had lost control, and egg on her face or no, she tried to convince the judge to delay my release, probably so she could have more time to invent some *other* falsehoods. She also opened the door to filing an appeal of Judge Mehta's order to the U.S. Court of Appeals to rescind the judge's order to release me![8]

"I'm not going to do that," Judge Mehta replied. "I'm not going to stay it at this point. Mr. Caldwell, I've got standards I'm supposed to apply under the law, and I think they justify your release."

At this point, he could have called me every name in the book as long as he sent me home to Sharon.

"Your Honor, thank you," is all I said.

"All right. Have a good weekend."

The official transcript chronicles that at 4:24 p.m. Friday, March 12, 2021, my life was spared.

***

Three very different scenes began to play out in three different locations. Two I am certain of and one is simply an educated guess fueled by some "inside baseball."

A world away, in Dave Fischer's office, Dave turned to Sharon and just said: "Go get him! Better leave now. I'll call you!"

After multiple hugs, Sharon was off to fight the legendary traffic from the Baltimore Beltway, onto the Capital Beltway and an additional two hours-plus drive to Orange County, Virginia, my Bethany. There to be reunited with her loving husband, a real-life Lazarus, who was being raised from the dead.

In the cramped Video Teleconference room, Officer Roberts unshackled me from the ring welded into the tabletop. We smiled warmly as he shook my still-chained hands with congratulations on a huge win. A shared outpouring of Praise to the Lord happened there and then. Guess he's a believer, too. The tension of this time together was released as if a colossal valve had been turned. He added that he hoped I could get all these bogus charges dropped quickly and that Sharon and I could get our lives back. I will never forget his smile. I wonder how big mine was.

As for Kathryn Rakoczy, I don't *personally* know that she had a hissy fit and tossed a coffee cup. There's no denying that the *mere formality* of another detention hearing had turned into a win for me, the fall-guy. A high-profile Ivy League DOJ prosecutor outdone in a legal face-off by a guy with a University of Maryland law degree!

***

With folded hands and head bowed, I prayed a long, grateful prayer. As ravaged as my body and brain were, my rescue would soon be complete. I felt that the judge had ruled and no one, not even a government lawyer, would dare to ignore his directive or delay its execution.

They had thrust me into worse and worse levels of Hell after stripping me of all personal possessions. I was leaving with cards, letters, a diary, sketches, and snacks from "Commissary." I needed a clear plastic garbage bag to hold it all.

Within about an hour, it was *my* nesting materials, towel, and throwaways that were cast into the main passageway. The last contribution to the Tom Caldwell Memorial Library, SHU branch, was also complete. We'll have to officially drop the "Memorial" part from the name designation by tomorrow, I guess.

Uniformed officers wandering past offered their congrats just as if they were relieved for me. My voice was cracking with so much emotion that I could barely speak except to mumble Praise to the Lord in response.

I was overcome with wondering if so many of these men I would never see again had been watching out for me as they could. Did they stay the evil intents of others more than I could ever know? Were most of the "staff" keeping the burden of my scapegoating hidden in their hearts, to be shared with family alone, far from this fortress where they might have been admonished for empathy and compassion? Wallowing in my own kind of misery, I never knew it could have been so much worse if not for these noble few, or perhaps many.

Two COs on-scene said they would gladly take me out front right away. No need to offer twice! Plopped into the wheelchair unencumbered now by any chains, my meager holdings were flumped into my lap. Brakes released, I was turned in a lazy arc toward my escape route.

One last time I gazed up at the cross and Sharon's name beside it that I had painted on these gloomy walls with blood from my wounds. My simple cave paintings born of heartbreak. They were now a pitiful marker of my suffering and of the cruelty here. With the wound-squeezings from my own tortured body rubbed into that bloody cross, I had truly left a piece of me in dungeon Number 4 of the dreaded SHU. I was forever changed.

There was one last thing to do as I thought of the humane respect and, yes, perhaps kindness shown me by the small handful of unwanted men with whom I had served an unjust incarceration. I called out loudly to Boo, hoping he might hear if he was still being held.

No response. What did I expect, anyway? Were we *chums*? *Buddies*? We were fellow inmates in a particular corner of Hell in Virginia. Condemned separately, we would be freed separately. Boo and I and everyone imprisoned here would continue to battle, each in our own way, a system intended to dismantle and crush us. That would be our fight: to resist. To overcome if we could. And to live. And we would do it on our own.

And never again speak to each other.

Buzz–snap, and the SHU was opened. A gust of air brought the unaccustomed sound of imminent freedom. With a smile on his face, my transport CO wheeled feeble me toward the door.

From somewhere afar off, sweeping along the stark passages, came Boo's booming voice that even now lives in my memory.

"Hey! Caldwell's getting out! Get your popcorn ready, boys!"

I was going home!

***

Clad in my own musty clothes, I heard Sharon's sweet voice on a SECURUS phone for the final time. I was excited but impatient at discovering she was still well over an hour away. COs turned their heads at my end of the I-love-you's she and I shared before ending the crackly call.

Officer Pollard told me about a visitor's area situated at the opposite end of the building, facing the parking lot. The people who zealously imprisoned me now wanted me out from under foot. Emboldened by assurances that I could wait indoors "over there," plastic bag in hand, I was buzz-snap-flushed into the cold rush of a biting winter wind.

My bag dropped to the pavement. I took a wide stance to guard myself from tumbling over backward, then gazed upward as much as my groaning neck would permit. With arms lifted high, I looked in wonder as if for the very first time at the bright stars of Creation in an oil-black sky. On trembling legs I breathed in the beauty of those twinkling dots, so magical even with the electric lights of the parking lot competing for dominance. Thank You, God, for this moment.

I drew in the air of a free man—a new man. One raised from a tomb. God the Father, the same Father who saved Sharon's life on our front porch, had rolled away a door as solid as any stone and brought me out. He had changed everything. I couldn't yet know all He had in store for me.

Hefting my plastic burden like a pitiful dollar-store Santa, I shambled in painful fits and starts in the direction the desk CO had indicated. In the large, sad waiting room with its cheap, molded plastic seats, my first hour-plus of supposed freedom was a lonely vigil. Freshly released from the gulag's maw, I was hopeful that each set of headlights captured by the glass doors heralded my lover's arrival in our aged SUV.

At last! I could just feel it somehow. This was Sharon pulling in! Head held high and with confident, though uneven, strides that belied each step's electric ripple, I made it to the pavement, smiling and waving to catch her eye. The headlights winked out and her car door flew open.

The relief I felt in my adrenaline-enabled stagger across the dark Death Camp parking lot and the tumble into the arms of my loving wife is indescribable. I wanted to tell her how much I love her and never ever stop telling her. We hugged so tightly and I could feel her heaving with emotion as she collapsed against me with a soul-deep cry.

We pulled just far enough apart to look into each other's eyes, then kissed deeply, again and again. The taste of her sweet lips, the touch of her skin, the softness of her hair as the wind floated it in a caress of my face. I never want to forget. Never. There were so many times I thought I would not see her again this side of Heaven. We held each other a long time and we praised God, thanking Him over and over. I had never been so grateful for the miracle of her embrace.

In a few minutes I was in the passenger seat banging down the medications Sharon had brought along. I flushed them down with my first drink of gritless, parasite-free water in almost two months. I confessed when she asked that I was indeed hurting, but being with her was the tonic I needed most.

Sharon is a very beautiful girl but she was wearing the sheer exhaustion of the day on her sweet face. I could tell she was nearly spent. I had made it to her arms by virtue of sheer adrenaline. She was just the same. My true-love was on the collapse-o-meter, but she showed unimaginable strength. She wanted only to pull from the parking lot before the bad guys came racing across the pavement with guns drawn.

On our drive, the conversation was exactly what you'd expect. Islands of proclaiming our love and how much we missed each other, floating in a sea of the retelling of happenings at the end of each other's video connection that day. In a rolling getaway car, I sat swiveled in my seat to keep gazing at her beautiful face in the amber glow of the dashboard lights.

Hours later, we returned to a humble family farm which was now a farm in name only. There were no more cows to dodge on our way up the gravel drive. My heart ached over the empty and lifeless fields. We crossed a cattle guard to a grassy slope with deep ruts left by the armored personnel carrier and a fleet of government vehicles that had excreted here their cargo of usurpers. The FBI had left structures in desolation. Buildings whose doors and door frames still stood damaged by their battering rams were illuminated by headlights. The places where simple possessions had been ripped from walls and boxes pitched contemptuously aside implored me in their ruin.

An SUV-dismount into the cold. Remembering: remembering the dreadfulness of the dark morning of January 19, when the Lord answered my prayer and kept the godless criminals from taking my Sharon's life. Everything was so quiet and still now.

***

Stepping through the door of our sweet home, could it be real? I had spent so many hours in suffering, sometimes not knowing what was authentic and what was not. They had messed with my mind so much I couldn't really comprehend that I was actually here. It hurt me to think of home most of the time I had been locked away ... to think of things so dear that I might not ever see again. It had all been too much.

Our hand-me-down sofa where they had kept Sharon under armed guard wasn't the same anymore. Where Christmas presents had been opened, where friends had relaxed and chatted, where Sharon would nap after long afternoons in the garden was different. It was replaced by the vision of armed specters looming above her as they looted and vandalized our simple home.

I was *home*. And it still *was* our home, no matter that it had been invaded and dirtied. For now the defilers were gone and we would survive and we would repair and we would rebuild with whatever strength we have remaining with the Lord's love and guidance.

Sharon lit up our Christmas tree, which still stood in the corner where we had happily decorated it the December before. It looked more beautiful than ever with its twinkling lights and hand-me-down ornaments. We smiled as we stood there hand in hand remembering. A member of our extended family had asked Sharon while I was in lockdown if she needed help reboxing the decorations and taking down the tree. A well-meant offer considering how stressed and overwrought Sharon was. But she never hesitated, saying matter-of-factly that she and I had *decorated* the tree together, therefore she and I would take the tree *down* together. When I was home again.

Though she was running on empty, Sharon hurried off to get us some water while I dropped the plastic bag of bad memories behind the ripped old couch. *My* couch, we called it, because its lumps and bumps were perfectly molded to the pressure points of my perpetually inflamed back bones.

I sat quietly as Sharon busied herself in the other room amid the clumping of cabinet doors and the wump of the refrigerator closing. I looked around slowly, drawing in the reality of all of the memories of this place that had faded in and out while I was in Hell. Can I finally relax and just be me again?

She gently comforted me as we sat for a while. We were so exhausted we were in a countdown to collapse. Before we could turn in for the night I needed a long hot shower. With actual soap. And shampoo. And freedom. Bathing in freedom.

I wanted to wash the dungeon off of me. Maybe the way everyone who's been violated wants to wash off the criminal and the incident. But you can't wash enough or scrub enough or peel away enough dirt or skin, not even if you scrape to the bone, to remove the memory of what happened or the memory of the ones who did this.

Perhaps, if they aren't too noticeable, the marks, be they bruises or cuts or a shattered spirit, might heal. Heal enough not to be the first thing people see when they look at you, even if *you* will always see it, always feel it. The personal struggle is to not be defined or limited by it. That's a daily fight. Maybe a forever fight.

At the bathroom mirror, I gazed at the pitiful image I had glimpsed a few moments before stepping from the steamy heat of a fresh-smelling shower. The shave foam was right where I had left it, so I began, razor in hand, the reclamation of my outward self. My shakiness made the razor unruly and disobedient. Supporting myself on the countertop, I leaned in to see sunken eyes that had changed into an unrecognizable olive-drab from the deep and happy brown they had always been.

I was staring at a stranger.

I just had to know, so I stepped onto our trusty bathroom scale to evaluate something that was quantifiable. Down 26 pounds. My first thought was for a weight loss program I'd recommend Nutri-system rather than Penal-system!

Sharon and I bedded down but even under multiple blankets I could not lose the bone-deep chill that had become as much a part of me as my own skin. The quiet of our refuge was a startling contrast to the racket of the madhouse. Now the only screams keeping me awake were the ones rattling around inside my head.

I tried to pray my way out of it with praise and gratitude. Sharon's hand finally slipped from mine as she rolled over to a more comfortable position and soon she was asleep, breathing softly and peacefully in our bed.

Come, let your brown hair, just lighted with gold,
Fall on your shoulders again as of old;
Let it drop over my forehead tonight,
Shading my faint eyes away from the light;
For with its sunny-edged shadows once more
Hap'ly will throng the sweet visions of yore;
Lovingly, softly, its bright billows sweep;—
Rock me to sleep, Sharon, – rock me to sleep!

— From the classic poem "Rock Me to Sleep"
... with apologies to Elizabeth Akers Allen

CHAPTER 6

Lazarus Man

"If you're not careful, the newspapers will have you hating the people who are being oppressed and loving the people who are doing the oppressing."

— Malcolm X

Man charged in Capitol riot plot to be released from jail

By ALANNA DURKIN RICHER March 12, 2021 AP

A man charged with conspiring with members of the far-right Oath Keepers militia group in the attack on the U.S. Capitol will be released from jail while he awaits trial, a judge ruled Friday after challenging the strength of the evidence against him.

The decision is a serious blow for prosecutors, who fought to keep Thomas Caldwell locked up, calling him a threat to the community and major player in the Oath Keepers' plot to stop the certification of President Joe Biden s victory.

"He has been perhaps the most honest, straightforward client I've had in 25 years, and I truly believe this man is innocent," Caldwell's lawyer, David Fischer told the judge.

***

When sleep released me, I blinked myself into a new reality. I looked around the bedroom in a panic, my brain at first unable to process anything around me. An altered state, remember? That's what I had entered as a defense mechanism against the horrors of brutal captivity. The sights, sounds, and smells of home were foreign to me. Everything about them and my place among them would need to be relearned.

I stumbled through the most basic of morning ablutions and limped through the great room, using the walls for support. I was met by Sharon with a lingering and loving hug, followed by a kiss and an inquiry about my possible desire for *lunch*. She had compassionately let me sleep the morning away, hopeful that I might play catch-up with the restorative sleep denied me for so long.

Near the kitchen, large windows designed for maximum morning and afternoon sunshine were overpowering for me now. I had not seen natural sunlight in nearly two months and it assaulted my vision and my brain so that I retreated to the curtained great room like some recently exhumed vampire. All manner of light would force me to wear sunglasses, even indoors, for much of those first days as a resurrection man.

I was deeply concerned that my manly hydraulics would never function properly again, and the persistent pain in my nads, though taken down a notch, was worrisome. Yeah, I probably needed to see a doctor about it. But that wasn't going to happen. The broken wrist would have to continue to heal by itself and it, along with the trembles, the gut problems, and the persistent leaking just a bit lower were things I must learn to live with for now.

What the heck to do about the gash on my ankle that would not stop leaking? I was gulping outdated antibiotics to fight the infection, but I needed to close the wound. My perpetually trembling hands argued against trying to stitch it closed with needle and dental floss. The office stapler was not a viable option. No, this called for a country boy's outside-the-box solution. I rummaged through the kitchen junk drawer until I found it. Generic super glue!

It was a painful challenge to twist my body enough to get both hands near the wound. A squeeze, a rake of the finger along the length to remove the ooze, then struggle with the glue to remove the cap. No easy feat to get the wonder substance flowing, but then it burped out way more than was needed. I packed as much into the open wound as possible, feeling it burn like molten lava.

It's really more art than science when you're trying to squeeze a wound closed without gluing your fingers to your own ankle. I was in uncharted territory, but when I did peel my fingers away, the split-tomato gash had become a pretty good-looking red line. Not too shabby.

***

With the hooks of the judge and the DOJ still deep within me, I was far from free of those ridiculous charges and irrational hatred. As part of the court's conditions of my release, I was forbidden to step outside our house, even onto the porch! Any departure from our home for medical attention, church services, or even to visit my lawyer's office needed first to be approved "well in advance" by the same authorities involved in my prosecution. The steps to obtain that permission were both unclear and decidedly <u>not</u> a priority for anyone not named Caldwell. I was prohibited from using the internet, social media, or even a cell phone. The list of exclusion and isolation decrees went on and on. A different kind of segregation confinement.[1]

I was alive, but I was not free. I was still theirs to twist and manipulate.

Dave felt that approval for in-person worship would eventually be granted, since prolonged denial of the freedom to attend church might be "bad optics" for the prosecutors. Justice, humanity, even common sense be damned, optics and the perceptions they create are what's important to the powerful in Washington, DC.

I was home and that's what mattered most.

***

A flood of kind and supportive friends and neighbors called and came to visit. It was all refreshingly satisfying to reconnect with the people we love during those first days of renewed life.

Sharon and I worked mightily to bounce back, at least on the surface, to the people we had been before. Friends listened in astonishment as I described sweat meat and the SHU and the people I had met, good and bad. I purposely made everything as over-the-top and light-hearted as I could, for their sakes and for our own. It was all so important to fuel recovery for Sharon and me.

I came to understand that it might be a good thing that the Lord had not answered my exhausted plea for a one-way express ride to Heaven. I'm not embarrassed about it because I was done when I asked. I was serious. He had taught me the succinct answer to the ageless question: Why doesn't God answer my prayers? The answer in this case: Sometimes you're praying for the wrong thing. Instead of just giving me what *I* wanted, He gave me what *He* intended.

I had no idea how deep down the well of altered brain chemistry I had been dragged during confinement and torture. Although I was still struggling physically and psychologically, the emotional healing modulated by Sharon and our friends progressed at a slow but steady rate.

For now, I would be content in my attempt to enjoy the colors and the visions, sights, and smells of being outside the confines of concrete block, metal chains, and steel doors. Sensory acclimation would come in small bites. I was free enough to enjoy home cooking seasoned with kisses and pressed down by warm, loving hugs. Each day was about the process of putting bad stuff in the rearview and embracing home. That was the task: recovery.

***

Sharon and I were able to hold hands and speak together tenderly as husband and wife. What a beautiful thing. But something had changed. We were both a bundle of emotions and raw nerves. It was impossible *not* to speak about the dreadfulness we had endured *together*. As I sat bleary-eyed one morning, Sharon ventured into our tiny home office and returned with a print-out of an online article she thought I should read. She left me to it and headed to recharge our coffees.

This article appeared on the author's blog as well as on the online news source *Conservative HQ*. I devoured it.

Free Thomas Caldwell. Now.
Written by: Diana West
Sunday, March 14, 2021 6:15 AM

Saw an amazing report, the next best thing to man bites dog: Federal judge raps sloppy, run-amuck US attorneys. Even according to *Politico* of the precious Left, this was a "setback" to the Justice Department's "widest ranging conspiracy case" related to the January 6 Capitol protest.

What happened is this: Judge Amit Mehta ordered the pre-trial release of Lt. Commander (USN, ret.) Thomas Caldwell, 66, to home confinement pending trial on numerous charges spun out of the DOJ fever dream that a handful of Oath Keepers militia (of which Caldwell is not even a member) conspired to lead a pre-planned attack on the Capitol to stop Congress from certifying the fraudulent 2020 election.

The reason the judge's decision is a "setback" is because Caldwell is the Justice Department's "lead defendant" in its fantasy of premeditated insurrection. How, in their hasty and error-filled indictment did Government lawyers conclude Caldwell was a leader of this supposed army of Trump rebels? Because Caldwell's social media handle is "Commander Tom."

That the moniker is just a relic of Caldwell's Navy days would be funny if the consequences of this sloppy prosecutorial overreach were not so serious.

Judge Amit Mehta said the fact that Caldwell never went into the Capitol with a so-called "stack" of other Oath Keepers rendered the government's case against the Navy veteran weaker than that against some of the other eight defendants in the case.

"There is an absence of direct evidence, at least, of planning by Caldwell to enter the Capitol building," Mehta said following a Friday afternoon hearing held by videoconference. "Ultimately, he did not enter the building."

> No evidence of planning, no entry into the Capitol. Then, why, oh why, has this decorated, twenty-year military veteran with no prior arrests been held without bond on conspiracy-related charges for two months in the first place
>
> Reading the *Politico* account, it becomes clear that what the prosecution is really targeting is Caldwell's *attitude.*
>
> Prosecutors had argued that Caldwell presents a risk because he expressed continued belief that the election was stolen even after Jan. 6.
>
> So do I.
>
> According to every poll I've seen, so does a large majority of Republicans. In our new post-Constitution day, this is a hanging offense, metaphorically speaking, for now.
>
> And the US Government seeks to punish Thomas Caldwell for what he *thinks* about it.

***

I hungrily read Ms. West's writings while wiping away tears at seeing the only truth regarding my unjust treatment ever appearing in print at that time. My eyeglasses kept filling up, forcing me to stop to dry them. I dared for a moment to hope that there were other real investigative journalists who would call out this terrorizing of an average American citizen and his dear wife. I imagined a flood of articles to raise a cry in the public square for my complete freedom.

Sadly, there was none.

Each room I entered bore witness to the desecration two months prior. Personal family photos were gone; every image of weddings, birthdays, vacations, treasured memories of places in time, of loved ones lost long ago had been spirited away on computers and flash drives by the FBI. They scooped up notebooks, personal medical records, and many of my creative writings, including funny short stories, post-it notes, jokes, quotations, and background notes for some of the screenplays I have written.

Shame on them all for what they do to innocent people like us.

***

After a few days at home I suffered the further indignity of being shackled with a bulky ankle monitor and geo-location device so that any time day or night, the Deep State inside the Beltway would be able to track and grab me on a whim. Now I was being monitored 24/7 and I had a Parole Officer to whom I must report.

Being required to pay for the privilege of being thus burdened by one of these leg-mounted people-finders was particularly onerous. The daily rate is four dollars and twenty-three cents. We would have to pay these clowns about $131.13 a month! How delightful. A maddening insult added to injury. I guess it beats ear tagging.

***

Empire Towers in Glen Burnie is one of those high-rise buildings along Maryland divided highways that houses everything from a sandwich shop to curious state and federal offices and Reiki wellness centers. Rising as a lone sentinel along a preferred "street outlaw" racing strip, it is flanked by two cultural icons: a car dealership and the local burger franchise. Within the Towers, the law offices of Fischer and Putzi could also be called the offices of the two Daves, reflecting the first name of the two top-notch barristers who call these unpretentious digs home base.

At last I met Angie, the charming and capable professional who would prove an indispensable team member in our life-and-death struggle against the corrupt DOJ. She had established for us a workplace in a sunny room with a bulk printer and two desks. The huge, ceiling-scratching window revealed an up-close view of the cockpit crew of aircraft on final approach to BWI Airport.

Dave Fischer's office boasted a huge wooden worktable topped by impressive piles of paperwork. Massive office bookcases strained under a load of reference volumes and other documents. Leather high-backed chairs faced his desk, which was strategically arranged for work and easy ergonomic transition from phone to computer to files.

Perhaps every lawyer, like many retired military members, has what we laughingly call an *I-love-me wall* adorned with memories and testimonials to professional achievement. Dave's was loaded with parchments bearing reverent witness to myriad academic and legal accomplishments. Something about his cool Southern style told me that if you asked him he might dismiss these framed testimonials as merely useful for covering leak damage to the wallpaper.

Dave was a modest but highly accomplished and widely admired professional joining a battle with eyes wide open. The smiles and jibes we enjoyed with Dave were relaxed and easy, sitting there in the comfort of his big office. I had been rescued, yanked from a terrible torment which I'd thought could hold me forever. There was so much to be happy about and, for what was too brief a period, we let it wash over us. Even the bad stuff was easy to poke fun at because, well, it was over. And that kind of terror would never be visited upon us again.

Wrong.

***

Dave had watched the clandestine recordings of my relentless interrogation and knew that I was being completely railroaded. Sharon and I spoke of our FBI experiences: from the lumbering destructiveness in the main house to the separate bumbling questioning we endured. Sharon would hear details from my shackled Q&A in bits and pieces during our times with Dave.

Together we reviewed parts of my interrogation on the day of my arrest:

FBI Special Agents Palian and Robinson continued to press me as I sat trussed up in chains in our once peaceful home. Palian's propensity for texting on his phone all this time was particularly annoying since we didn't seem to be getting anywhere.

"My back hurts. I'm supposed to take medication, I haven't had it," I stated once again. "It's been a couple hours now."

"No, no, no. Let's get your medication then. Let's stop this second. I don't want you to not have your medication. We can pause. We don't even need to stop, we can pause," Palian jabbered.

But the inquisitors did not pause.

"But I mean, guys, come on," I shot back. "How many times you gonna make me ask?"

The agent tandem, now well over an hour into my questioning, were anxious to press forward and continue to deny my medications, apparently thinking that the distress I was in might give them an advantage of some kind and make me "squeal."

"Let, let me ask you," the lead agent began again. "We're gonna finish up here so we do need to get you that medication. There's no ifs, ands or buts about that. Umm, and we're gonna get that to make sure it goes with you, just in case."

I retorted, "So *when* are we going to see my medications? Okay. So, what do you want to show me *now*?"

At his most devious, Palian stumbled out with, "So, well, I, I want to say, at any point, you know, I've got something here. ... Did you make it inside the Capitol on that day?"

"No."

"No? Okay."

This is where Agent Palian turned his laptop computer screen around so I could see 11 thumbnail photo images that I'm almost sure were some of those I took on January 6. He clicks on, and then expands the now infamous picture published worldwide (with no royalty paid to me, I might add) alleging it was from inside the Capitol. Surprise! The government lied.

Now came the moment Palian had waited for his entire FBI life. The moment he would show me a picture he falsely swore to a federal judge was a screen-capture from a video made inside the Capitol. This is his great "gotcha" moment! In his mind's eye, he can already see his commendation hanging on his office wall.

"Are you guys in that picture at all?" he demanded. "This is not photo shopped. Is that your wife right here?"

"No."

"That's not?"

"No."

"Okay." Then in the most condescending way possible Palian taunted with, "I'd be happy to give you my glasses if you need to look at anything else."

"I said *no*."

I felt like asking him if he was deaf or just stupid, but what purpose would that have served?

Palian pressed on. "Did you take this picture?"

"That's the plywood walls built underneath that scaffolding that I told you about an hour ago. It's a little tunnel there for safety, remember?"

"All right, so this isn't really *inside* then?" he replied, shooting a worried glance at his partner.

"No."

"Right," Palian responded, not knowing what to say next.

"We good? You seem disappointed," I continued. "When you get to the top of the stairs, underneath that scaffolding, right? They've built these plywood tunnels so people don't drop stuff on your head from up high above."

"Yep," said Robinson. He clearly *got it*. At long last. But not so his partner.

Palian was incensed now as he said accusingly, "That's not Sharon? Right there!"

"No."

"Right," said Palian absently. He was clearly now at a loss.

Impatiently I added, "That's not Sharon! Have you *seen* my wife? She's *hot*! I don't know *who* that cow is!"

Robinson, to his credit, could barely contain his laughter.

"Okay. All right, fair enough. It's hard to see from that angle," said Palian, trying to regain control of the grilling.

I wasn't backing down now and continued, "Yeah, but you see the plywood seams on the left there?"

"I can, I can see how that would be what you're talking about."

I tried to drive the point home. "This is a *safety* tunnel. See how the plywood seams on the left are running vertically ... ?"

"Vertical! Right there!" said Robinson, as he touched the picture on the computer screen for emphasis. He was trying to be helpful but only drew a dagger-glare from Palian, causing him to clam up.

You should have seen Palian's face drop.

"And the *nail* pops?" I said.

"Oh ... yeah," Palian responded, looking at the photo as if it was his very first time.

"Whoops, you all right?" I asked.

"Yep. Umm my glasses, that's all right ..."

The video recording and the transcriptionist captured my verbal reaction as well as Palian's to his glasses *falling off of his face in his shock!* Oops. There goes that commendation, boys. Not to mention the *I'm proud of you!* he might have gotten from his wife.[2]

The rest of my shackled interrogation was a slow, sucking, toilet-swirl for the FBI wunderkinds. I had done immense damage to their non-case against me. The fact that this entire thing was an amateurish farce did not stop them from violating our rights. There was no thought of unshackling me, apologizing, and walking away. Not with his DOJ masters pulling the strings and giving Palian instructions via text all the while.[3]

Guilty until proven innocent.

I was anxious to push back against the DOJ phonies. I saw them for what they were, and I bristled at their willingness not only to break the law but to intimidate citizens through physical and emotional pain. Never underestimate the power of a threat of violence to one's family members or the threat of long-term incarceration.

I cannot tolerate a bully. My visceral reaction to injustice might be traced to being picked on as an undersized youngster whose classmates at each level were often a full year older and bigger than I was.

Then again, it could just be the manifestation of a pathological rejection of tyrannical, immoral authority based upon unresolved childhood trauma. I'm not sure which.

***

One day as I sipped coffee at the breakfast table, I picked up the landline phone and called the jail where I had been held and asked for Medical. Sweet Lydia could not have been nicer and recognized me instantly. Along with her best wishes and those she conveyed on behalf of several COs by name, she was only too happy to send me the documentation I now requested from my incarceration.

This was the first of the flow of official paperwork which documented milestones and incidents in the lawfare campaign against me, beginning inside those forbidding walls. It would prove critical that I gathered documents before the Federal Government and its agents had time to falsify, alter, or destroy them. Which I suspected they would do. And I was right. I knew neither the Feds nor the prison industry in Virginia could be trusted. Only time would reveal the depths to which they would stoop to deflect responsibility and cover what should have been their shame.[4]

That simple phone call was prompted by divine inspiration, as we would soon learn.

***

Our first virtual *Status Conference* established a regrettable pattern of subterfuge and stalling by Assistant U.S. Attorney Kathryn Rakoczy and the DOJ. These teleconference remotes seemed little more than an opportunity for her grandstanding, with a generous amount of schmoozing of the judge. It was a "kick the can down the road" approach to trial and would have been more than I could bear if still locked away in Hell. The defense lawyers had no choice but to go along with every postponement because the government *would not* produce evidence required to prepare a thorough and vigorous defense.

Where was the evidence for defense review and speedy trial prep? The Feds held all the cards. It was the same for all accused within the net of January 6 as it was for me. All of our own exculpatory evidence had been scooped up during the attack on our home and was now inaccessible for my defense. Even before my arrest, government goons had shut down my social media accounts, forcing us to rely on *their versions* of my Facebook postings and all other communications. All incomplete, of course.

The judge in our case, Amit P. Mehta of the let-me-go-home hearing, had made a determination that the investigation into the events surrounding the government's narrative of J6 was so complex that the DOJ just didn't have sufficient time to fry its victims within the time limits demanded by the Speedy Trial Act. He ignored our rights and delayed our ability to clear our names until sometime in the distant future. So much for due process and guarantees under the 6th Amendment to the Constitution.[5]

Like me, most other defendants were arrested on the flimsiest of pretenses and with no actual evidence at all. For the Feds, there needed to be time for the DOJ to invent something to support a prosecution, even a totally fake one.

A quick dash to a federal courtroom was absolutely the last thing the DOJ wanted.

The Federal Government's propensity for the repeated reinvention of the wheel was never more evident than in our forced dependence upon the DOJ for the production and presentation of so-called evidence. Rather than utilize any of the huge menu of software programs commercially available for a systems-related task, they elected to take the expensive and foolish approach of contracting to develop brand new proprietary software using taxpayer dollars. Another calculated delay.

Legendary beltway bandit Deloitte was awarded $6.1 million, with a possible total contract of $16 million, to build a new information system supporting the prosecution of thousands of Americans, including me. When Rakoczy said they were hoping to have the system operational in 6 to 9 months, I leaned over to Dave and asked him to tell the judge that if he would lift my restrictions, I would build it for them on-site in three months for the bargain price of three mill. I could have *done* it, too.[6]

Dave didn't relay my offer to the judge.

I knew from my years on active duty and in the world of government contracting that the DOJ would do everything possible to slow-walk the delivery of information to us, and Deloitte would be either a witless serf to them or an active member of the collusion. Contractors like Deloitte remain highly profitable by dragging out the process, not by remaining agile and responsive. It comes as no surprise that delay after delay in providing discovery would be encountered—repeated holdups that would gobble up well over one year. More kicking the can down the freeway. [7, 8, 9]

The upshot of the DOJ software calamity is that it would always create colossal headaches for defendants like me who were caught in their flypaper. Two years-plus later, defendants already falsely *convicted* would learn that the DOJ had in fact deliberately withheld videos, pictures, and other data, much of it supporting their innocence. By then it was too late to change their fate.

This is only part of the unvarnished reality of due process denied.

***

There was a lot of anxiety in our home now. Lots of sleepless nights and worry. The fatigue was so overwhelming that some days I could barely function, flaked out on the couch in withdrawal from our dire circumstances. Even though I knew that it would please our attackers no end to think that they were making our lives so miserable, there were many days I just couldn't get beyond a worry-induced paralysis.

The false portrayal by federal officials had destroyed my reputation and standing in the local community and nationally. The DOJ propaganda flowed through the media hose to poison the minds of so many. Even people with whom I was acquainted who were supposedly part of the local Church family had become the most incessant gossips and seemingly couldn't wait to trash me on chat board sites and elsewhere. It all led to an incredible level of anxiety, depression, humiliation, and an ongoing sense of vulnerability.

Being ostracized was one thing, but it didn't hold a candle to the fear for our personal safety. The hate mail flowing our way, uninvited people coming up the driveway coupled with the raw memory of violent attack by the FBI made me feel that we were sitting ducks. We had no ability to defend ourselves in the public square or on our property should the hate-speech in the press manifest into physical confrontation on the street or at our home. The street arm of the Democrat hate apparatus was hard at work.

***

The first dribbles of soft-copy discovery schmutz from the government were dodgy password-protected flash drives containing PDF files of warrants and receipts for things seized along with the deception-filled criminal complaints authored by the government. Later we were able to find evidence of the infuriating lengths to which the Feds had gone to invade our privacy and devastate our lives. The digital nature of life in America these days lends itself to all manner of intrusions, and it made things quite simple for the DOJ and all its subsets to violate our rights.

Even before they impressed me into the dungeon population gang, they obtained our phone records and identifiers from AT&T for everybody either Sharon or I had *ever* called. Every business, every creditor. None of this had anything to do with the so-called January 6 case, but why should the DOJ or AT&T care?

On false pretenses, DOJ prosecutors were at once granted access to the Google email accounts for Sharon and me, and again just prior to the government's military-style assault on our farm. This led them to my complete email account history, including folders for saved things, all unsolicited advertising sent to me, every receipt for any purchases, all political contributions, and every email I sent and received. Ever. Going back decades. And all my personal contacts, *including relatives.* Those folks were now also being violated and would soon be harassed.

The same DOJ that bristles at the mention of their politically motivated prosecution campaign was *very* interested in any political contributions our household had made. They even grilled me about such contributions during a portion of the FBI inquisitorial period that was "redacted" from the "official" transcript of that event in two separate places—but, thankfully, *not* from the copy I saved before they doctored it and reposted it to the evidence website. [10]

The DOJ contacted our credit card companies and demanded a complete history of our transactions and payments made over several years, first informing them telephonically, then electronically, that I was a *terrorist.* That was the word they used: "terrorist." The wokeists at these banks were only too happy to supply in multiple formats to the FBI/DOJ alliance everything they asked for, and then summarily *cancel* our credit cards.

Take note, all Discover Card members. We found out about the credit card thing only when our card of choice was repeatedly rejected in the check-out line at the local Walmart as we stood there with a cart full of groceries and a long, impatient line behind us. This was the woke joke: Discover Card. Kathryn Rakoczy had reached out to Discover with a subpoena for a card not even in my name. The card in question was one opened by Sharon many years before we had even met. Not *my* card. *Her* card.[11] The one she used to pay the bills at her Mother's Elder Care facility. *Sharon* has never been charged with anything!

Do you think Discover Card cared one whit? The report in reply to the subpoena showed zero adverse information.[12] That didn't stop Discover Card from abruptly cancelling our card if not at the direction of, then certainly in partnership *with* the DOJ. The people at Discover Card wouldn't even discuss their decision with us.[13] What had changed? Over twenty-five years of customer loyalty. Thanks for nothing, Mrs. Caldwell. We don't know you.

And let us not forget USAA! United Services Automobile Association. You know, the people who bombard us all with heartwarming commercials about how they just *love* service men and women and all veterans. They even hired a likeable ex-football player as a paid spokesperson for their commercial barrage. Yeah, they cancelled our USAA Visa card, too, after a give-and-take with the DOJ. Guilt by accusation. Thanks for your sacrifice, veteran. Now drop dead. [14]

The FBI and the DOJ contacted Experian and other credit agencies, destroying our pristine lifelong high credit rating.[15] Now it would be harder, if not impossible, to borrow against the family farm to pay mounting legal fees.

At the Social Security Administration, a place where some believe expediency and customer service go to die, it seemed a flash-precedence imperative that my disability payments be halted. Thus, while still reeling from the effects of the gulag, I got the dreaded benefits cancellation letter, which contained the words "we should have stopped the Social Security benefits beginning January." That was accompanied by a demand that we *repay* them many thousands of dollars that we did not have. This demand was wrong and completely illegal, of course. The only possible reason for their demand was direction from the DOJ. We were so outraged! [16]

Having toiled in public service for most of my adult life, I held active security clearances up to and including Top Secret Codeword. The DOJ took steps to destroy my eligibility for any future security clearance through targeted slander and letters directed to clearance-adjudication authorities. The written documentation we uncovered was unjust and heartbreaking.

The DOJ contacted every active-duty Navy and Joint Military Command still in existence at which I had ever served to officially inform them that I was a terrorist and that I was the target of a full counterterrorism investigation. This accomplished the dual purposes of ensuring that I could never gain employment at any of those places again, even in what the DOJ considered the improbable event I should escape their grasp, *and* making sure that each command informed their members that contact with or support for me might be grounds for their dismissal. [17]

Isolation. This was a lockup of a different sort.

All of the above and more was done with notable enthusiasm and giggly delight. The DOJ and the FBI held irrefutable evidence of my innocence.

But they didn't care.

Chapter 7

Outrage and Treachery

Cellebrite is the primary tool used by the Feds to extract from your phone all contacts, SMS messages, pictures, videos, audio files, and even stuff you have deleted and thought had disappeared. Cellebrite is an Israeli company, rumored to be the brainchild of enterprising ex-Mossad (Israeli secret police) agents, possibly with clandestine seed money. The DOJ, when railroading people during prosecutions, also use Cellebrite to superficially meet the requirement of providing "evidence" to defendants.

NSO, Cellebrite's parent company says the software "*transforms* the data from phones with a code that scans and rewrites the data to another computer or device." The keyword here is "transforms," meaning *changes the data during this transfer and even afterward.* That's correct. *Changing* it to what the FBI and the DOJ *want* it to be. Not just in form, but in *substance.*[1]

Matthew Rosenfeld, the genius software guru known online as "Moxie Marlinspike," states that Cellebrite makes it easy to *"rewrite the data, even that saved from* previous *analyses and extractions."*[2]

It was only through this compromised and invasive government software that we could access any of the so-called discovery evidence the government would slowly release to us. They had the computers, phones, and electronic records of the lives of every defendant caught in their J6 trap. No one charged could access that information on their own, not with every company and organization acting as an arm of the Feds.

Although the DOJ had provided me with a Cellebrite extraction of supposedly everything in my phone, it was almost impossible to find certain information using the cumbersome Cellebrite interface and reports. How are you supposed to prepare for a trial and present exculpatory information in your defense when it is hidden deep inside a mound of digital gobble-dee-gook? Or not given to you at all? The FBI appeared hesitant to let us look at my phone in person, but once we put in a request through the court, well, I guess they had to let us see it.[3]

I would never have my smart phone returned to me by the government, but with Dave Fischer at my side, I held and inspected my phone one day at an FBI complex in Manassas, Virginia. Under the watchful stare of an FBI babysitter, we were able to view the data and information in my phone and confirm that valuable exculpatory evidence was, in fact, still there.

Its forces arrayed against me, the DOJ thugs must have thought I would fall in line and simply do what some of their other victims had done when confronted with phony evidence: squeal for mercy. But I did *not*. Their reaction was to become enraged like horribly spoiled children who didn't get a pony for their birthday. And to triple-down on the lies and pressure.

***

Less than a month after I had been raised from the dead, Dave Fischer had worked out a strategy for us to go on the media offensive, which I had been anxious to do. Our hopes were dashed when he phoned shortly thereafter to tell us the judge in our case had called an "emergency" meeting of counsel.

A guy named Michael Sherwin, who had been the "Acting" U.S. Attorney for the District of Columbia on January 6 and who was a key player in the events of that day, had garnered quite a bit of attention. Some have described him as a pompous unapologetic acolyte of the twin paragons of legal corruption, William Barr and Eric Holder.[4, 5, 6] He had given a television interview, on a major network, broadcast in prime time, in which, among other things, he portrayed himself as the architect of the legal response to events on Capitol Hill on January 6. And as a bit of a hero, at that.[7]

Sherwin cheerily proclaimed on camera: "I wanted to ensure and our office wanted to ensure that there was shock and awe, that we could charge as many people as possible before the twentieth, and it worked because we saw in social media posts that people were afraid to come to DC 'cause they're like: if we go there we're gonna get charged."[8]

His words were simultaneously infuriating, disgusting, and revealing. Here was a taxpayer-paid so-called lawyer, who clearly admits that *he personally*—and his "office," the FBI, and any other forces he could assemble—wanted to arrest "as many people as possible." Thus he conspired to use force to simultaneously deprive large numbers of citizens of their Constitutional rights and, through the use of intimidation and fear, control millions of others.

His interviewer served up what you might call a "high hanger" right over the plate to an itchy Sherwin ready to send a soaring soundbite over the fences. The talking head specifically asked whether people should be charged under the Civil War-era Sedition Act, accusing them of attempted overthrow of the government, thus spilling the beans on future action scripted and planned for implementation in the fullness of time.

Sherwin said, "I believe the facts do support those charges, and I think that as we go forward, more facts will support that."[9]

Sherwin referred to the former President as "the magnet" who brought people to the Capitol on January 6 and claimed Trump made people feel compelled to take action. He was saying President Trump was responsible for any misdeeds committed that day.

"Maybe the president is culpable for those actions," Sherwin said.[10]

Sherwin's televised performance-art shone a white-hot spotlight on the true and final goal of the Deep State and media's January 6 operation: eliminating the chance for President Donald Trump to ever be re-elected to serve our Country as President.

In the hastily called status conference after Sherwin's remarks, Judge Amit Mehta put his best "I am appalled" face forward and wagged the verbal finger at all of the law school grads concerned with the case, though the comments could only have served the purposes of the inquisitors, with whom the judge shared an office building.

He went on to say, "[A] second media event was a story that appeared yesterday in a *New York Times* article that was titled, 'Justice Department Said to Be Weighing Sedition Charges Against Oath Keepers.' That article attributed two anonymous sources that the Department of Justice is evaluating sedition charges in this case; and specifically, the article named three of the defendants in this case."[11]

One of the yappers among the prosecution army had talked to the Times. The fuzzy feline was officially out of the sack now.

"These types of statements in the media have the potential of affecting the jury pool and the rights of these defendants, and the government, quite frankly, in my view, should know better," said Judge Mehta.[12]

They *did* know better, your Honor, and they did it willfully. They're unscrupulous, not stupid. For the DOJ, tainting the jury pool was just the next box to check. I believed even then that they counted on the trial never moving from the District of Columbia because the government could not take the chance that anyone might be acquitted.

"No matter how much press attention this matter gets, let me be clear that these defendants are entitled to a fair trial, not one that is conducted in the media," said the Honorable judge.[13]

I wholeheartedly agree with you, your Honor: We ARE entitled to a fair trial. I also state on the record that I could never be high enough or drunk enough to think we will actually receive one.

Good old Sherwin was the guy who *personally* signed a 22-page court document which argued that I must remain in forced solitary confinement. It contains so much blatant falsehood that to this day it is difficult to read, knowing the suffering his self-serving delusions caused and *still* cause for my wife and me.[14]

Sherwin's braggadocio and this new explosion of negative press scrutiny surrounding January 6 caused lawyer Dave to shut down our plan to go public. We would need to wait.

***

While the threat of life in a cage hung above me like a sword of Damocles, Sharon and I continued on, trying to regain the joy of life we'd once had in abundance. Notwithstanding Roman philosopher Cicero's parable about people being incapable of happiness while constantly apprehensive about impending death, we managed to laugh every day.

I don't know that this is illustrative of the triumph of the human spirit or anything as noble as that. We have never felt the victor's elation of accomplishment or conquest. Sharon is a realist, and even in the early days of my extraction from prison, she knew that this struggle against the darkness would be long and painful for us. Physically and spiritually.

I hoped she was wrong.

Sharon and I enjoyed our Bible reading and study period each morning. It was a pleasing and encouraging way to begin the day, and we found that our plans and responsibilities became jumbled and frustrating if for some reason we were forced to put off or even skip this time together in the Word. The Bible, then a devotional, then daily prayers from a wonderful book given to us by Teresa, one of Sharon's cousins, all were a natural and important part of our daily lives. I was learning and being inspired. And I was encouraged.

Sometimes I was even shocked when I discovered passages that seemed written specifically to gain my attention.

From Psalm 42: 10-11

10 My bones suffer mortal agony as my foes taunt me, saying to me all day long, "Where is your God?"

I flashed back to that dirty Virginia backroad and the taunts from my abusers of "Where is your Sky Daddy?" The recall of that day made me shiver again so far removed from the time and place. Sharon read the words of my attacker aloud from the Psalm and as quickly as the dread remembrance was ratcheted up, the words of comfort, instruction, and hope which followed pushed it away. I was not the only one ever to be injured.

11 Why, my soul, are you downcast? Why so disturbed within me? Put your hope in God, for I will yet praise him, my Savior and my God.

Exactly what kind of evil were we fighting, anyway? I dreaded the answer I knew to be true.

There is no way to overstate the importance of our Faith, particularly now that we were fully engaged in a spiritual war. Considering the awesome powers of darkness arrayed against us, it is nothing short of a miracle that I was released through an earthly legal action we knew only happened through intercession by our Lord and Savior. That simple truth was plain to Sharon and me. We wondered if anyone else would recognize it.

After my experience in that tomb in Orange, Virginia, many things happened to me and for me. One of the most important was that I was understanding the New King James Version of the Holy Bible like never before. My spiritual eyes were now opened, never to be closed or averted again. The impact of this was incalculable.

Besides the fact the DOJ could count on the coddling good graces of the judges to whom they were pandering, prosecutors also had a plethora of tools to assist them in every endeavor. Their assertion that other critical arrests of people involved in J6 were *imminent* was justification in their view for keeping people locked up.

The foundation of the DOJ fantasy was that keeping people incarcerated in pre-trial detention (virtually all of them with zero criminal history) in violation of their Constitutional rights would thwart "ongoing criminal activity" just waiting to spring into another "attack on democracy!" All that the prosecutors had to do in order to continue this subterfuge was, with some regularity, arrest someone else, *anyone* else, and add them to the list of the indicted.

That is exactly what happened, and it is an irrefutable matter of public record, regardless of any DOJ spin that doubtless will follow this telling.

One device used to smack the defendants and Lady Justice on the noggin is called a "superseding indictment." The superseding indictment mambo amounts to charging an additional person or wordsmithing a current version of any indictment, and perhaps adding a charge here or there against one of the detestables being persecuted. This never-ending stream of documents would take the name of First Superseding Indictment, Second Superseding Indictment, and so on.

The DOJ illusionists had adopted the Salem witch-hunt rules of engagement through their characterization of the January 6 inquisition as an "on-going investigation." This meant that each time a count or a person was added and a new version of the indictment was submitted to the court, the trial was kicked down the road another 90 days or so. The perpetual revision of a start date for a trial provided the prosecution with carte blanche to subvert any actual justice or speedy trial requirements time and time again. It was bad enough for us; imagine the horrors of this tactic for those continuing to rot in pre-trial detention. Awaiting a trial with no foreseeable start date. This practice is not widely known, but it happens all too frequently in our so-called legal system.

It's just that nobody before me has ever told you about it.

This entire process is part of the punishment.

The inexorable advance of the powers of darkness was maddening to watch. I knew all too well a feeling of helplessness from my time in the Gulag. I was feeling it again. But I still believed in the justice system and the American way, which I had defended all my life.

What a dope I was.

I suppose the court couldn't easily justify denying my requests to make the multi-hour drive to meet and work with my lawyer. There were long, tiring hours of contemplation spent behind the wheel driving home in the dark from Dave's Northern Law Office in Glen Burnie, Maryland. Often with Sharon slumbering in the passenger seat, I had time among the wearying headlights and taillights to wonder what was happening to us and how much we would be forced to endure.

I also had lots of time to consider what I was learning from the daily study of God's Word. What was the intent of all of this? God does not set about to hurt His people. He did not do this thing to us. I'd read many references to God accomplishing His plan in His timing, not our own. I sometimes worried I might drop dead waiting on the promise.

The Bible says He has a plan for us all, so it must be true. If a prophetic "word" has been spoken over me, then when will I move into my destiny?

What's He waiting for?

I know I have changed in many ways since this began, especially in terms of having a personal relationship with Him. Could it be that there's something *else* He is trying to work within me? Could that be the holdup? Is the holdup *me*? Oh, man! Is there something in my life that's delaying the miracle?

As these thoughts spun around in my head, I kept piloting our old car capably homeward through pitch-black nights.

***

Everyone starts somewhere, and not everyone who likes the prospect of farming or being on the farm was born into the farming experience. I am a perfect example of this. I was in junior high school amid a gaggle of friends I had known for nearly a decade when one terrible day my parents said matter-of-factly that "we" were moving. Before I was even aware of what was happening, the groundwork for an escape to the country and the first of several cataclysmic upheavals in my life had begun.

Anyone who has ever faced being the "new kid" in high school knows what a turbulent time this can be. It was very distressing for me to leave the school chums I had grown up with and the neighborhoods and soda shops I was familiar with to enter a world in the country where I was a stranger. I left a place that was comfortable and where the future seemed well charted to become a freshman among the cliqued-up social hierarchy of a rural high school where I *was* no one and *knew* no one.

Compounding my sense of loss and my feelings of being adrift in a strange land and a stranger way of life, was that I was an instant farm kid but, alas, quite clueless. My Dad had spent a period banished to his uncle's farm near Slippery Rock, Pennsylvania, as a child and "knew enough to be dangerous" in the farming department. He and I learned a lot through trial and error. Lots of error. I think back now to digging post holes by hand and bottle-feeding baby calves. It seems a lot more idyllic than it did at the time.

But I learned.

I often say that I couldn't wait to leave the farm, and, as a daydreaming teenager, that was certainly true. I also say for comedic effect that I joined the Navy to see the world. I saw it, the bad guys shot at me, I didn't like it, and I came back!

When I wasn't stationed on the other side of the world, I always tried to schedule my vacations during peak harvest times so that I could be on the farm to help. Even though I was a Navy officer, I wanted to help my folks cut and bale hay, build fences, cut and stack firewood for the winter and tackle the myriad other major chores. While other single officers were taking trips to Acapulco or Sydney, I was doing stuff like helping birth baby cows! Here is a helpful hint to the would-be gentleman farmer: If you have to reach inside to help turn the unborn baby cow or pull it out during the birthing process, make sure you take your wristwatch off *first*!

Now, after an incredible trauma, I was at our little homestead once more alongside my loving wife.

But I could not escape the lingering sense of dread. How long before the demons snatched me away again?

***

Those first spring and summer seasons since being raised from the dead of the Central Virginia Regional Jail were a swirl of activity on the farm. Even the simplest things—the budding of a tree, the return of birds I knew to be seasonal visitors, the eruption of the spring peepers—seemed so amazing. I could feel the Presence of the Lord and the magic of His Creation in the wind easing through the leaves. There were times when I thought I would never again experience these wonders. If they had their way, the bad guys would make certain this would be the last spring, the last summer of country life for me. It was so unfair that Sharon and I should have even these most modest of pleasures overshadowed by worry and the massive weight of anxiety brought down upon us by people in a three-letter federal bureaucracy.

As the DOJ dawdled, the increasingly frustrated judge in our case called for more remote go-to-meeting style *status* conferences.

If I had to hear one more time about how "diligently" the unethical government lawyers were working to make so-called discovery information available to defense counsel, I felt I would throw up right there in Dave's office.

Then one day, it happened. Assistant U.S. Attorney Kate Rakoczy opened her yap once too often. And Dave stepped right up.

Pontificating before the judge about the efforts of the prosecution team to date, she spoke of perhaps doing some "reverse proffers" with the defense. As she paused to take a breath, Dave struck like a cobra impatient with the bouncy antics of the annoying, slap-happy mongoose.

"Your Honor, Dave Fischer here for Mr. Caldwell. We would be anxious to participate in a reverse proffer with Ms. Rakoczy as soon as it could be arranged."

She had stepped in a steaming pile, what a scientist might call a mass deposition, of her own creation.

And she didn't have the right shoes for it.

A *reverse proffer* is the act of the DOJ presenting to a defendant in the presence of his or her counsel the so-called facts which they intend to use at trial to obtain convictions. There can be any number of situations in which such a thing might actually support the pursuit of truth and justice. This was *not* one of those times.

Now the government crew was on the hook because of Dave's request, and on the record before the judge, no less. Dave thought to use this reverse proffer to gather some intelligence on the DOJ plot to frame his client. There was absolutely no downside to this, since Dave and I needed not say a thing before, during or after. It was to be conducted by teleconference, which was fine since I didn't want to be in the same room with any of those people.[15]

The FBI's Palian was advertised initially to be a participant, but that is not what the DOJ had schemed. The so-called evidence in the reverse proffer was displayed in PowerPoint projection-style while Rakoczy appeared on-screen in a visible "box" (which seemed appropriate). The "box" for Palian was curiously blacked out to support Rakoczy's preposterous contention that he wasn't part of the event at all.

I instantly knew this to be a bit of FBI *tradecraft*. Palian was there all right, most likely alongside one or more of the "specialists" the FBI keeps in the basement for such times as these. At least one "body language" expert would pay close attention to the real-time image of Dave and me on the screen to watch for physical reaction to DOJ verbalized *stimuli*. This might tip the government wonks in real time to any hot buttons they might push. Like a "tell" in poker. Please don't forget that I am educated and used to work for the FBI despite prosecutors' claims to the contrary.

Virtually *nothing* shown in that hour-long, droning, Rakoczy sleeping pill of a *proffer* was destined to be presented in any trial which might come. It was totally made up in an effort to help convince the judge that the DOJ was doing something professional.

Now Dave took charge.

"Do you have any evidence that my client entered the U.S. Capitol building, participated in a plan to enter the Capitol, or to stop Congress from certifying the Electoral College Vote?" he asked.

"No," was Rakoczy's nervous response.

"No," Dave Fischer accusingly repeated.

"No, but the investigation is still ongoing and we expect ..."

With her response, Rakoczy in effect admitted that prosecutors had lied during three detention hearings and two grand jury proceedings already. "No," she said, telling lawyer Dave they had no evidence of what they had charged me with.[16]

But the *judge* would never hear about it. Dave tells me the defense can't just talk with the judge. Regrettably, that kind of service-to-justice stuff only happens on television.

> *"Some people don't want to hear the truth because they don't want their illusions destroyed."*
>
> — Friedrich Nietzsche, scholar, philosopher, philologist

The world may never know the truth of what Kathryn Rakoczy had to do to be assigned to the fake *Russia Collusion case*, a plot to overthrow a duly elected President. That was a huge professional opportunity for her.[17] Bending and even breaking rules and violating ethics to further the leftist agenda is, after all is said and done, the essence of the DC ethos.

Some on the chatboards of her profession found it odd she was added to the *Mueller Team*, engaged in the political conspiracy to falsely portray President Donald Trump as a *Russian Agent* which wasted tens upon tens of millions of taxpayer dollars. Rakoczy joined the project having been an Assistant U.S. Attorney in DC working misdemeanors and street crimes.[18] True, she had been elevated for a respectable amount of time to *violent* crime cases, possibly in an attempt to establish some kind of powerful *bona fides* for her.

In this image-conscious town, Kathryn Rakoczy was best known for marrying a co-worker and professional mentor and then having the wedding ceremony at the Whittemore House, the home of the Women's National Democratic Club in Washington, DC. This got considerable ink from none other than the *New York Times*.[19] A political headquarters, not a church. You don't see that every day, and it raised more than a few eyebrows in DC. So much for any attempt to portray fairness and political neutrality in professional ideation and activities for dear Kate. This is not *my* assessment. This is straight from lawyers being catty about fellow lawyers on their blogs, websites, and in online articles.

Mueller wasn't investigating street crime, so it stands to reason both that assignment and this one to the January 6 thing could have been a favor, payback, or a type of pay-for-future-play. Among Rakoczy's legal brethren it was mused that any of these could explain her being plucked from the crowd for two anti-Trump assignments in a row when there were others who had significantly better resumes along with the right schools. Nothing against an American University Law Degree, they argued, but many in the legal fraternity across this land and inside the capital city speak of such degrees as if they can be had by slitting open the latest coupon mailer.

The Oath Keepers and the Proud Boys social clubs had been selected as J6 targets during the previous summer, a decision involving an FBI tool named Steven D'Antuono. He was fresh off the laughable Gretchen Whitmer operation in which the Bureau faked a kidnapping of a leftist Michigan governor with national-level political aspirations.[20]

D'Antuono was the big shot of the moment and assigned to the highly coveted and financially profitable FBI *Washington Field Office* to work his magic once more against "militia groups." In his Whitmer fairy-tale plot, "rife with wrongdoing by undercover agents and informants,"[21] the "mastermind" was a homeless guy sleeping in the basement of a vacuum cleaner store. In my case, the alleged perpetrator was a permanently disabled veteran who wasn't even a member of either of the target organizations.

The brain trust arranged for a backwater Virginia detention center to be on the hook for "Caldwell." The U.S. Marshals Service established that all-important "plausible deniability" by never actually booking Caldwell into the system at all. That's right. A federal prisoner never processed by the Feds! Not in Orange, Virginia, or in Harrisonburg after my roadside abuse. Diabolically cunning. This avoided any electronic paper trail of federal responsibility. No Bureau of Prison fingerprints, DNA swab, files in the "cloud," nothing. Ideally, in their devious scheme, he would die in lockup, a victim of a heart attack that his pre-planned mistreatment virtually guaranteed would bring about, what with the denial of critical prescription meds and the Gitmo-perfected assault on the body-mind connection in solitary confinement.

I could imagine that within minutes of my body going into rigor, Kate Rakoczy could be in co-defendants' faces with her own version of *The Godfather's* "offer you can't refuse." Blame it ALL on the dead guy and we'll go easy on you. She could deal out the hard felonies to people and wring every bit of usable pseudo-confession from them like squeezing stale beer from a frat house bar rag.

However, there was a co-worker—rather, a rival—looking over her shoulder.

Enter Assistant U.S. Attorney Jeffrey Nestler, a relentlessly self-promoting University of Penn Law grad and Merrick Garland acolyte. He had gotten some great coverage from those bastions of repetitive misinformation, *POLITICO* and *National Public Radio*. This was for his lead role in the very first jury trial for a J6 defendant, a gentleman named Guy Reffitt, which ultimately resulted in a guilty verdict. It was a slam-dunk case in which the target had been done in by the willingness of his misguided son to wear a wire and goad him into venting his frustration over an apparently "stolen election."[22]

Blasphemy to the Biden Administration!

Nestler was being fast-tracked for a judgeship and desperately needed a win over this Reffitt guy who, like me, never went into the Capitol building on January 6. In the end, Reffitt was convicted based almost solely upon what most clear-headed folk would consider Constitutionally protected free speech.[23]

Nestler was Rakoczy's senior in the pecking order and seemed to some mostly concerned with basking in his own imagined glory. There had never been any doubt that he would take the reins of the very first J6 jury trial, and now he was lining up another high-visibility prosecution against the Oath Keepers. This was guaranteed to provide an inexhaustible number of opportunities to strut, bluster, and, of course, give interviews. His facetime to date put him well on his way to acclaim as the new darling of the liberal Left.[24]

Nestler definitely had his methods, not all of them admirable in my view. For example, when the defense attorney in the Reffitt trial pointed out that video evidence had been *altered* to benefit the government, Nestler simply scoffed and insulted the guy. It's helpful for a prosecutor to have a sympathetic jury. He won the jury's support by shouting at them during his closing arguments and telling them they *must* convict. Reffitt was found guilty and received a sentence of seven years plus.[25, 26]

Nestler had perfected the game plan to take down the defendants of January 6. No *evidence* needed to convict. Only heretofore Constitutionally protected free speech. Just words.

Nestler was certainly aware of Kathryn Rakoczy's progress in doing the mundane dirty work of document creation and stalling the efforts of defense teams to gain access to exculpatory data. In due time he would shove Kate aside and take center stage in his next off-Broadway starring role as the Grand Inquisitor.

Of course, Kathryn Rakoczy couldn't be blind to all of this. *Main Justice* movers and shakers were lined up to make the pleadings paperwork happen quickly and efficiently. If she acted fast enough, she might force some plea deals and stand alone as the woman who had taken down the Oath Keepers and saved the very "foundations of democracy" without so much as a single jury trial. With a bit of luck, she just might steal some public acclaim for herself.

But there was a problem.

The problem wasn't that she needed to railroad an innocent man in order to take that triumphant victory lap, although I probably was the ideal patsy—a guy she and her compatriots openly referred to in the halls of the Justice Department as "that asshole Caldwell."

You might say that Kate's problem was that the U.S. Marshals and their surrogates in a country cooler couldn't do one simple thing right. I did *not* break or plead for mercy while in their custody, as they expected. Nor did I die, as they probably hoped. Without me in detention, there was no guarantee I couldn't fully recover. Worse yet, unlike so many other J6 deplorables, I would be able to work closely with my defense attorney to sift through the dumpster loads of material with which the government burdened the accused. So severely restricted were the jailed that they would be lucky to have an hour or two on a janky, marginally functional laptop computer while in stir. And that only on an intermittent basis. I, on the other hand, could sit and search the obfuscation pile for as many hours as my aching body and burning eyeballs could endure.

Kate Rakoczy and the entire J6 prosecutors' clown show might be found believing they were surrounded by incompetents, from Palian to U.S. Federal Marshal Sweet-ums, and on and on. Why the hell did the judge have to let me out? And don't try to say it's because he smelled a rat or thought I might be what I actually was: a scapegoat to be sacrificed to the DOJ juggernaut.

For the DOJ, it goes back to Palian's decision to sit there and listen for three hours to me tear the government's case apart on the record, one woozy statement of fact after another on the day of my arrest. How many times did she tell Palian that morning to get moving? With nudging phone calls and texts, too. She was on the phone playing status ping-pong with him for hours.[27]

She positively must keep the transcript of that interrogation away from a jury.

It made a heck of a lot more work for Team DOJ, but they had unlimited money and eager coolies to assign to the task. I might not have dropped dead under their pressure, but they could be trying to make me *wish* I were dead.

Keep the pressure on and hold back on the evidence. Check.

Contact our banks and get our credit cards cancelled. Check.

Ruin our credit. Surveil our friends. Check and check.

Call the third-party payment provider called "Stripe" in San Francisco to ensure we can't use the crowd funding sites other people use for legal fund donations. Check![28]

Isolated, doxed, and blocked.

DOJ scamps were churning out press releases on the agreed-upon schedule and endeavoring to bleed us dry. Just maybe the DOJ was laying bets on how long Sharon and I could afford to pay a $400-per-hour defense team on my measly military disability payments. They kept me under relentless surveillance so they might violate me at a moment's notice and return me to lockdown, as the Feds did to my ride-along friend from the Virginia hellhole.

And now the reverse proffer! Kate Rakoczy had been careless to underestimate David Fischer, never thinking for a moment he would put her on the spot in front of the judge. No big deal, just a headache, as underlings quickly produced some nonsense PowerPoint presentation. And all the while there I was chuckling at her inflammatory readings, and Mr. Fischer sitting stone-faced, forcing her to admit there was no evidence![29]

From here on, DOJ lawyer Kathryn Rakoczy would have to step it up while counting on the one person whom she could trust and whose star was clearly on the rise: herself. She would take control to sink those Oath Keeper people for good. Starting with "Caldwell." Her fingerprints and her name are all over the documentation of my persecution.

***

NEWS & POLITICS

Did the Feds Lie About January 6? Navy Vet Capitol Protester Says So and Wants His Case Moved Out of 'Trump-Hating' Capital

BY VICTORIA TAFT 9:31 AM ON JULY 08, 2021

The attorney for one of the men at the "protest gone wild" at the Capitol Building last January has called on the federal judge to move Thomas Edward Caldwell's trial out of "Trump-hating" Washington, DC. Caldwell was the first of the Capitol protesters to be arrested. The coverage of his arrest set the tone for media coverage of all other arrestees in the Department of Justice's "shock and awe" plan to root out alleged "white nationalist" militancy. Caldwell's attorney says that's the problem because it's untrue.

Attorney David W. Fischer filed a motion to move the trial to the Western District of Virginia where there are fewer people who "despise many things that traditional America stands for" and who have less "petulant intolerance for those with differing views." He notes that only 5% of Washington, DC, residents voted for Trump and they hold him in such contempt that they believed the fake news that he was a Russian spy.

> Prosecutors have delivered *four* versions of their claims in *four* superseding indictments against Caldwell, each less histrionic and myth-making than the one before.
>
> The motion for the change-of-venue is a near-complete takedown of the efforts undertaken by federal investigators and prosecutors to poison the jury pool and media coverage, which, let's be honest, isn't hard. *It's such a scintillating read that it could be a movie.*

***

Immediately after the January 6 hoax had been perpetrated, the ruling class had cordoned off the U.S. Capitol building with imposing high black-wire fences and concertina wire. It made me wonder what the Iroquois maiden adorning the Capitol dome thought of it all. Storm trooper look-alikes stood ready to thrash compliant Washingtonians into submission, though the masses were all too willing to be locked down once again. It worked during Covid, it'll work now. An impulsive "everybody's doin' it" reaction: relinquishing personal liberty out of fear instilled by a bunch of professional liars and manipulators in government and mass media.[30]

Unnecessary panic was instilled in all residents of the District by flooding the city with a declaration that another attack by *white supremacists* could be imminent![31]

The art of the mindscrew. A deliberate tainting of any and all potential jurors for the outrageous political show trials to come. Fear served up steamy-hot to the masses.

The judge in my case, you will recall, claimed outrage over Sherwin and the government's televised comments regarding the case for their potential as a corrupter of the jury pool. Four months afterward, he chastised all defendants and defense teams for even the *suggestion* that the bright, intelligent, and highly educated citizenry of the District of Columbia could possibly be anything less than objective, open-minded, and completely fair—even to those they had been propagandized to hate. He said there was no proof to support a claim of bias, and he denied our motion to transfer venue to another jurisdiction outside the District of Columbia.

Our defense team decided a professional poll should be conducted, the results of which might bolster a future argument for change of venue. The judge wanted proof of bias, and a simple and honest poll conducted by the pros might provide it.

***

Never fully coming to grips with how urgent my hip problem was, especially having been dragged along and beaten while a guest of the State, I pressed forward with daily life on the farm. As time advanced, I was frequently catching myself cringing and clutching at grinding pain deep inside. By late spring 2021 I should have been lined up for corrective surgery, a total hip replacement. Instead, believing that I would have my day in court at virtually any time now, I held off. That was a bad health choice.

The very real prospect of being in recovery from surgery while being attacked day after day in a courtroom seemed like a special level of torment. It behooved me to try to avoid it. In those days there was the slightest chance the DOJ would act honorably, as grownups, and simply drop the false charges against me. Of course, monkeys could fly out of my pocket, too, but it's similarly unlikely.

Given what Sharon and I had endured this year, simply making it to my Leo birthday-time was an amazing blessing. So much so that I offered no curmudgeon-style protests as Sharon and our local family unit swirled about in the planning of a backyard picnic birthday party and the chance to relax with those we loved and trusted. Our dear neighbors took it upon themselves to haul and erect the party tents, grab tables and stereo speakers, and coordinate food and beverages, all while telling me, the walking wounded, to stand back and watch the magic happen.

Large, joyful gatherings for any occasion tend to end too soon and certainly before I had spent enough time (whatever enough is) visiting, laughing, and story-swapping with every single person who had come. This sixty-seventh birthday shindig was no exception, as merriment and laughter flowed easily and agreeably over us all.

For perhaps the first time this year, Sharon and I could look at our home and our yard and not see the apparitions, the paper cut-out figures of those who had invaded and defiled it. Instead, it was squealing children running after lightning bugs and spinning sparklers while evening shadows crept in. Lawn chairs and cold drinks in Solo cups with oldies from the 60s and 70s made everything just about right. Friends helped ensure that we held fast to our joy. This remains a blessed memory, even now.

America as it used to be. And will be again with God's help.

***

The year 2020 had brought Americans to the grim reality of violence in the streets of many cities and towns, all unchecked and some seemingly endorsed by municipal and national leaders. Homes and businesses were torched, people were attacked, and fear for personal safety was everywhere. Hitting particularly close to home was violence directed at Christians and conservatives, some of it captured on video as elected officials and their families were subjected to threats and violence on the sidewalks of our Nation's Capital. Most notably following what had been a joyous 4th of July celebration at the Ellipse, a park-like area at the south White House grounds.

I had never heard of Stewart Rhodes or the Oath Keepers service organization until a chance meeting just after the contentious November 2020 elections. As its Founder and Leader, he explained that the Oath Keepers was dedicated by charter to helping their local communities in times of emergency and natural disaster. Now his group was stepping up as volunteer protective escorts for conservatives at public gatherings, since it sometimes appeared that local police were not inclined to stop assaults upon conservatives. Cowards such as the paid anarchists of Antifa tended to melt away when no longer given free rein to physically attack the elderly and families with children.

A very large rally in support of President Trump was being planned in Washington, DC, which came to be known as the *Million MAGA March*. When the March was announced, the Oath Keepers and who knows how many other groups resolved to come to DC. Mr. Rhodes asked me as a Virginia farmer if I knew of any property near the city where members of his group could camp out on the land. This way, they could attend the rally together and not have to pay outrageous DC hotel prices to stay overnight. Several farmers local to our area volunteered to allow them to camp for the weekend on their property.

Sharon and I agreed to offer our property as a camping option for these out-of-towners. We had sufficient land and amenities, including outdoor water fixtures and a small outbuilding with some heat, to accommodate a small group.

The Oath Keepers I met were the type of folks I have tremendous respect for: military veterans and former and current law enforcement officers. One of their number introduced himself to me as a current member of the FBI! A close friend of mine *knows* this same gentleman. That's right, an FBI guy living in Virginia was among the handful of Oath Keepers I met, and he told me how great and noble they are. His glowing endorsement convinced me these guys are legit and respectable.[32]

But there was a bit of contentiousness within this band, leading Oath Keepers members from North Carolina, people who represented the vast majority of those who camped on our farm, to withdraw from the club and become independent. When they left after the *Million MAGA March*, I stayed in casual contact with a few of these good veterans. When I meet nice people, I like to stay in touch and I looked forward to perhaps seeing them again someday as they departed, soon to christen themselves the *Carolina Guard*.[33]

Although some members of the North Carolina group attended the events in Washington, DC, on January 6, none were ever charged by the DOJ with any wrongdoing. Just like me, they had done nothing wrong, and I was the one caught in the DOJ "rush to judgment" or perhaps something far more sinister. It would be reinforced time and again that prior to my arrest, no formal investigation of either them or me had ever been conducted by the FBI.

Which meant the DOJ had a problem.

Which in turn meant that prosecutor Kathryn Rakoczy had a problem.

Again.

Without proof I had done anything wrong on the run up to, during, or even after January 6, there needed to be some creativity in order for her career-boosting prosecution to work.

The decision was made to turn the government's attention to the break-away group of Carolina Guard members who had been identified as having had some type of contact with me, up to and including on January 6. This would bring two totally innocent gents who, like me, had done nothing wrong relative to the insurrection fantasy, directly into the DOJ's sights: Doug Smith and Paul Stamey.

The plan was for the DOJ to lean on these two "rednecks" in order to dig up any dirt they could on me and, in the process, potentially add other people to their expanding prosecution hit list. In addition to DOJ attorneys Kate Rakoczy and Katherine Bowles, the hunting party included FBI Agents Michael Palian, Sylvia Hilgeman, and Clint Morris. They would interrogate one man and then the other during what sometimes is called a proffer. This was nothing more than a pressurized Q&A session under oath and on the record, designed to squeeze useful, even self-incriminating, statements from their targets.

Chapter One of the North Carolina comedy of errors was begun with the aggressive questioning of what one DOJ co-worker had laughingly dubbed the "President of the Head Injury Club for Men," Doug Smith. Better known as Ranger Doug by his friends, he was an Army Ranger, leader of men, and had been grievously wounded under enemy fire. Another whom the DOJ viewed as a hillbilly whose only chance to get out of Dogpatch was to join the Army. No one at *Justice* could comprehend why someone would want to volunteer for the military anyhow.

It must have been painful for Rakoczy and her entourage to slog through those lost hours of the Smith interrogation, seeing how Smith time and again failed to deliver the desperately needed dirt on me or anyone else. Not just that, but Smith stated under oath and on video that the most important aspects of the phony prosecution of me were simply untrue.

Also untrue, as told to the band from DC, was the notion that I was ever an Oath Keeper, let alone a leader. I was never part of any plans regarding January 6, none of it. Smith stated that it was *he* who assigned an underling in the person of Paul Stamey to be the Quick Reaction Force, or "QRF," for his group of *former* Oath Keepers. The DOJ, unfamiliar with any and all things military, had falsely told the world that the QRF was intended to attack the Capitol for evil intent at the behest of then President Trump. Mr. Smith was the first to clarify that the QRF was simply a phone recall roster for use by Stamey to stay in contact with Carolina Guard members and the forty or so female and male retirees traveling by bus to DC in their company to hear the President's remarks that fateful day.

Using a list to call people's cell phones to direct them back to a bus for return the same day to North Carolina is not a crime. The DOJ's folly was being exposed. Now Rakoczy was faced with an additional grim reality: Smith himself had directed Stamey to find out where my wife and I would be staying prior to the event so that Stamey could stay there, too. I never "chose the hotel" for the Oath Keepers, as the DOJ accused, and was no more than a well-liked veteran and a phone and text buddy of Stamey.[34]

Particularly annoying to the DOJ pack was that Smith told those assembled that it was *he himself* who formulated the quickly abandoned idea of a boat to cross the Potomac River for evacuation of injured people should there be a mass-casualty event caused by Antifa and Black Lives Matter anarchists. Not so far-fetched considering the mob violence of the summer and fall of the year 2020. No one at the DOJ had ever known that Oath Keeper community operations, most noticeably the successful one to protect private property during riots in Louisville, Kentucky, involved having a boat standing by. This "boat thing" was the linchpin in the sadistic propaganda campaign against me in the global media.

Smith himself could come to Washington to clear things up and Stamey could do the same. You got it all wrong, he stated.

Less than a month later, the DOJ, unable to find a way to legally force Paul Stamey and his lawyer to journey to DOJ Headquarters, was compelled to head south once more. The DOJ had accused me of "contributing a firearm" to the mythical QRF, which was not true. What *was* true was that I had inherited a number of antique firearms when my father passed away. One such was very unique and from a manufacturer no longer in existence. I would not dream of trying to fire such a thing in its neglected condition. Thinking that my new buddy Stamey might like to see it if the opportunity presented itself, I took it with me to our Virginia hotel for a bit of show-and-tell.

Of course, Special Agent Palian continued his important part in *Operation Screw-Up*.

Palian's interview style might have been thought of by any government attorney as a waste of time when the DOJ held all the cards. Whip up a fuss about *guns*, something DC jurors have been propagandized to fear, and we'll really have something, they might have thought!

Now here's Palian on camera during Stamey's proffer, *giggling* with Stamey about how non-threatening Caldwell's ownership of an inoperable "wall-hanger" .22 caliber antique rifle was. Unbelievable. A decoration, not a weapon for overthrowing, interfering, or anything else.[35]

And the supreme show-stopping Palian video comment of all: "Let's face it. Is that even a *firearm* at all?" He and Stamey broke into laughter as if they were giving each other wedgies in the boys' locker room![36]

Rakoczy finally lost her cool and angrily growled at Stamey, "What you're saying doesn't *jive* with our *opinion* of the case!"[37]

Oops. Something she must remember to have removed from the video tape, although Stamey's counsel, Joseph Traficanti, took notes just as he often took control of the interrogation.

There is a name in professional psychiatric circles for people like these DOJ-types who cannot conceive that they might be incorrect about anything. It's a part of a narcissistic personality, experts say.

For the DOJ, multiple portions of the Stamey proffer video would have to be marked for deletion or obscuring. The latter was much easier because the transcriptionist could simply type the word "unintelligible" in place of the targeted word, words, or phrases embarrassing to the *federales*. This was a much better tactic than slicing an entire section from the video file, since a jump in the image was a marker that something had been done post-recording.

Tried and true, this technique was also used with the record of the three-hour marathon Caldwell questioning on the day of my arrest by simply indicating that the last ten minutes of this event produced "no relevant statements" or that the batteries in the recorder had run out. The transcriber can only transcribe what he or she hears, right? Cut the video and voila! Add the disclaimer onto the end of the transcript and the poor bastard in cuffs is done for.[38, 39]

Falsifying evidence. Commonplace at the DOJ.

For the Feds' plan to work, neither Stamey nor Smith could ever be allowed to testify at trial.

It was a shocker when we saw via discovery how far Rakoczy and her colleagues had gone to urge members of these same Carolina Guards to invent lies against me under oath. In the face of threats against them, though they were clearly afraid under the badgering, their recorded and fully truthful proffers before the DOJ zealots were enormously brave. The interrogations of Doug Smith and Paul Stamey in particular, an Army Ranger and a Marine, respectively, were fully exculpatory of me and quite a find, hidden as they were within the mounds of jumbled so-called evidence. Things were definitely looking up![40, 41]

Their testimony is really going to help us. For our defense to have the best chance, all we have to do is get them to DC!

***

Solitary confinement in excess of fifteen days for any reason is called torture by the United Nations and most civilized countries other than the U.S. It's addressed head-on in The Mandela Act.[42] That's because it does permanent damage to people. That's also precisely why the DOJ does it. Why did Congress bother with hearings about inmate mistreatment involving Taliban and Al Qaida mass murderers? The label "ill-treatment" has no meaning when it involves abusing *Americans* who may or may not have voted for a particular dude for President.

One thing for certain is that someone who has committed a crime has a specific burden to carry during the years snatched from him or her through incarceration in concrete by those in authority.

It is equally true that on wrongly condemned shoulders rests an entirely different load, whose effects, both physical and psychological, are unique and long lasting.

Those unlawfully imprisoned like me will never be the same. *Never*.

My confinement was a colossal attack on the lives of both Sharon and me. All the negativity, stress, and anxiety corkscrewed deep inside me at the Central Virginia Regional Jail hypogeum was virtually unshakable upon my release. I was suffering mightily and I had fallen subconsciously into a series of coping mechanisms, which not only did not relieve my continued suffering but added to the stress upon Sharon and upon our marriage.

I regret to say that I frequently pestered our hardworking counselor, Dave Fischer, to demand from my accusers this file or that, this picture set or that video. I wanted to go aggressively after the DOJ, its agents, and the jail itself to demand accountability and evidence from them before they could destroy it in order to cover up their crimes. It was only in these times that I was capable of focus; a consuming single-mindedness of purpose akin to *living by the feud*. I didn't make it easy on Dave or Sharon, who had to deal with my anxiety day after day.

I was so convinced that I knew what was best, what would work, and what we should be doing. I struggled to exert some control when in fact nothing was in my control. When you believe you are dealing with a very real attempt by evil people to take your life, you either have to become obsessed or give in to hopelessness. At least that's the way I saw it in those troubled days.

I needed to find some peace.

One afternoon while digging through the mass of electronic files dumped upon us defendants, my eyes fell upon an unusual sight. From the internal memory of my smartphone was presented the image of a tiny, pink, collectible toy which was one of a popular toy group called *Shopkins*. Years ago, Sharon and I delighted in our niece's story of her adventures with this adorable, 1-inch-high cartoonish figurine resembling a vacuum cleaner. It is one of scores of collectibles that gave her joy and many hours of harmless fun.

The image was found in a password-protected hard-drive painstakingly created and mass-duplicated by the DOJ, which they claimed held irrefutable evidence against me to be presented in a court of law. How a tiny child's toy could be considered by the misguided DOJ as proof of my guilt of anything is stunning. Yet here it was, I mean *she* was: her image shared with every lawyer in the DOJ and every defense team held fast by the J6 dragnet. Marked as evidence.

I was confronted by the frightening prospect that since Kathryn Rakoczy kept swearing to the presiding judge that there was an "ongoing investigation" and that more arrests were imminent, some judge might soon sign a warrant for the capture of the inch-high J6 conspirator *Vicky Vacuum!*[43]

While I was being worked over in prison, with heavy heart Sharon set out to establish a web presence for possible donations on the platform GiveSendGo. Although even now people accused in J6 cases use this platform to raise funds for their defense, as far as I have been able to determine we were one of the only J6ers who were *de-platformed* and unable to use this site to raise funds. The reason for this is that their third-party payment provider, Stripe, refused to process credit card and other donations received from people who wanted to help us. Sharon appealed to Stripe, to no avail. They indicated that no formal appeal of their decision was possible and did not provide a logical reason for their decision.[44]

In the indomitable spirit of "I am woman, hear me roar!" Sharon researched, problem-solved, created, and fine-tuned a first-rate website of our very own. She found a hosting company and everything else we needed. It was hard, exacting work. Perhaps we could use this website as a vehicle to share our true message with Americans befuddled by the propaganda and lies tossed about regarding me. The words of Psalm 27 would shape Sharon's efforts and appear on our site:

Psalm 27: 12-14

12 Do not turn me over to the desire of my foes, for false witnesses rise up against me, spouting malicious accusations.

13 I remain confident of this: I will see the goodness of the Lord in the land of the living.

14 Wait for the Lord; be strong and take heart and wait for the Lord.

The long hot summer of Sharon's labors on this and the efforts of so many other good people to keep us afloat and courageous were coming to a head.

We were ready with our website to go "live."

CHAPTER 8

We Are Not Alone

October 4, 2021

There was nothing we could do to staunch the flow of self-serving hogwash from the prosecutors to the misinformation feed-trough-humping press. We had endured in stoic silence until the time was right.

Now Dave Fischer played his card. He reached out to the most trusted man in television: Tucker Carlson.

My restrictions on movement from our home prohibited travel to the studios in Washington, DC, and so it was that a broadcasting team, capable of satellite uplink, would make the overland pilgrimage to the countryside and conduct Mr. Carlson's live on-air interview with us in the tranquil confines of our home.

We would have our moment. We had asked the Lord to help us say only the things He would have us speak to Tucker Carlson's worldwide audience. Mr. Carlson was gracious and he was angered by our treatment and our story of government malfeasance. The star that evening was the star of my heart. Sharon was as beautiful as ever and spoke with such grace and clarity. She crafted and displayed a hand-made sign with the address of the website that she herself brought into existence. It showed our website address, www.saveourfarmva.com, where viewers could learn more about our situation, and also donate to help us with legal expenses if they felt moved to do so. We felt that the sign was a necessity because it is difficult to explain, in a few short sentences while on camera, the horror we had experienced and fully describe what we were facing. The time with Tucker seemed surreal, and it changed everything.

Kara McKinney, whose *Tipping Point* program appeared on The One America News Network (OAN), was another honest journalist anxious to have us with her on camera. But as part of the conditions of my release from the Death Camp in Orange, Virginia, I was prohibited from utilizing zoom calls or similar technologies that would enable me to be shown on-screen. Instead, Sharon and I "appeared" as voices on a crackly land-line phone, layered over still photograph images we had captured during our happy, non-violent day in the Nation's Capital.

Kara graciously afforded us a chance to share much more of our story than we had any right to expect, and her thought-provoking interaction led the shocking revelations to flow naturally. Days after the blessing of that night's show, she went on to engage in a spirited on-air dialogue about our situation with nationally known author and journalist Julie Kelly, who, like Kara, was infuriated at our mistreatment by the government.

From the very beginning of the January 6 propaganda, Tucker Carlson and Kara McKinney were the strongest broadcast media voices asking the hardest questions. That put them both directly at odds with the government's deception machinery. We will forever be grateful for their genuine concern and, frankly, personal outrage at what we were enduring. We tried to take the high road and politely referred on air to the heinous, rabid attack on us as a "rush to judgment.[1]

Those two quiet, starry nights at our home provided us such hope in a wilderness of pain. The Lord had led us in His time, not ours, to an opportunity to speak directly to our fellow citizens, however briefly. This was a *good* thing.

Surely, this bad dream might soon be over and truth and justice would reign once more.

***

Being nursed back to health *physically* is a challenge. The psychological effects of torture are far more difficult to reverse than people might think. The reality of my world after resurrection was to exist in the clutches of both the cruel GPS tracking monitor and an entire government weaponized against me. The mental and physical tortures were still underway. How could there be recovery until there was exoneration? Only then might I be able to find out what the Lord wanted Sharon and me to do with the remnant of our lives.

Renewal and freedom seemed unattainable. A mirage. Not to be accomplished by our own hands.

A funny thing happened on our trail of emotional highs and lows. The Lord dished out a heapin' helpin' of blessings in a most unexpected way.

From the printer, Sharon had taken a handful of sheets and handed them to me excitedly. I wobbled to a spot at the kitchen table. I have no distinct recollection of what she said at that moment but the message was clear: Americans were speaking out and reaching out.

Taking my battered old reading glasses from their hard case, I carefully hooked them over my ears as I thought absently that this was the time to clean their bi-focal lenses. Well, maybe later, and I sank stiffly onto my chair; the one that seemed perfectly made for people whose spine was held together with metal and more than a tad of God's sustaining power.

The tiny print documented the first two hundred Americans who rallied to our aid! From near and far, from cities and towns big and small. They reached out to us and so many with very personal notes of prayer and encouragement. I could hardly believe their words as I let my eyes rip left to right along page after page:

Lawrenceville	GA	The Lord Almighty is with us; the God of Jacob is our fortress.
Spring Hill	TN	Praying for you dear courageous folks. May God bring you through this storm.
Charleston	SC	Good luck and Godspeed! Terrible what you both have had to deal with. What country do we live in?
Brookfield	WI	May God lead your path to victory!!! Thank you and your wife for your service!! God bless!!

Bridgeport	WV	From one disabled service-connected vet to another; we have your back!
Dallas	TX	May God be with you!
Hunts Point	WA	God is with you; we are with you...don't lose faith.
Portland	OR	Keep fighting! Jesus loves you!
Butler	PA	God bless you in your fight…
Clearwater	FL	We will pray fervently for your family…
Roseville	CA	God Bless You and thank you for staying strong America needs to hear your story and your bravery.
Arlington	WA	What the government is doing is obscene. Keep up the good fight…..
Ocala	FL	I am so sorry you all are going through this travesty! My heart breaks for you which is why I am donating. Hang in there! Praying for you as well. God bless you both!!!
Batavia	OH	May God bless you mightily. You are treasured and loved. Thank you for your service!
Conroe	TX	“Be strong and courageous! Do not be afraid for the LORD your God is with you wherever you go” (Joshua 1:9) God Bless You! Your family is in my prayers.
Henderson	NV	Please be strong; millions of Americans support!
Prescott Valley	AZ	This is spiritual warfare. Out of many; one. We are with you; in solidarity!
Dallas	TX	Prayers and Blessings to you and your family!
Blue Ridge	GA	We pray for added strength and courage for you to continue to stand firm during this trial.

Wild Rose	WI	God Bless you and your sweet farm! We're praying for you all!
Germantown	TN	If God be for you; who can stand against you?
Fort Myers	FL	GOD BLESS YOU VETERAN TOM CALDWELL AND WIFE! As I started to hear your testimony through Tucker Carlson Tonight Fox News this compassion started to grow in me towards your family of what happened on January of 2021 and this nation. I humbled myself to the LORD as I started to listen to you and your wife; at that same time and for the past 2 days I had excruciating pain in my left hand to the point that I couldn't even move it and as I prayed for your family and this nation I got healed! The LORD told me to bless you with this offering.
Naples	FL	We wish you the best. You and your wife are national heroes! Praise God! Praise Him for this Blessing of love.

All of the pain and worry, all of the pent-up emotional soup that had been locked away inside me bubbled up. I struggled to control its release.

Here is the answer to my question the day I was brought forth from a man-made hell. *Here* is the America and the Americans I had never met but whom I nevertheless loved and gladly served and sacrificed for on active duty. They are here.

Jesus showed us that it was not only *He* who was *with* us. Not just *He* who is *like* us.

We are not alone.

I was glad that Sharon had left the room.

I wept.

***

I guess anyone who's ever been emotionally battered to what they thought was the point of no return will relate to the rush of our despair turned to gratitude. Our financial resources and our emotional ones were at the straw-in-the-empty-glass stage, and likewise so much of our situation sucked.

Support was thundering our way online from beautiful, caring people we had never met. It brought us renewed strength. Strength. I had forgotten what it was. We'd been given a moment to share the truth in a heartfelt and direct way. Here is the response. The desperately needed gifts, the many sensitive and poignant messages, built a new pillar for us to lean on in our weakness. I say the Lord had energized a force of angels, because these people were like angels to us. All who have ever felt the deep well of loneliness and been helped to climb out know exactly what I mean.

We were now the recipients of more family support and love than most persecuted people will ever know.

We were infused with hope. Hope that the Lord would continue to carry us through this valley and end the bad times soon. The gathering of hearts that linked up with us through the speed of modern technology kindled inside a reassurance of the eternal nature of our Heavenly Father. They stirred a remembrance of the promise of His Grace and the encouragement to maintain Hope. Hope is something that good people share and nurture. And what the enemy fights hard to squash.

Unbeknown to us, a rising pile of blessed mail soon fully covered Angie's desk at the Fischer and Putzi Northern Law Office. I suppose like Santa Claus near Christmas, she was in a way overwhelmed by it all, but unlike those hopeful Christmas-gift letters, this mail asked for nothing in return. We were surprised to receive the bulging overnight delivery box she sent us and were unprepared for what lay within.

In our hands we held an outpouring from every state in the Union. We were instantly connected to the lives and hearts of so many more brothers and sisters we never knew we had! They lifted us up through each personal message, story, scripture passage, and heartfelt profession of tender concern for us. Sharon and I were nearly bursting with gratitude for the joy, the smiles, and even the tears brought by these postmarked treasures.

Late at night, sleepless and alone with my thoughts, I would read them again and again.

I was prohibited by the intractable "court" from utilizing the internet or any social media, so my personal response to our online family was for now blocked.[2] But there were no orders stopping me from responding to *postal mail*. Beginning there and then, regardless of how badly the wrist of my writing hand had been smashed on that lonely side road somewhere outside of Orange, Virginia, I wanted to write back with our thanks for each and every precious bit of correspondence.

Maybe it would prove impossible, but I would give it a try.

In the weeks that followed, we were back to being dominated by the numbing trudge through endless DOJ nonsense. Reviewing forms and reports and muck and spreadsheets of nothingness. All generated by the J6 vengeance machinery. I longed for a disconnect. My mind wandered back to the beautiful people whose correspondence kept coming. I might get physically exhausted sometimes, but I never tired of reading them and answering them.

And then something amazing happened.

People began to write back!

Christmas of 2021 was one of renewed joy. More joyous than some might expect, given that there was zero money for presents, no possibility of online shopping or treks to the local mall. Our focus remained upon the true meaning of Christmas and the miracle of our being together for one more celebration of Jesus' birth. For Sharon and me, the gift of being with each other was the greatest present this year, and our joy and love for each other couldn't be wrapped up and set beneath a tree.

Sharon and I were prayerful for a revival in our country. A renewal of truth and decency, of respect and compassion for people and for love which would overtake the culture of cold-hearted hate and persecution that symbolized our society. The Lord was with us in our tribulation. There were still so many things to be grateful for.

***

The New Year 2022 brought the next iteration of the fiction-laden superseding indictment containing newly invented conspiracy charges, including *Seditious Conspiracy*. First revealed by U.S. Attorney Michael Sherwin's slip of the lip in March 2021, it was a nod to a Civil War-era concoction used to label, libel, and jail political enemies. The tactic, employed with enthusiasm, was designed to fan the flames of the January 6 *insurrection* story, which had been losing steam.[3]

Most Americans had moved on from the government's tall tales. They had figured out that it was a big nothing but were oblivious to the fact that many were still suffering and hundreds were detained in cesspools like the infamous DC Gulag. Those same Americans were actively obstructed via a media conspiracy from hearing of the shameful treatment of prisoners and the willful disregard for their human and civil rights.

The Injustice Department's paper-chase, by dropping multiple charges and adding others equally insane, created a course-correction in our efforts at presenting a concise, fact-based legal defense. When I was denied release on the day of my illegal arrest, magistrate Joel C. Hoppe had parroted the nonsensical raving that I was involved in a *conspiracy* to interfere with this or that. Poppycock, of course, but suggesting what the DOJ masterplan might be. A gaff by former Acting U.S. Attorney Michael Sherwin on television removed all doubt.[4]

I remembered what one of my brother exiles in lockdown had said about how the government would lean heavily on conspiracy charges against someone, especially if they really couldn't prove anything. All it took, he explained, was a paid liar, a government employee, an inmate or someone being charged who was looking to lighten his own sentence. The lowest of the low were these. Inmates called each a *creeper*.

The government has a limitless supply of creepers. Sometimes, these creepers were FBI agents all too happy to spend a day hanging out in a courtroom and lying under oath as they were taught to do as part of *COINTELPRO*.[5]

COINTELPRO is a devious little FBI hold-over from the Hoover era whose cover story was that of the FBI counter-intelligence program. Hence the acronym. But in reality, it was and still is the FBI political warfare program. It is covertly and illegally focused upon infiltrating, disrupting, discrediting, and jailing those considered subversives or Enemies of the State.[6, 7]

Originally, it was J. Edgar Hoover himself who assigned such a designator to any individual, group, or movement. Doctor Martin Luther King, Jr. and Muhammad Ali were labeled as enemies, so I'm in pretty good company! With Hoover gone, it could be that the political wonk of the day who occupied the FBI's directorship position was now branding people, although he likely had a boss, too.

The FBI in partnership with the DOJ-proper has routinely abused the legal system to target their enemies of the moment. Documented tactics used by FBI agents over the years under this program and its subsets include perjury, witness harassment, witness intimidation, and withholding of exculpatory evidence.[8, 9, 10] As if that were not enough, these people who are supposed to be officers of the law are *required* to provide perjured testimony and testify to the accuracy of fabricated evidence as a pretext for false arrests, prosecution, and wrongful imprisonment.[11, 12]

Looks like *COINTELPRO* is alive and well and still targeting "dissidents," which in this case means anyone *they* (to include all of the DOJ and the methodically structured federal judiciary) perceive to be opposed to, or engaged in questioning of, the prevailing political winds. And right now, the typhoon-strength blow was coming from the leftists and their operatives in every branch of government, every Agency, Administration, and Department.

That sinking feeling is your life-long security and Constitutional-freedoms snuggie being steadily pulled from your body.

***

All prosecutors, especially federal prosecutors, are predisposed to avoid trial, whether before a jury or before a judge (the latter called a "Bench" trial) for any number of reasons. First, a trial means that they might actually lose, which would make the prospect of a trial as toxic as the drinking water in prison. They might lose because they can't always be certain they can control the jury or the judge.

Besides, a trial is so time-consuming it would interfere with the most important things for prosecutors, such as brown-nosing anybody who can help their careers, planning their future in politics, bedding as many junior clerks, interns, or other loose people as possible, and golfing with judges and others who are politically connected.

Oh, sure, winning a jury trial could pay off some time in the future after prep and motions and delays and the trial itself. But plea deals pay off right now! At least for the prosecutor.

Through bullying, threatening, manufacture of evidence, and utilizing a whole raft of other dirty tricks, prosecutors can pressure a defendant into admitting all *kinds* of things he or she never actually did. Over and above feeding both the narcissistic and prideful bent of some prosecutors, it provides a win that stays a win since it is virtually impossible to appeal a plea bargain once it has been accepted by the court. There isn't even a mechanism within the law for the victim to recant or to pursue an *appeal* of such a thing!

It takes a real knack to instill enough fear in people to convince them to agree to a multi-year federal jail term for something they didn't do. Then again, such a deal doesn't look so bad to someone held in a gulag. Especially if they've been convinced they could get twenty years to life if they're tried in Washington, DC.

Just as the hero, Paladin, from the 1950s hit television program *Have Gun Will Travel* said: "Ambition without morality is a dangerous thing." I guess Paladin was warning us about DOJ prosecutors.

***

Months removed from the dungeons of the SHU, I still never sleep through the night. I have no idea what restorative sleep is any more. That must be for somebody else. I'm ultra-sensitive to stimuli that most people would take in stride, such as fluorescent lights and buzzing or electrical humming. Loud noises make me jump. That's something new. Flashing lights give me migraines, and the cold ... the cold. I can't bundle up enough to fight back the cold. I have problems concentrating, and once I start thinking about something, particularly regarding the case and the injustices, that thinking becomes downright obsessive. I've been told it's all a result of solitary, known worldwide as torture.

I can't imagine I am the only one who is experiencing problems like this after the government has turned its brutality against their bodies and minds. I have no concept of what it takes to endure solitary confinement for years; such people must have an astonishing inner strength. I shudder to think of their emotional scars. There is a special septic tank in the underworld awaiting the people responsible for condemning others to places like those that I have seen.

I would look directly into the vapid, soulless, and scheming eyes of exactly those kinds of people many times in the agonizing months to come.

***

I don't know if FBI Special agents, or if anyone for that matter, called to the witness stand in an effort by federal lawyers to obtain an indictment must swear to tell the truth, the whole truth, and nothing but the truth. So help them God. Through the process of discovery, my tiny defense team was afforded only glimpses, not a full transcript, of the grand jury proceedings which resulted in an indictment of me for crimes I never committed.

On the outside chance that government witnesses *do* have to so swear, then on January 27, 2021, while I lay bleeding in a freezing dungeon, FBI Special Agent David Lochner perjured himself before a secret grand jury. Of course, he wouldn't have done that if someone in the hastily established "Capitol Siege Section" of the DOJ hadn't drilled him and told him what to say. No Fed lawyer ever lets one of their witnesses take the stand without an exhaustive rehearsal of what would be asked and what answer was expected. At least in this circumstance, Lochner was keeping with the FBI laziness credo of doing no investigative work and merely chirping from the stand what he was told to like a pet store cockatiel. There were lots of eager little beavers to help Kate Rakoczy in the directed deception of the jury involving this agent, including a nobody junior attorney calling himself Ahmed Baset.[13]

The Feds were using a dubious bit of re-engineered audio they received from National Public Radio for their twisted purposes. It was alleged to represent a recording from something called Zello. Zello was best known as the push-to talk walkie-talkie type communications software of choice for Antifa and other anarchist organizations in the U.S. This so-called *Zello evidence* was not merely one audio file but was in fact a blend of *multiple* such files, slickly edited, with fictitious timestamps.[14]

Zello was presented to citizens sitting in judgment on the grand jury with no such caveats and exists on the record to this day as a totally manufactured and false exhibit presented for the dual purposes of obtaining an indictment and forestalling any possible release from captivity for an honest man: me.

FBI Special Agent Lochner told the grand jury, presumably under oath, that the voice on the Zello audio recording directing the movements of Oath Keeper members was mine. It was not true. He never met me, never interviewed me. He never performed a forensic voice analysis on the recording. He did no research. FBI Special Agent Lochner played his part in the framing of me with noteworthy enthusiasm. His testimony seems to be the very *definition* of perjury. No amount of later waffling or obfuscation could ever have made the grand jury panel unhear his solemnly delivered words.[15]

Just wait until we get this guy Lochner on the witness stand!

***

The government continued its slow dribble of information to us. They were bleeding away the days until the judge would set a trial date before dropping a huge data-dump onto the heads of the defense team. Reliance on the crumbs of useful information buried within terabyte detachable hard drives from the prosecution was our cross to bear.

This was when I found the audio recordings of nearly every phone call I had made from the Virginia prison. Included in these calls were Constitutionally protected and privileged attorney-client conversations and those with my sweet Sharon. It was necessary to relive those days of trauma once again by listening to each and every one.[16]

It was hard to understand as I listened to them, how some of those recorded personal conversations with Sharon, now shared across the DOJ and multiple defense teams, could have been so upbeat. They revealed my attempts at silly *jokes* about the ill treatment and the rancid food-substitutes and the squalid conditions to cheer her up. In Dave's office, when I asked her rhetorically how I could possibly have joked while in the belly of the beast, she just says, "It's because that's who you *are*. That's how you deal with things." Laughter is good medicine, and in this case it might keep loved ones from worrying as much as they otherwise might.

The survival instinct is strong. And laughter blocks pain. Even in a hellish, chthonic Virginia dungeon.

***

How on earth could I have come to be on the dastardly DOJ's radar at all? Revelations through discovery provided the answer.

At the time I initially met several members of the Oath Keepers group, I met a delightful young lady named Jessica Watkins, who was affiliated with them. She is an Army veteran who served with a Ranger Battalion, the kind who fought *actual* terrorists in the sandbox of the Middle East. Her home was in Ohio. In keeping with the teachings of the Holy Bible found in Romans 12:13—"Share with God's children who are in need. Practice hospitality"—as she left to return home, I offered up my cell phone number. I suggested she use it should she ever be in the neighborhood again and find herself lost, broken down on the side of the road, or in need of a place to stay overnight. She keyed my number into her contact list.

People who know nothing about the military, which includes everyone in the DOJ, are not aware that veterans routinely refer to, or address directly, other veterans by their former ranks. For instance, Bob Smith might be *Lieutenant* or *Lieutenant Bob*, Fred is Master Sergeant Fred, and so on.

So casual was our acquaintance, Jessica's and mine, that after she walked away, she couldn't even remember my last name. She *did*, however, recall that I was a retired Lieutenant Commander in the U.S. Navy. So the phone entry became not Tom Caldwell, but Commander Tom.

Through discovery, we found some minor data and reporting regarding this lady, including images of her smartphone contact list. Lo and behold, there was my number, displayed below the large-type entry: *Commander Tom*.[17]

When the FBI seized her smartphone in January 2021, they began to scan her contacts. Less than two hours later, FBI Special Agent Michael Palian, with absolutely no actual investigation having been conducted, conned a federal judge named Meriweather into signing an arrest warrant for me, labeling Thomas Caldwell as *Commander Tom*, Commander of the Oath Keepers.[18]

With not so much as a cursory tip of the cap to requirements mandated by law, Palian opened a case against me based entirely on a fictitious representation of predication. *Predication* is supposed to be a clear and supportable statement of fact that justifies the opening of a federal law enforcement investigation of a U.S. citizen.

Palian's predication, found on federal paperwork, was that I was the "Commander" of the Oath Keepers and that I had "led an armed force inside the U.S. Capitol" building on January 6, 2021. In my case, the FBI found it more expedient to mislead a federal Magistrate through sworn affidavit than to do any real investigative work. Palian's statement of predication was a lie.[19]

The engineered events of January 6 created a feeding frenzy, and seemingly every FBI special agent nationwide wanted in on the action as well as the career boost and accolades sure to follow. One FBI guy named Steven Duke, with absolutely no impetus other than perhaps a phone call with Special Agent Palian and maybe another with Special Agent Justin Ellers, pounced on the notion of "Commander" Tom like a sled dog in heat. All on his own, Duke opened a *terrorist* investigation of me and even holds the distinction of being the one to assign a unique case number to my unjust persecution.[20]

Palian and the DOJ prosecutors *knew* their claims about me were untrue even before they hauled me off to what they likely anticipated would be the remainder of my miserable, short life in January 2021.[21]

***

The federal gaslighting machine was working overtime, and the propaganda over January 6 was everywhere in the DC region. Our little legal team was thoroughly convinced that no jury would find in favor of January 6 defendants, and we were not the only ones who thought so, as the disturbing number of accused who were taking plea deals will attest. Fear is a very real thing. How do you fight the lies of a monstrosity with seemingly absolute power?

Dave felt we could bolster our argument for a change of venue with a new professional survey of DC residents, the only potential jurors as things stood now. Lawyer Dave, in conjunction with other defense attorneys on my case, worked to engage another professional polling company to conduct a more revealing and targeted survey.

Thus, we hired Inlux Research and Analysis to scientifically determine the level of prejudice Washingtonians harbored against defendants in the upcoming "Oath Keepers" trial. They developed and conducted a professional community attitude survey (CAS) not only in DC but in three other areas of the country, including the Eastern District of Virginia (just across the Potomac River), the Eastern District of North Carolina, and the Middle District (Ocala area) of Florida. This would allow for comparative analysis.

We were filled with hope for a fighting chance if only we could obtain what we believed were our Constitutional rights: a chance to meet one's accusers and, more importantly, a jury of one's peers. I may have been born in Washington, DC, but few inside the city limits would remotely consider me one of their "peers."

The following comes verbatim from the Inlux Key Findings:

"Results from the Study show that the DC Community's attitude is unique among the Test Areas—and is decidedly negative toward the Defendants."

"The study shows that the DC Community is saturated with potential jurors who harbor actual bias against Defendants. 91% of

DC Community respondents who answered all of the prejudgment test questions admit making at least one prejudicial prejudgment on issues related to the case(s), while the other Test Areas admit doing so at rates from 49% to 63%. This bias is not only more prevalent in the DC Community, it is more intense. In fact, 30% of DC Community respondents admit they *have already made every prejudicial prejudgment tested for in this survey*—double the rate of the next highest Test Area."

"72% *of respondents said that they are likely to find defendants guilty*—even when given the choice to answer, 'It's too early to decide.' "

"Members of DC Community claim *high levels of personal impact and perceived victimization*."

"82% of DC Community respondents who answered all of the personal impact and victimization questions *reported feeling personally affected."*[22]

The same community that the judge stated with certainty would be fair and impartial revealed they have a prejudgment rate much higher and more intense than any other test area in the country. That's the bottom line.

It would not be a great leap to conclude that the survey has identified a deep desire on the part of the respondents to exact a measure of payback.

Dave Fischer labored over a twenty-three-page legal pleading and submitted it to the judge. On the heels of this *third*, yes *third*, and by far most finely focused of the three separate surveys proving jury pool prejudice, an undeniable conclusion of bias was at the forefront of Dave's straightforward request. The propagandists had succeeded in tainting the jury pool. This was exactly what Judge Amit P. Mehta had once said he had been concerned about. Here was the proof Judge Mehta needed to support movement of the trial outside DC.[23]

Judge Mehta rejected the findings of the InLux survey.

He would not move the show-trial to make certain of a more impartial jury. Not even to nearby Alexandria, Virginia, just across the Potomac River, where prejudicial feelings were far, far lower, as this last of three surveys proved beyond doubt.[24]

Allowing even the potential for an unbiased jury was more than the DOJ could bear and an unwarranted gamble with no upside for them.

Tom and Sharon Caldwell during the celebration at the Inaugural Ball for President Donald Trump in Washington, DC, January 2017

Smiles for the new president at the Inaugural Ball in 2017

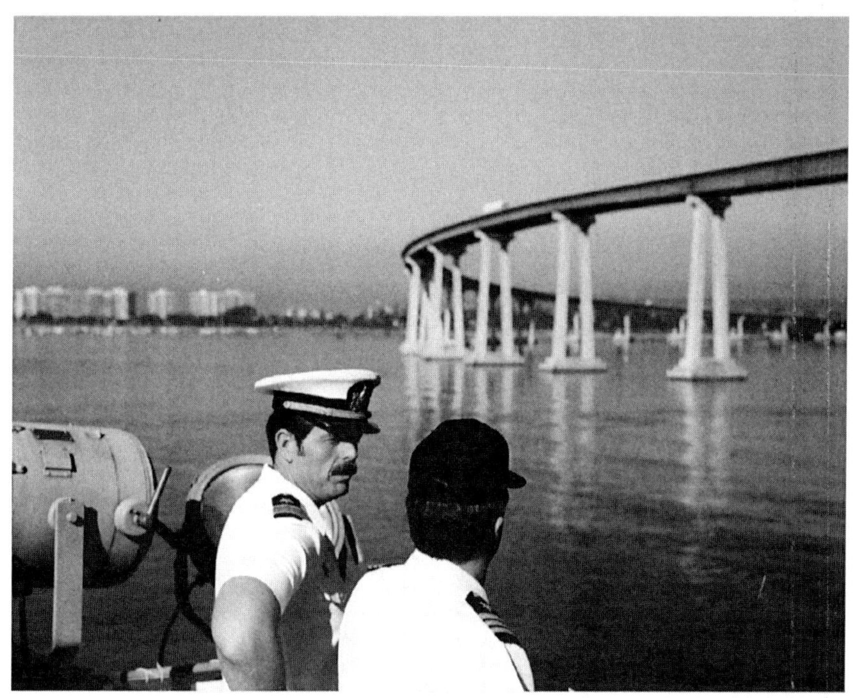

Underway aboard USS Bunker Hill CG 52, San Diego, California

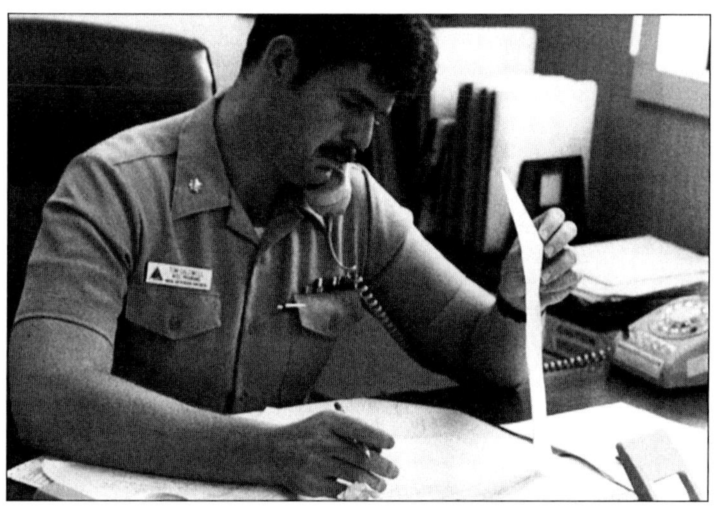

The burden of life as an officer: paperwork!

Left: Tom on his Virginia farm with Desiree the horse and Otis the goat. Above, Tom holds a trapped groundhog, soon to be released back into the wild.

Photo by Sharon Caldwell

Tom and Sharon on the farm. Don't forget ear protection!

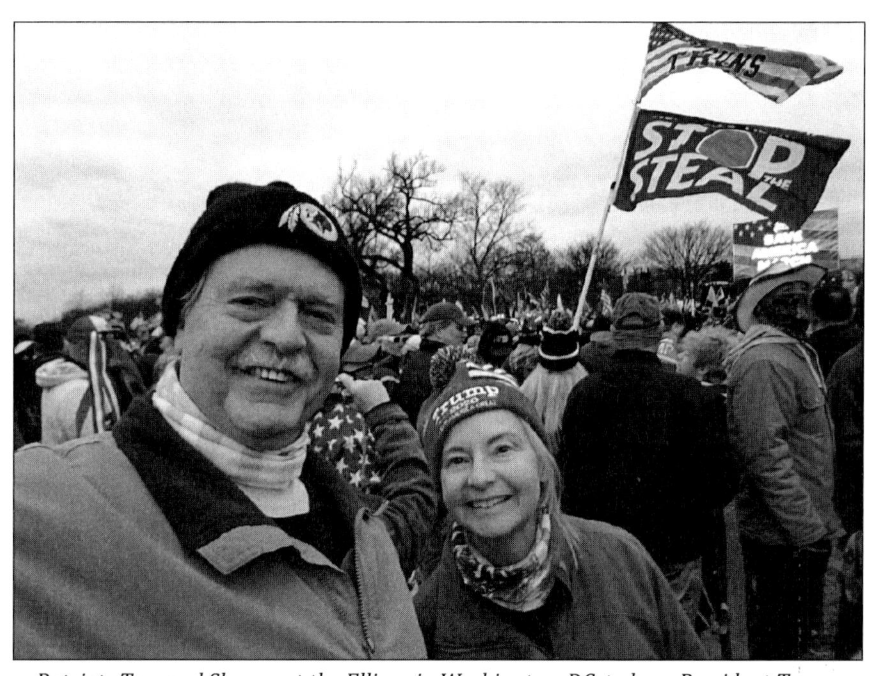

Patriots Tom and Sharon at the Ellipse in Washington, DC, to hear President Trump speak on January 6, 2021. Below: sitting at the Peace Monument

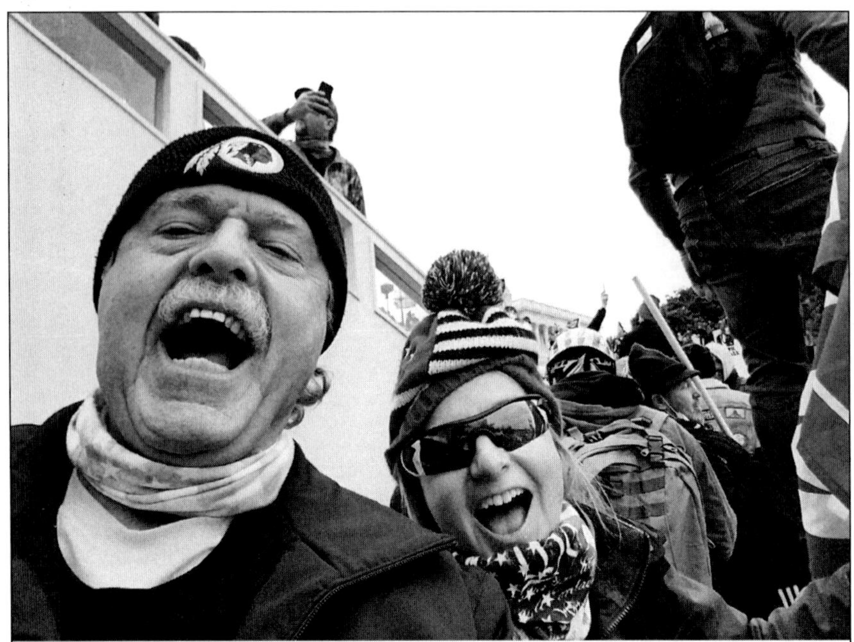

Tom and Sharon sing along with the crowd at the U.S. Capitol on January 6, 2021
Photo by Tom Caldwell, all rights reserved

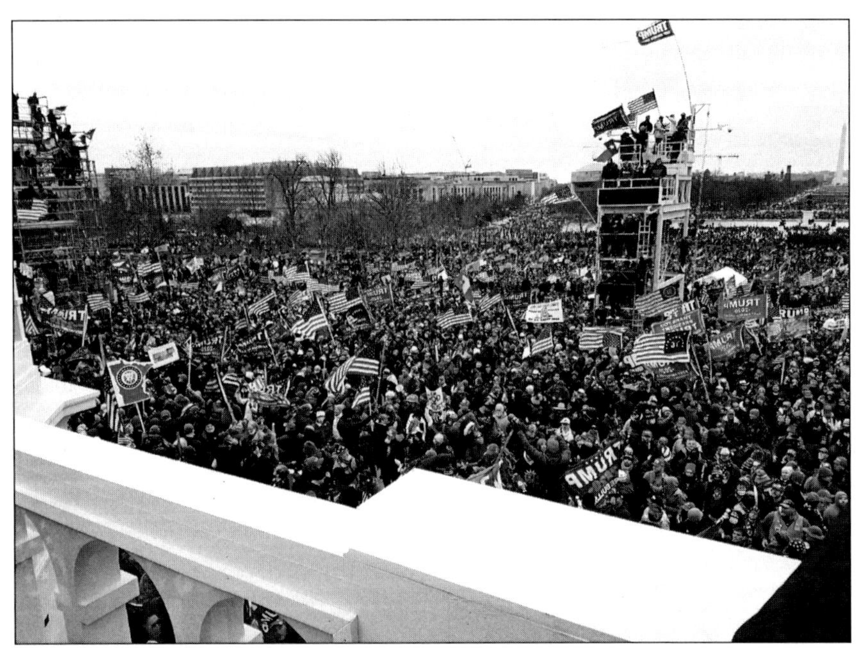

A peaceful crowd gathers at the U.S. Capitol on January 6, 2021
Photo by Tom Caldwell, all rights reserved

Tom and Sharon standing strong together on their empty farm in 2022
Photo by Samira Bouaou/The Epoch Times

Empty barns, empty farm: Tom surveys the damage after the FBI attack
Photo by Samira Bouaou/The Epoch Times

Chapter 9

A Secret Tribunal

"Whenever you have a group of individuals who are beyond any investigation, who can manipulate the press, judges, members of Congress, you're always going to have those within our government who are above the law."

— Steven Seagal as Nico Toscani
in Warner Brothers' 1988 movie "Above the Law"

The E. Barrett Prettyman DC Federal Courthouse is one of several official buildings that has been expanded as the insatiable appetite of the bloated Federal Government gobbles up resources that could be better utilized for the benefit of our citizens. Right about here was where the Masonic Hall used to stand. Called Jackson Hall for President Andy, it was a Greek Revival style building whose cornerstone was laid about 1845 and which saw lots of notable events but alas has gone the way of the dodo. Another architectural treasure lost, its place taken by a boxy structure designed with little imagination and existing now as an edifice where no vestiges of decency, spirituality, or Christian morals exist.

The ballyhooed Oath Keeper trials into which I had been wedged would be held in the laughingly named Ceremonial courtroom, in part to accommodate a legion of liberal reporters expected to swoon over the prosecutors' fiery rhetoric. There never seemed to be fewer FBI people in attendance during trial than required to fill out an intramural basketball team, plus subs. No wonder in our country zero *actual* crimes were being investigated by the Bureau.

Truly independent observers or those present expressly to support defendants were seated on the hard wooden benches to the right as one entered the courtroom. It was appropriate that the propagandists, the prosecutors' co-workers, and prosecution groupies (a real thing, sadly) would fill seats on the left, as leftists do.

To move from the bench seating, one pushed a low, saloon-style swinging gate. Sectional tables arrayed perpendicular to double-doors at the rear of the courtroom were the spot where the principles would work each day. The leftmost table of three was for the prosecutors (imagine that), and there was tiered seating for the jury just beyond.

In the middle was the defense lawyers' table and at the far right was the table designated for the condemned. Here is where we the accused were squished together along with additional defense team members unable to find a seat at the grown-up table.

Upon each table sat black handset telephone devices to allow the judge and the lawyers to have arguments over objections or exhibits. That is, whenever the prosecution wanted to talk about something without the jury being able to hear. This would take the place of the *sidebar*, where counsel approaches the judge to discuss things up close.

I was the only one of the five falsely accused individuals in this very first Oath Keepers trial—the one the prosecution *must* win on all counts—who was not forced into lockdown during breaks or returned to the DC Gulag each night.

In a pre-trial masterstroke, Dave Fischer had secured a small workspace in the courthouse to begin the battle to save my life. It was equipped with some rickety furnishings and light fixtures, a few of the latter actually in working condition. There was no cell service inside the room and too few electrical plugs; entry was controlled by a push-button cipher lock system for the illusion of privacy and security.

The attorneys for all four of the Oath Keepers with whom I was tried were content with piling into a singular workroom, perhaps to better coordinate their defense. There is a chance they were anxious to let Team Caldwell go it alone. Maybe since I was an outsider, meaning *not* an Oath Keeper, they saw no need to coordinate all that closely with Dave Fischer.

The crafty prosecution gang had set up its rec-room in a space immediately adjoining that of the combined defense, which, notably, shared a non-loadbearing wall. The walls of these workrooms were akin to those of a Chicago southside flop house, in terms of sound abatement. It was the result, no doubt, of a government contract let to the lowest bidder. Eavesdropping advantage: inquisitors.

The door to each workspace featured a slotted lower panel allowing conversations from within to spill into the hallway. I had already seen that DOJ mouthpieces wouldn't hesitate to do anything possible to scuttle the defense. Even something unethical and, yes, even something illegal. That explains their lingering outside the Combined Defense Workroom on breaks, listening to conversations underway, and vigorously tapping on their phones all the while. I know this because I had to walk past them to reach the men's room.

The September 2022 trial commencement date found us still forced to wear those idiotic Covid masks inside the building, and I couldn't wait to rip that respiration-blocker off my face whenever possible. It restricted my breathing like the Training Masks used by UFC fighters to deprive their bodies of oxygen while they work out. They deprived my tired old body of oxygen, too, much to my detriment.

Washington, DC, is a two-hour drive even in good traffic from our home, and it simply wouldn't do for me to be late to court for any reason, even if some knucklehead had caused a pileup on the toll road. Tardiness would be just the excuse necessary for the judge to throw me into that portion of the city sewer system nicknamed the Gulag. There really was no choice at all in the matter so we would have to stay in a dingy motel near Crystal City, Virginia, each night in order to ensure my appearance bright and early for persecution each day.

We did everything possible to keep our remote living costs down, including schlepping with us from home each week bottled water, breakfast bars, and the makings for peanut butter and jelly sandwiches with which to sustain us on the long days and worried nights far from home. We set up camp there along the banks of the polluted Potomac and prayed for the best. Perhaps we could snatch a day and night back home on the weekend before the legal battle would be rejoined on Monday. That early morning start required us to check into the motel late on Sunday for a tortured sleep and an early wake-up, gulp, and go.

The derisive term I overheard in the halls of the DOJ was that Sharon and I were "those people." Meaning the kind of people who believe and say out loud that the Lord will provide a way somehow. Yes, I'll proudly claim that designation, thank you. He moved many a member of our far-flung family to help us in this desperate time of financial and spiritual need.

The first major cluster we had to deal with was called jury selection. For this trial it would have been less like an outtake from the movie *Jackass Five* if, in my opinion, the DOJ weren't making it up as they went along. Even a legal giant like Dave Fischer with scores of federal jury cases to his credit was less than pleased, and the other defense counsel were borderline apoplectic.

More like a twisted Juror Draft Day operation, the prosecution and the defense would be permitted a certain number of selections of people they *did*, or else *did not,* want to be on the actual final jury for trial. There were hassles and wranglings about all of this, most notably on the defense side.

The government had a detailed strategy to manipulate and control members of the jury before, during, and after this all-important trial. Part of that involved the trial start date, chosen to overlap the ongoing "January 6th Select Committee" hearings, a Congressional exercise in self-gratification for the larger purpose of influencing the mid-term elections.

One of the more peculiar revelations for me about DC residents being considered for the jury was their nearly universal exposure to crime, even violent crime, on a personal level. I stopped counting after the first two dozen or so potential jurors offered up their experiences with carjackings, break-ins, auto theft, armed robberies, grand theft, assault, petty theft, and more. When asked if those experiences would make them less than open-minded, they naturally all answered in the negative. I'm not saying I don't believe them. I got the impression that crime was an accepted part of life for people living in a run-down city.

If I had been the victim of crime, I would have moved with a pledge never to return. Not so for the District's population.

What I *did* have a problem with was their near-unanimous claim of having virtually no awareness of who the Oath Keepers were or any charges against them and little knowledge of things "J6." And if they *did* admit to having heard any of the 24/7 stream of preposterous hit-piece reporting on the Oath Keepers, me, or J6, they swore, with dripping reassurance, that they above all others would be absolutely fair to the accused.

The DOJ was banking on the notion that these had been transformed into a people incapable of being fair to those charged by the chief payroll source within the city limits: the Feds themselves. Many clearly were eager to get even with Trump and *Trump people*.

This was the first time I got to see Jeffrey Nestler, the pre-eminent pint-sized prosecutorial protagonist in the DOJ passion play. For his loyalty to the Left, he was given the ridiculous title "Senior Assistant U.S. Attorney, Complex Conspiracy Unit, Capitol Siege Section." Gag me with a rake. There are multiple misrepresentations and outright puffery right in the job title. This didn't bode well for the pursuit of truth and justice.[1]

Nestler compulsively *sneered* more than spoke my name before the jury during trial. This was not unique to him; this derision was part of the framework embraced by every government lawyer and was particularly galling. While the transcribers of the courtroom action did their best stenographer act, they could never capture the nuance or the smarminess of the words from people like Nestler.

Suffice it to say that every single thing Nestler said about me in his opening argument was an absolute lie, and if he had tried that with someone else in the previous century, perhaps somebody with a senorita or Harley Davidson tattoo, he might have ended up as a stain on the sidewalk instead of a stain on the record of the American Justice system. I have spent a great deal of time around livestock but never have I seen as much absolute manure as was spewed from the oral fantasy-cannon of Jeffrey Nestler.[2]

If he were not so obnoxious, one might actually feel sorry for him, since he apparently suffers from significant memory issues, perhaps the indicator of early onset dementia. You see, in the weeks and days that followed, he would tell lies that effectively contradicted lies he told during this opening diatribe and other rants delivered even later.

Part of Dave Fischer's trial strategy was to demonstrate to the jury that not only had I done nothing wrong, but that the government had done no investigation of me whatsoever before they attacked our farm and violated my rights and those of my wife. When confronted with irrefutable evidence of my innocence, the people at the DOJ and its subsets kept violating their professional oaths, even inventing phony "evidence" to support their own pipe-dreams. Lawyer Dave went quickly to work.

On the afternoon of October 3, 2022, Day 4 of the political show-trial and day 622 of our miserable persecution, Dave Fischer addressed the jury in what was called the Defense's opening arguments. I breathed deeply and said a prayer, asking the Lord to help him say what the Lord would have him say in order to reach the jurors, even the ones already hostile to me without any knowledge of the facts in my case.

There was so much good stuff that we had waited for nearly two years to present in public, and these reminiscences are just scraps from the opening presentation by Dave Fischer.[3]

"May it please the Court, your Honor," he began. "Ladies and gentlemen, the government explained to you Mr. Caldwell's role in the conspiracy theory that they're putting forward. They are claiming that Mr. Caldwell was the coordinator of a QRF, an armed force that would be called upon to attack the United States Capitol. They're claiming his role is just that one thing: the coordinator of a QRF, ladies and gentlemen. But ladies and gentlemen, Mr. Caldwell is NOT a member of the Oath Keepers!"

"Mr. Caldwell did not direct or participate in a QRF! Anybody who has served five seconds in the United States military or in law enforcement knows that a quick reaction force, or a quick response team, reacts to emergency situations. By definition, a quick reaction force would not be used to *attack* anything, including the United States Capitol."

"Not one single, solitary person they, the FBI or the DOJ, have interviewed has said that the QRF was meant to attack the United States Capitol. So any suggestion the purpose of a QRF was to attack anything in Washington, DC, on January 6th is an absolute *abject lie, 100 percent,*" Dave stated emphatically.

Dave Fischer had the jury's full attention as he continued: "There is not a single, solitary human being who has said that Thomas Caldwell had any plan to go into the United States Capitol on January 6th. So why do they keep suggesting that? *This is the biggest bait-and-switch in the history of the American justice system, what they're doing here!"*

Dave quoted language from the government's own documents as he continued. "Let me be *specific.* The *specific* thing the government *specifically* said about Mr. Caldwell was that he *specifically* masterminded and concocted a military-style plan to *specifically* train up a band of tactical fighters to *specifically* attack the United States Capitol. This plan *specifically* began in early November of 2020. And it was *specifically* aimed at attacking the United States Capitol for the *specific* purpose of stopping the Electoral College certification. Could I be more *specific*?[4]

"Ladies and gentlemen, that's what they were saying 20 months ago about Mr. Caldwell! So here's the bait-and-switch: *Now it's Stewart Rhodes they're claiming this about!* Now, Caldwell is just some little guy here who coordinated a QRF? It's hogwash!"[5]

Over repeated prosecution interruptions and objections, the judge let most of Dave's opening continue, piling up many of the facts later proved in court. Such as:

- I never brought firearms into the District, as the DOJ claimed.
- I never entered the Capitol Building.
- I never battled with police.
- I never climbed over or moved barricades.
- I never conspired with anyone to break the law.
- I broke no laws.

"Ladies and gentlemen, the FBI—you think it can't get worse?" Dave asked the jurors. "When they went out to Mr. Caldwell's farm, they did not realize that Mr. Caldwell *used to work for the FBI!* They didn't know that! He was a GS-13 for the FBI! They wouldn't even confirm that until over two months later! They called him a liar! *That's* how thorough their investigation was when they named Mr. Caldwell the number one suspect in January 6th."

You could have heard a pin drop as he continued, "... and I'm sure you're probably thinking that the FBI went out the next day and said: 'Hey, we screwed up, and we told you that we're arresting a guy who plotted and planned to take over the United States Capitol. In fact, he's an elderly veteran who did no such thing.' But, of course, ladies and gentlemen, they didn't do that."

Dave leaned on the lectern and spoke clearly. "Instead, what they've done for the past 20 months is try to dig up evidence to support their theory instead of letting evidence take them to a person who's guilty. That's what they've been doing for 20 months! For 20 months!"[6]

Then Dave moved on to the three-hour voluntary interrogation of me by Palian and Robinson.

"But the one thing Mr. Caldwell has *not* been charged with is lying to the FBI. Think about that. It's a defense lawyer's worst nightmare to have a client speak to the FBI. 'But I'm innocent,' he told me. The FBI had Mr. Caldwell on the hooks. He's under arrest and they're pressuring him and he's talking and he's talking. After three hours, with the *number one suspect* at that time in January 6 right in their very midst, and he's talking, guess who ended the interview? *The FBI ended the interview!* Ladies and gentlemen, I suspect they *knew* they had it wrong!"[7]

Jeffrey Nestler spewed: "Objection!"

The judge fired back: "Overruled."

"We're in Washington, DC," Dave continued. "It's a different culture here, different from the culture where most of these Defendants come from. And they, the bad guy lawyers, understand that if they put inflammatory things before you, that they can do that and it will cover up the fact that they have *no evidence.*"

"Ladies and gentlemen, I'm not going to come to you five weeks from now, begging you to find a reasonable doubt as to whether Mr.

Caldwell is guilty or not. I came here to clear his name. And that's why I'm talking today."

Dave Fischer had put the government back on its heels, and they were visibly pissed off about it!

The jury was taking notes. Literally.

***

> *"We are the victims of a foul disease called social prejudice, my child."*
>
> — Academy Award Winner Thomas Mitchell's Josiah Boone in the John Ford movie *Stagecoach*

I felt very much alone in that godless misery of a courtroom as they launched their attacks against me. Sharon was prevented from being there to support me. Ostensibly, this was because she was going to be called to testify, and as Dave explained it, the court (meaning the judge) was desirous that witness testimony not be "influenced" by any statement they may have heard.

What a crock!

You see, the *government* witnesses and consultants were under no such restriction; FBI agents, key performers in this sham, routinely perched in Row 1 inside the swinging gates. They listened intently to the direct testimony, cross-examination by defense attorneys, and re-direct without their presence being challenged by the judge in any way. Even though they themselves would testify during this same trial.[8] Dave Fischer's protests were brushed aside by the judge.[9]

Cell phones or laptops in hand, FBI agents could record and even broadcast the proceedings to places and people unseen. It was yet another advantage rendered to a prosecution methodically using a marked deck and playing with house money. All the better to make sure the government's conspiracy advanced smoothly by ensuring each agent only confirmed what the previous one had said.

Dave complained about this once again, and Nestler in his arguments before the judge slipped up, even admitting that FBI agents were in another location, actively monitoring the action within the courtroom![10] The judge sided with the government, naturally. The FBI special agents would continue to follow the action.

***

I can't overstate how destructive to my defense was the unilateral decision made by this judge to conceal from the jury the contents of my candid interview with the FBI. Dave was allowed to mention that there *was* such a thing, but he was ordered not to enter into evidence the actual substance of the interrogation!

The judge also went so far as to decree that no audio or video of this interrogation could be presented to the jury. Nor would he permit excerpts from the transcript to be presented or even discussed in their presence. I imagine if there had been anything damaging to my defense which had arisen during the questioning it would have been front and center, fully a part of the case against me.[11]

Enter FBI Special Agent Michael Palian, the person who swore out affidavits against me, obtained an arrest warrant for me, grilled me while I was shackled in my own home, and lied to me consistently during my interrogation. He of the tag team from my arrest day was presented to the jury as the person who would offer detailed and damning testimony against all defendants throughout the trial.

Palian's appearance was clearly off to a flying start during direct examination by the prosecutors, having been heavily rehearsed. This pre-testimony scripted dry-run is government standard operating procedure, as we would learn during testimony by Special Agent Moore later in the trial.[12] The smug, self-anointed "Quarterback of the January 6 Investigation" had just weathered a first cross-examination from one of Stewart Rhodes' attorneys.

Now it was Dave Fischer's turn.

Mr. Fischer asked Agent Palian, "And you would agree that it would be the best practice that when you do an investigation into a crime, that you take your time, be methodical, interview lots of witnesses, go through evidence before you make a decision whether to charge somebody. Would you agree with that?"

"No. No, I would not agree with that!" Palian responded.

"You would *not* agree that it's the best practice to methodically investigate, review evidence, interview people before you make a determination whether to charge somebody?" This was more a repeat of Palian's words than a question.

Then Dave continued, "Okay. Now, just because you can charge somebody, doesn't mean that's the best practice. Would you agree with that?

"Again, it's a hypothetical. I don't know if I'd—I can't opine on that," Palian stalled.

"Sir, are you suggesting that the *accuracy* of an investigation cannot be affected by the amount of *time* put into the investigation?"

Palian snorted. "You use this term "accuracy." I'm not sure what you even mean by that. Can you define "accuracy" for me?"[13]

Dave's response began with, "Well, I think it's clear....but I'll move on."

Special Agent Michael Palian of the FBI believes that it is not FBI *best practice* to perform a thorough investigation before charging someone with a crime. That he swore under oath he has no idea what "accuracy" means to an investigation is chilling.

"Based on the large number of interviews you've done, and based on your review of all these social media and communication devices, you haven't come across one single solitary human being who has told you or your investigators that Mr. Caldwell planned to breach or attack the United States Capitol on January 6th?"

"We've not come across a person that has told us that; that's correct," testified Palian.[14]

"And, sir, you also have not come across one single solitary human being who has told you that the purpose of the QRF with the Oath Keepers around DC on January 6th was to attack the United States Capitol, correct?"

"Correct," Palian responded.

Next, Dave asked, "Mr. Caldwell—he sat down with you and Agent Steve Robinson; is that correct?"

"Correct."

"He answered all of your questions over a period of almost three hours, correct?" Dave continued.

"He answered the questions," Palian responded.

"He even signed a consent form for the FBI to be able to go into his barn, which the FBI didn't have authority to do; right?"

"That's correct," Palian stated.[15]

Full disclosure here: They had already broken into the barn *and* our detached garage with a battering ram prior to my signing. I had seen this when I was shoved into a government car. Why *not* sign the form?

Dave pressed onward with, "you asked him a number of questions over a two-to-three-hour time ... and to be clear, in this case today, he's not charged with lying to you, is he?"

"No," admitted Palian, "he's not been charged with that."

"During your interview, you warned him—you said it was a crime to lie to the FBI; is that right?"

"Correct," the agent responded.

"And you asked him a number of times whether he went inside the United States Capitol, right?"

"We asked him a couple times," Palian toyed.

"Sir, I showed a picture yesterday in opening argument that I represented was a picture that *you* showed to Mr. Caldwell, where you believe he had gone inside the United States Capitol. Do you remember seeing that yesterday?"

"Yes."

"Sir, during your interview with Mr. Caldwell, did you present him with a photograph and tell him that you believed he was inside the United States Capitol in the photograph?"

"Yes, we—believed that."

"And would you agree today that *you were mistaken*?"

"Yes," Palian admitted.[16]

"So bottom line: to the interior of the Capitol, you have no evidence that he damaged any property."

"Correct."

"And to the exterior, you have—you have no evidence of that either?"

"We have no evidence," Palian admitted once more.

Dave Fischer continued, "When you arrested Mr. Caldwell, you charged him on a charging document called a criminal complaint. In fact, that criminal complaint was taken out specifically before Magistrate Judge Meriweather, and it was signed on …"

Rakoczy interrupted: "Objection!"

The judge brushed her aside. "It's overruled. He can answer that."

What Palian did next was stall, as he was being instructed through Rakoczy's hand signals, while pretending, regardless of how Dave framed the questions, to have neither knowledge of nor familiarity with documents he had signed and presented to a federal judge.

Dave Fischer would have none of it. He handed Palian a copy.

"Sir, if you could take a look at that document, and if you have had a chance to refresh your recollection, let me know when you're ready." After Palian's head nod, Dave continued, "So you'd agree, 3:42 p.m. on January 17th of 2021 is when *you* were granted the criminal complaint against Mr. Caldwell, is that right?"

"Yes; that's correct," Palian responded.

"In order to obtain that criminal complaint, *you* had to go to a magistrate judge and file an affidavit; is that correct?"

"Yes."

"And *you* typed up an affidavit—I think it was about 13, 14 pages long; is that fair enough?"

"I think so."

"Subsequent to that affidavit and criminal complaint, you sought an *amended* criminal complaint *after* your interview with him; is that correct? On January 19th of 2021."

Palian delayed in response to another hand signal to do so. The prosecution was desperate to halt Dave Fischer's cross-examination momentum. After Dave gave him a copy of this second document with Palian's signature upon it, he continued the line of questioning.

"And after reviewing that document, does that refresh your recollection, sir?"

"Yes."

Dave Fischer continued to walk Palian's testimony forward. Palian and the jury could see where this was headed.

"Sir, you just testified that you had *no* evidence that Mr. Caldwell destroyed any property inside or outside the Capitol; correct? Is that correct?" he asked, incredulous.

"Correct."

"Okay. And, sir, you'd also agree that on January 19th of 2021, you charged Mr. Caldwell with a felony: *destruction of government property*, correct?"

"Yes, that's what it says," Palian admitted.

"[But] you indicated before you had no *evidence*—you said he did not go into the United States Capitol on January 6th, 2021!"

Palian responded with, "He *didn't* go into the Capitol on January ... " Then he broke down with, "I'm so sorry!"[17]

I nearly jumped out of my chair as his words stunned the courtroom. "*I'm so sorry"?* Is "I'm so sorry" supposed to make my wife and me feel better, Mr. Palian? This should have been the slamming of the door on this persecution of me, but the judge did not agree.

Dave forged ahead: "Sir, you would agree that you were able to determine *after* your arrest of Mr. Caldwell that he's a retired Lieutenant Commander in the Navy; is that correct?"

"Correct," Palian answered.[18]

"Well, sir, what was the plan that Mr. Caldwell had that you accused him of at the time of his arrest? What was the plan he was the commander of?"

"Objection!" blurted Rakoczy.

"Overruled."

Palian fired back, "He was at the minimum coordinating and, in my opinion, leading the QRF!"

"Well, sir, you didn't even *mention* anything about any *QRF* in your initial charging documents against him?" Dave asked.

"Nope," said Palian.

"So in fact you knew nothing about the idea of a *QRF* when you arrested him, correct?"

"That's right."

***

I want to be as gentle here as possible, but Palian is a guy supposedly trained as both a "scientist" and a "law enforcement" professional. I respectfully suggest he could use a refresher in investigative techniques, critical thinking, and decision making. The following concept, which spans both of his professional areas of so-called expertise, is helpful to examine here:

Correlation does *not* mean *causation*.

This basic scientific principle means that just because things might appear to be on parallel paths or are happening at the same time, it does not mean they're related. It does not mean that one influenced the other or that one caused the other.

Jumping to that kind of conclusion is what's called a questionable-cause fallacy of logic. A fallacy, also known as *paralogia*, is the use of faulty reasoning in the construction of an argument that can invent a false connection between things.

If you collect data for monthly ice cream sales and monthly shark attacks in the United States each year, you will find that the two variables are *correlated*. When ice cream sales are up, shark attacks are up. Summertime. Does that mean that eating ice cream causes shark attacks? How asinine would that idea be? One does not cause the other. Thus, there is no *causation*. But the DOJ's fallacy of logic would bring about the arrest and prosecution of all sellers of ice cream for battery and even murder for the carnage inflicted by sharks.

Congratulations! If you have just read and followed the undeniable logic of the above, you are desperately needed in the Federal Bureau of Investigation. Hopefully, they will have thousands of job openings soon.

Ladies and gentlemen, this is the "*new*" FBI.

On cross-examination, Dave Fischer had exposed and discredited the testimony of the "Quarterback." In so doing, in about an hour, Dave had demonstrated through the prosecution's own chief witness that the case against me was rotten to the core.

The jury couldn't have missed it.

The evening of Dave's triumphal discrediting of Palian, I had my first positive feelings about the trial in a long time. We had achieved a victory in that small skirmish against the bearing of false witness against me. In our old car that evening, I spilled as much info to Sharon as I could. She was hungry for good news. How were we to know that this happiness, even elation, would never be felt again during the entirety of the trial?

The prosecutors knew they had suffered a beating with the "you're full of it!" stick applied by Dave Fischer in the courtroom. Their malevolent stares at me and at our team spoke volumes.

One of the consequences of making the prosecution look as dumb as a bag of doorknobs was the hysterical backlash it spawned. The very next day after the Palian dismantling came the "Get Caldwell" campaign in which the entire focus of the prosecution had become me and me alone. Hour after hour, mine was the only name in the maws of the accusers. Nestler and crew needed to convince the world once again that J6 was *all* my fault.

The collective gaze of my fellow defendants felt like waves alternating between "poor guy" and "glad it's not me." Given the incredible hatred churning within that cold, confined space, who wouldn't cling to a moment's respite from personal attack? None of us was under any illusion about the demonic forces assembled against us.

What did Boo tell me long ago and far away through the concrete walls of the dungeons in the SHU: "Caldwell, you're a gimpy, white, veteran, country-boy who loves Jesus. You got *no* chance against those bastards."

And the equally prescient: "You're everything they hate!"

While the prosecution was berating defendants, the political January 6th Select Committee hearings were underway. Not only was it presented on live television, but this same group of politicians daily issued lengthy press statements. Excerpts from the proceedings were run relentlessly on all local television and major cable networks. This was designed to shape the beliefs and perceptions of the viewers, including jurors.

When it seemed as though the prosecution might be losing steam, even Joe Biden got involved in decrying the actions of the Oath Keepers in particular, in essence instructing the jury to convict me and everyone else. The clamor created was so intense that the judge directed, in the jury's absence, a half-hearted discussion of what could be done so that someone might not successfully argue about this blatant attempt at influencing the jury, thus causing a mistrial or the overturning of guilty verdicts on appeal.

The manipulation attempt by multiple facets of government was foreseen by David Fischer, who had argued early on that the trial should be held in a different city entirely. But just as in that argument, any discussion of how these latest developments created an unfair advantage for the prosecution was also summarily dismissed by the judge.[19, 20]

This is a matter of record.

What chance at justice and fair treatment does anyone have?

***

I was so consumed by the maddening fight for life that I was not able to evaluate the progress of the trial in a detached way. We wished we had been given access to the transcripts of each day's recorded statements and testimony in a timely fashion so that we could review them and counter the lies therein point by point. Access was slow-walked by the government, as was their revelation of the next day's evidentiary exhibits to be presented. By design.

The government sent to the defense at about midnight each night some or all of what they called *exhibits* slated for presentation before the jury the following day. Even presuming that Dave and his legal assistant, Kim Bommersbach, stayed up that late in order to receive them, it would not be until the next morning in our workroom that we could see the DOJ hooey, leaving us less than an hour or so, insufficient in anybody's book, to develop a concise refutation. It is never ideal to be solely reactionary in a conflict between good and evil, but that is the state we found ourselves in. Not frantic, but deliberate. That was our approach lest we get overwhelmed.

There was no actual evidence against me, so it had to be invented. The trial was rife with examples, perfected by Michael Sherwin a year earlier, of the reliable DOJ tactic of extracting one sentence from a paragraph and pairing it with a response to something different, thus creating an invented running conversational exchange that never happened. Slides attributing comments made by other people but falsely presented as mine were another outrage to endure. Repeatedly.

But some chicanery simply stood out from the rest.

It is more accurate to describe what the prosecutors had prepared each day for the courtroom as props rather than exhibits or evidence. These were carefully chosen or constructed memes to be used in creating or enhancing a desired effect. They were not "evidence" at all, although they did provide proof positive that the Merrick Garland attack dogs were certifiable.

Somewhere within the bowels of the federal courthouse, refugees from a 7th Grade science fair had created a series of Hobby Store poster boards. They provided an evolving backdrop for use by the talking head accuser of the day. *Fraudulent Government Exhibit 1530* and its evil sibling *Exhibit 1530.1* displayed a cascading wiring diagram of names of people, most of whom I had never met. To support the preposterous claim that I was a member of the Oath Keepers and in charge of their imagined QRF, there was my face heading a list of folks claimed to be the "highly trained fighters under my control." Most of them just old men.[21, 22]

One version presented me as the number-one guy behind the actual leader of the Oath Keepers. Another purported to show the communications channels each individual used to communicate with others within the Oath Keeper organization. Of course, it showed I was not on a single one, but the Fed lawyers rushed past all that. Still a third version, one shown to the jury but never *officially* entered as an exhibit demoted me from Top Banana in the mythical Quick Reaction Force to number 9 in a list of 13.

The prosecutors would continue to swear, with no evidence at all, that I had conspired in some way with *someone* to do *something* bad. They saw the jury as a gullible Jack in the fairy tale about a Beanstalk, whom they might convince to buy their magic beans.

***

Fraudulent Government Exhibit 6740, entitled "Call Detail Records," was created by the government to support the notion I had directed the movements of defendants by phone on January 6. The government witness, prepped and led by a junior lawyer named Louis Manzo, solemnly testified under oath as to the accuracy of the exhibit showing multiple phone calls between me and one defendant at what they thought was a critical point during the day's "attack."[23]

It stood until later in the trial when one of the defense attorneys in our multi-defendant case stepped in. When confronted with actual phone company records, not a phony compilation of rows and columns generated from thin air, the government's witness emphatically stated the calls in question never took place. Never happened. She admitted the exhibit and previous testimony had both been false. False exhibits. False testimony.[24]

Their efforts vacillating between diabolical and absurd, the "Justice" Department had me wondering each day when they might produce dancing sock-puppets to fuel the fires of prosecution.

A daily problem throughout the trial was dealing with the constant, baseless, personal attacks. Hour after tortuous hour wedged into a stifling trial cloister, I had to listen to the foulest of lies and just sit there and take it. Most normal people when they are insulted will either leave (not an option) or confront their tormentors verbally or physically (inadvisable). I was able to hold it together for the most part, but day after day it began to build up, like pressure in a steam boiler that was redlining to a critical failure of equipment and components.

Who *wouldn't* feel that way?

How can you defend yourself against a legion of lies? How can you escape undeserved and endless wrath?

Something had to give. Then I remembered what Sharon had encouraged me to do in those early days of my torture within the Central Virginia Regional Jail, Isolation and Sadistic Punishment Division. When my neck pain reached unimaginable levels, as it had done once again, she told me to pray the Lord's Prayer.

So I did.

During his opening ravings, Nestler had presented 20-year FBI veteran Palian as the shining star who would give powerful testimony during many trial appearances against all those at the defendants' table. I would never put words in Dave's mouth, but I think our lawyer was motivated and anxious to unravel the government's case directly through Palian and finish the job he had started at Palian's first appearance in court.

Now, however, the *Quarterback* had been benched.

In a complete reversal of the prosecution's pinky promise of explosive attestations yet to come, the government had seen enough of Special Agent Palian. Never again would he be entrusted to provide testimony against these defendants. The DOJ decided not to risk another fumble by their star Quarterback. If they could stop the turnovers, the *game* of convicting the guiltless could be won by making it tougher for the defense to elicit usable statements from government witnesses.

Dave's cross-examination rendezvous with Palian had become nothing more than *ignis fatuus*: a wisp of light in the dark. Dave's instinct to go directly after Palian in his first chance to question him was correct. There would never be another chance.

Next came the unveiling of an updated government game plan. The best offensive strategy for the prosecution became *stovepiping*.

In stovepiping, each special agent was fed information from the top down, as if it were poured down an old-fashioned log cabin stovepipe. They would know only enough to serve as a talking head while exhibits, many dubious at best, were put before the jury by the prosecution. Nearly clueless FBI special agents were shoehorned into freshly vacated Palian witness spots in the schedule. Many of these bit players in *Circus Minimus* would swear they had no idea about any of the actual evidence save for one small sliver here or there poured down their section of stovepipe.

Either they had never bothered to learn anything about the case or *feigned* a lack of knowledge, thus testifying to little or nothing when cross-examined by defense counsel.

In a federal courtroom, you can't just stand up and say, "You're a lying sack of poop." Especially if it's true. In federal court, the system is so rigged in favor of the government that once embroiled in a trial, your chances of escape, even if you're completely innocent, fall quickly toward zero. That's why over 90 percent of federal cases end in plea deals to limit the pain to defendants' families and stop outright threats. Just ask General Michael Flynn.

Dave Fischer taught me a lot about the federal system. In his over 20-year career, he had seen the majority of federal prosecutions succeed. But that was typically because there were years of actual investigative work, evidence-gathering, and planning taking place before charges were brought. In theory, this was an effort to make sure *actual* bad guys were brought to justice. Prosecutors would rather not go to trial, but if they must, they know they should have a genuine *case*. There had been no investigation of me; hence no case, only a rush to judgment.

In the meantime I still had to sit there and take it, just as I took the sadistic abuse in prison. I just got pounded. Slide after audio-visual slide, prop after prop was shown. The pain was increased as many government witnesses, often FBI personnel for whom reading was *not* fundamental, stumbled through the reading of exhibits, each in their own halting style. It was like listening to 5-year-olds with badges and guns trying to read the encyclopedia aloud.

From the multiple defense attorneys at work in the Oath Keepers case, Dave received the shared questions from my co-defendants that amounted to, "What is *Caldwell* doing here? He's not one of us. He didn't do *anything*!"

The DOJ's efforts were the continuation of a hoax while stoking the fires of outrage and revenge. It's important to remember that, at least in this case, no evidence was actually necessary because this trial was not about guilt or innocence.

This trial was about assignment of blame.

***

The effects of trial spilled over from the workroom to our tiny hotel room each night. This was a desperate, exhausting time for Sharon and me. But it was wonderful to share even a meager dinner of peanut butter and jelly sandwiches with my sweet wife, so badly did I miss her each day. We munched absentmindedly while conducting trial prep and review in support of Dave Fischer. Sleep was elusive, and when we went back to our farm at the end of a long week of being battered, we literally collapsed. A day later it was time to start packing again to return inside the toilet bowl ring which is the Capital Beltway.

Every morning before driving to the courthouse, Sharon read aloud from the Holy Bible in our morning Bible study time.

My eyes burning from lack of sleep, I closed them gently and let her sweet voice make the Word of God come alive. Months ago, we had embarked upon our quest to read the entire Bible in one year, and thus we would have daily passages from the Old Testament, New Testament, Psalms, and Proverbs.

Now I fought mightily not to regard this time as simply a calm before a calamitous storm. I would much rather have studied and prayed than walk into that abominable place festering with dirty lawyers, crooked federal law enforcement, and shameless press-pass stooges! I found it difficult to pray for those people, then and now—but I try. Perhaps our prayers might help to set them free.

On the darting drive through commuter traffic, with coffee in foam cups, we would listen to worship music on CD. Even in heavy traffic, this time in worship ended far too quickly for us both.

A stop at the light as we reached C Street. Into my pocket for the dumb China virus mask mandated in the District, perhaps until the end of time. Turn right on green, then ease up in the double-park position while depressing the auto's flasher bar mounted below the radio. Check all mirrors, then a kiss or two from Sharon and we exit our respective doors.

I waited for her to come around to the driver's side and, before she slipped behind the wheel, get one more kiss from the woman I love before donning my jacket. I heft my shoulder bag containing the previous night's work and a laptop, then grab my pockmarked and scratched cane to help me through the troubling walk to the grim building's revolving door.

Of we five being persecuted in this edition of the Patriot Inquisition, I was the only one who, by the grace of God and the courage of the judge, was *not* locked down each evening in the infamous cesspool known as the DC Gulag. Consequently, at my daily arrival and exit, I was the lone target for the clamoring cluster of paparazzi, videographers, and people with signs and filthy epithets.

This trip was painfully repeated day after oppressive day over weeks, then months.

I wasn't always the first one in the workroom Dave had claimed for us. Dear Kim Bommersbach, Dave's assistant, was an early arriver and a vital part of our defense team. In the courtroom, she sat at the right hand of Dave Fischer while I was not allowed to sit with either of them. It was Kim who would keep track of exhibits and testimony, serve up copies through the unreliable audio-visual link, and support cross-examinations during the inquisition. It was Kim who would chase down a copier and run exhibit and discovery taskers in the workroom for Dave even while testimony was underway. At a pause in the action, she would comfort and encourage me while sharing insight of trial chats and strategies she'd had with Mr. Fischer during the proceedings.

Kim was more valuable than a second lawyer in the courtroom for us. Dependable, innovative, and deeply committed to our defense, Kim knew every single piece of material produced by the government prior to trial and organized the growing piles of defense exhibits we used to counter their evolving slanders and fantasies. She and Dave became ever more earnest in their efforts and more disgusted daily by the fabrications and deceptions of the government lawyers. All while Sharon and I were being ground down.

Dave did an amazing job pushing back at the DOJ in cross-examination. The system, however, is designed so that government lawyers *always* get the last word in what was called re-direct. In those instances, often buoyed by a court-ordered break in the action, they would merely re-tread the ground previously trodden, leading their witness to recant the truthful answers Dave had elicited. This left the most deceptive government spin with the jurors before moving on.

The judge never took anyone to task for changing their testimony again and again.

I think it was the French playwright and poet Moliere who said, "Those whose own behavior is most ridiculous are always to the fore in slandering others."

So true.

***

We were dealing with a multi-tiered system of justice, no doubt about it. I was taken aback when a person who identified himself as being from the Washington Post phoned our wall-mounted kitchen landline as Sharon and I chafed under armed guard on the morning of January 19, 2021. The guy from that exemplar of malicious misinformation masquerading as a "news" paper was jonesing for a quotable to fill out his day's column. He wasn't going to get it from us, but you can't blame him for trying. Jeff Bezos has a lot to be proud of. As a native Washingtonian, my opinion is that the Post is unmatched. I mean that sincerely. You see, in my opinion, if you desperately need to paper-train a puppy or pick up a sidewalk poopy, you just can't beat the Washington Post!

The Post, which was pre-briefed by the DOJ about the planned military-style attack on our home, would print and distribute their pre-approved false narratives about me for years in a slanderous dump certain to support a lawsuit from us should we pursue it.

National Public Radio dutifully spread the government-approved make-believe about me just as the battering ram vehicle caressed our front door that fateful morning. They had gotten advance word that I was a target. People having their morning granola and coffee knew about the forces drawing battle lines on our pastures at the exact moment that Sharon and I slept peacefully. Though a late afternoon rewrite of the reporting called me only a *leader*, the pre-dawn version painted me as the commander of the Oath Keeper extremist and *white supremacist group*. The tainting of the local jury pool and the national consciousness had begun twenty months before my trial, and even in the pre-dawn darkness the day of my arrest![25]

There was so much hype surrounding the so-called Oath Keeper trial it was impossible to escape it. The gallery in the courtroom was teeming with reps of the national press corps, all of whom seemed part of the power play aimed at me and the other defendants. To accommodate the crush, an *overflow* room for reporters had been established. From here, reporters could actively monitor events underway before the judge while rubbing elbows with FBI Special Agents, who themselves were keen to follow the testimony so as to better coordinate their answers on the stand. To their eternal shame, the media almost never reported on Dave's motions or challenges to the court and its questionable actions. When Dave embarrassed the prosecution or made their witnesses look bumbling and untrustworthy, there was never a mention in the press. As far as I have been able to determine, only the plucky Investigative Journalist Steve Baker crowed about these daily victories.

The FBI people and DOJ lawyers not on duty in the ceremonial room basked in the fawning attention of the media reps, some of whom were little more than pimply recent college grads. There were few actual journalists present and reporting from the courthouse each day, save for the likable Steve Baker. For his persistence in writing the truth, and for his very presence at the Capitol on the 6th, he would later find himself mercilessly prosecuted.[26]

The judge's decision that the jury would not hear the mountain of evidence of my physical injuries and the fact I had been deemed service-connected disabled by the VA facilitated the erroneous reporting of an MSNBC employee named Ryan Riley, fresh off a nine-year stint at the *Huffington Post*. His completely invented so-called reporting that I had no injuries whatsoever and was in fact moving easily around the courtroom without my oft-needed cane was an even bigger lie than those he committed through omission of the daily victories we received via sworn testimony at trial. Not once did he report on the startling revelations that fractured the government case against me.

Once, this same Riley fella got a little too cheeky with Dave Fischer in the hallway of the courthouse. Dave faced him down over a recent falsehood presented under his byline by MSNBC online. After Lawyer Dave called him a "damn liar" to his face, Riley ducked into a men's room, and I have not seen him since. He could still be hiding in a stall there for all I know.

Chapter 10

Deception Most Foul

During this time, DOJ lawyer Jeff Nestler ruled the inquisitors' table and a spotlight made for only one: himself. His career as a prosecutor had been entirely before the Superior Court of the District, and he was installed through the good-old-boys' network as the head of the Major Crimes Section, responsible for investigation and prosecution of "serious" violent crimes and so-called "local economic frauds."[1] DOJ Headquarters, or *Main Justice*, had now tapped him to snatch the proverbial prosecutorial pigskin away from Rakoczy. He loved every minute of it.

I knew I should continue to pray for the prosecutors, particularly Nestler and Rakoczy, and for the compromised federal agents who are their accomplices. I should pray for them to come to know Jesus and I have and still do when I think about it. If they knew Jesus, they could never conduct a false prosecution this way. Not against anyone! Not even for the promise of a six-figure cash bonus following "successful" guilty verdicts drawn from a taxpayer-provided fund controlled by the DOJ itself. Yes, that's a real thing. Bonus money in exchange for guilty verdicts. How can any citizen expect justice in a place where prosecutors are monetarily incentivized to get convictions no matter what?[2]

> *"The moment you allow someone to lie and make money and face no consequences, the obvious result is that they will lie and make money and face no consequences."*
>
> — Dr. Keon West, American Social Scientist

When your torment is otherworldly, even demonic, there is no place where you can create your own safe harbor. Nowhere to find on your own a fortress from the ungodly. Here I sat in that awful place and I knew I could only find refuge in the Lord.

I prayed, eyes closed and palms open, speaking silently to God in order to feel what many might call a hedge of protection closing in around me. The weight of the injustice here was too much to bear, so I sent words on high—whatever my heart told me to say at the time, and always my heart was so heavy. The shaking tachycardia and the icicle-plunged-into-my-heart feeling were back. A return to that hellish crypt in Orange, Virginia. The stress meter was pegged, but I still had the capability to speak with the Father, knowing that He would hear me.

I depended upon taking refuge with my Redeemer beginning early on during that ten-week show trial. I could feel the condemnation of the multitude, especially DOJ employees of all types, to my impudence at *praying* silently in what they must have considered *their* temple sanctuary. "How *dare* he?" I heard them grumble about it. I heard them grumble other things, too. Their outrage rippled through this coliseum where, as it felt to me at that time, nearly everyone had come to see the end of me, thrown to the lions.

***

I enjoy movies and I always have. That's why I learned the craft of screenwriting as a storytelling vehicle. I enjoyed the toil and the challenge even if my finished works went nowhere but into a cardboard box. Voltaire is quoted as saying, "Writing is the painting of the voice." I never imagined my writings, including short stories or texts with friends and acquaintances about wild characters and story ideas, would ever be denounced as something threatening or dangerous. I never dreamed that notes, doodles, scrap paper scribblings, jotted-down one-liners, or even political satire could bring the threat of death first to my wife and then to me. That, however, is *precisely* what happened to us in this former land of liberty.[3]

Extracts from these simple, personal things were among what was chopped up and served at trial and through the media as a type of manifesto showing me a "danger to the community."

I'd never be so puffed-up as to call myself an artist, though I have a creative bent. Writing is my expression and release. I have been blessed with a fantastic life filled with wonder and joy and friends and challenges, travel, and a wide range of human emotions. It has provided what for me is a treasure trove of stories. I am a product of every experience, good or bad, every place I've ever been and the myriad acquaintances, unforgettable friends, brothers, and sisters I have known along the way. Aren't we all?

It's not surprising that creative people of any type, working with any expressive media, should become the targets of a despotic regime or sect. Isn't the Creator Himself minimized, mocked, and ridiculed by these same people? History has taught us if we are willing to look and listen:

Today's masterpiece is tomorrow's heresy.

Today's citizen is tomorrow's enemy of the State.

***

The government prosecutors renewed their attempt to tie me to a non-existent plot to use a *stockpile* of heavy weapons to attack the Capitol. On Day 12 of trial, October 17, 2022, FBI Special Agent Sylvia Hilgeman, presented as the *QRF expert*, was cross-examined by Dave Fischer.

There was a collective gasp in the courtroom when, during cross, Hilgeman was unable to locate the Ellipse and the White House, where President Trump's remarks were delivered, on a map of our Capital City.

Gently, Dave Fischer began again, "Okay," he said, pointing to a map. "So if I were to tell you that *this* is the White House and *this* is the Ellipse, does that ring a bell?"

"Oh, yes. Yep," Hilgeman responded.

"Okay," Dave continued. "Which direction on that map would the Capitol be?"

"To the east."

"Okay! Fair enough." Dave now wanted to speak to her just-delivered direct testimony for the prosecution. "Where you pointed up here, M Street in your earlier testimony, you would agree that that's going in a different direction from where the United States Capitol is?"

"I don't recall any messages that the QRF were specifically for anything at the Capitol," she interrupted.[4]

Stop the presses! The QRF expert has said she had no recollection of messages connecting the QRF, the completely imaginary Quick Reaction Force of "specially trained insurrectionists," to the U.S. Capitol!

Dave appeared stunned. "I'm sorry? Are you ... you're saying the QRF had nothing to do with the Capitol?"

"No," she stated matter-of-factly. Then she explained, "I didn't see *any* messages [saying] *that* would have been the destination of the QRF." [5]

Dave pressed this revelation. "Well, you understand the government's entire theory was the QRF was for the purpose of attacking the United States Capitol. Right?"

Special Agent Hilgeman, the QRF expert, asserted, "That is *not* my understanding."

The jury was shocked.

Louis Manzo for the prosecution could not contain himself: "Objection!"

The court: "Sustained."

What? The judge stopped our lawyer from getting Special Agent Hilgeman to further destroy the government's case! The judge supported the stoppage of testimony of the government's own witness that was *favorable to the defense*!

Mr. Fischer turned to the judge. "Your Honor, could we get on the phone?"

Whereupon the following proceedings were had at sidebar outside the hearing of the jury.

"Your Honor," Dave began, "during the opening argument, Mr. Nestler *specifically* said that this QRF was to *attack* the Capitol. I have the transcript!"

The judge responded in an offhand way. "Okay. If that's what he said. You've probably got a better recollection than I do. Mr. Manzo?"

Manzo began his pandering with, "We would disagree with that unless we saw the transcript. And talking about the legal theory of the case ..."

Dave cut him off. "Your Honor, what it says is: [Quote] 'You will hear evidence during this trial that these five Defendants reached an agreement with each other to stage an arsenal of firearms, including semiautomatic rifles, just across the Potomac in Arlington and to physically prevent members from meeting and certifying the election as they descended upon DC to attack not just the Capitol, not just Congress, not just our government, but our country.' [Unquote]"[6]

Manzo retorted forcefully, "And we would *disagree* with Mr. Fischer's assertion that the QRF was to attack the Capitol! The QRF was *available*." [7]

The stunned judge replied, "I'm sorry?"

"The QRF was available and *then* there was an attack on the Capitol," Manzo stated with assurance.

The prosecution's Louie Manzo has told the judge that the QRF was not to attack the Capitol! Louie! Did you forget that this is the very foundation of the made-up case against all of the defendants, especially Caldwell? Opposition by *force* with *guns*! Didn't you read the email? Or did you just slip and speak the truth? How will we ever get Caldwell *now*?

The judge may have been incredulous, but he still *blocked* the jury from knowing what Manzo had said, even after Dave made additional pleadings later in the trial for the jury to be made aware.

This should have been a boost. The judge's decision to withhold it from the jury left it a bust.

Those at the prosecutors' table were chattering like chipmunks now as Hilgeman looked to the other FBI agents, straining to see their hand gestures. Turning in my swivel chair to watch them, I felt like a new-age Leo Durocher stealing the other team's signs from the dugout at Ebbets Field!

Whereupon the proceedings began anew in open court.

Dave resumed his questioning after being cautioned by the judge: "Agent, are you aware that the government's theory in this case is that the purpose of the QRF was to attack the United States Capitol?"

Hilgeman responded emphatically, "No! The purpose of the QRF was to support an attempt to keep Biden from taking power in whatever form that took."

"Well, the Electoral College certification was meeting on January 6th at the United States Capitol. Correct?"

"Correct."

"So the QRF wasn't meant to invade the Department of *Labor*. Right?" he inquired.

Hilgeman answered, "I think the QRF was meant to *occupy* DC."[8]

Huh?

FBI Special Agent Hilgeman while on the witness stand further destroyed the government's case. She said her informed opinion was that the mythical QRF was meant to stand around in DC, not attack the Capitol building! But the world would never hear about it. And the judge would not dismiss the case, certainly not the case against *me*. The damage to the government's case against me *should* have been undeniable. But the DOJ and the perverted legal system it directs live in denial.

Mr. Fischer let go one more question: "And to your knowledge, there never was a boat that was in the Potomac that was put there by Mr. Caldwell or any member of the Oath Keepers?"

"Not that I'm aware of," Hilgeman stated with authority.[9]

Game. Set. Match?

Not exactly.

The government's case is hooey and certainly the jury *must* see it! Right? I need only to continue to endure, leaning into the Lord all the while, and to the best of my ability help Dave Fischer and Kim whenever possible.

Fear is the enemy of Faith, Tom.

And the trial dragged on.

***

In the early days of this secret, untelevised tribunal, I felt very much alone, banished as I was from what should have been my seat beside my courtroom defense team of Dave and Kim.

I looked at the chuckling hooligans of the prosecution.

I prayed earnestly: "Abba, Father! Is this the abomination that causes desolation standing where it does not belong that is spoken of in the book of Daniel and the book of Mark? They have no business in a place supposed to represent justice but where references to You, Father, Your Commandments, and Your Word have been expunged. I pray protect us all with the Shield of Faith in You."

An unintended consequence of my otherwise miserable day-to-day circumstance was the opportunity to meet Ms. Cynthia Hughes, the fearless Lady who founded and runs to this day the Patriot Freedom Project. She is dedicated to helping not only J6 defendants but the families of the accused, the wrongly sentenced, and the over-sentenced. These loving families were ruthlessly torn apart and often driven into financial ruin and despair. Many were hounded and outcast in their communities by people and institutions programmed to baseless hatred and cruelty. Cynthia works to the point of exhaustion, especially inspired by the suffering of the innocent children wounded by the actions of the DOJ coven.

Cynthia told me to think of her as Sharon's surrogate of loving support in this demonic place, and in the few moments we could share on breaks, we became friends. Her hugs were precious comfort in this dreary courtroom.

The fact that Cynthia Hughes has suffered disgusting attacks from none other than taxpayer-supported National Public Radio speaks volumes about the good she is doing with precious few resources.

***

One evening at the conclusion of court, I limped down the hall, my cane tick-ticking along. Rounding a corner for the downhill leg to a workroom for a rest, I froze at spotting the DOJ's nattering nabobs of deceit, exiting their room in high spirits. As one of the unclean, it was easy for me to disappear in plain sight because to them, I did not exist as a person.

Nestler had bopped a few steps in the direction of my intended path, and his chattering posse popped one after another from the room like so many hatchlings from the nest. With disdain, he watched until the last of those, manpurse clutched tightly, doused the light by which they had communed. That's when Nestler and his minions presented a visual I will not forget.

With a hand gesture and an "All right, let's go!" to his underlings, Nestler pivoted on his buster-brown sized treads and marched down the hall. No one strode aside him but instead fell into line, trailing behind in nearly perfect single-file. I couldn't help but be struck by the E. Barrett Prettyman Federal Courthouse version of the momma duck waddling with babies in pursuit, perhaps off to gobble an evening meal of worms.

Beyond the sheer hilarity of the scene playing out before my eyes, the best takeaway was watching several of those following him openly mock his gesture and his stride to the amusement of their fellows. Such was their respect for the "star" of the government team. With a grin overtaking my face, I reasoned that perhaps these others weren't beyond redemption yet.

I've heard it said that the more wicked people are, the more ridiculous they appear when you truly look at them.

The conga line soon disappeared near the building's central elevator stack. I detoured from my planned workroom collapse for a now-urgent appointment in the rest room. The vintage lavatory boasted antique urinals, the kind with the quaint brass foot pedal flush attachments and another Truman-era comfort room throwback: the way-too-low porcelain throne.

Urging a cockroach away from his path toward my lowered trousers with a flick of a shoe, I raised my eyes to see that in this place, the timeless tradition of writing on the walls and doors of individual stalls was still observed. In less-than-optimal reading light I could see nothing so amusing as off-color limericks or memorable one-liners.

I was struck instead by something scratched into the paint of my cramped booth: twin, slightly overlapping scratches of the letter "V."

I flashed to another place where not long ago I had encountered this very same scrawl: inside Segregation dungeon 101, Orange, Virginia's Political Prisoner Death Camp and Day Spa. Recognition hit me with the clarity of another kick to my privates, and I now remembered with a similar jolt exactly what this symbol was:

It was an apotropaic mark!

Also known as a witch's mark.

For those unversed in such things, it's more accurate to call it an *anti*-witch mark because this category of magical symbols and patterns has been used for centuries to protect people from witchcraft and evil spirits. They are symbols of the ancients and were prominent in the belief system of peoples throughout recorded history, especially following the crucifixion of Jesus Christ.

Scant feet from my face someone had scratched the double V, for the Latin "Virgio Virginum," an entreaty to the Virgin Mary for protection. In that solitary confinement pit and now here where they are still trying to claim my life, someone as despondent as I had pulled out all the stops to thwart the dark forces.

I don't believe in coincidence. This particular witch mark appeared in Orange, Virginia, and now Washington, DC, for a reason. It's because Satan is the berserker in both places. And believers must keep pushing back. Or else all will be lost.

I thanked the Living God that I already had my own powerful amulet: a simple cross on a chain, the symbol of my Lord and Savior and His sacrifice for all! He is the Only One who could defeat the depravity entrenched in this building and in the chests of the inquisitors.

***

The prosecution fought for weeks prior to trial against having my status as a 100-percent service-disabled veteran mentioned during court proceedings. They railed against the jury being informed. Heck, the X-rays alone showing the myriad metal implants holding my body together are the stuff of Frankenstein's lab! Chronic pain and reduced mobility are the kinds of things many veterans deal with every day.

Revelation before the jury of my injuries and operations could have undermined the absurdity that I had led a force of "highly trained fighters" to "storm" into Congress and halt the Electoral College certification.

The judge agreed with the prosecution that we could not show anything from the ten boxes of medical documentation, including decades of Veterans Administration records. Nor could we speak to the details of my physical limitations or have expert witnesses appear to testify about my constant debilitating pain and other medical issues.[10]

Chalk up another victory for the prosecutors.

***

One day prosecutor Louie Manzo presented phony *Fraudulent Government Exhibit 1510.8*, a portion of a lobby video from the hotel at which Sharon and I stayed the night before the president's speech. While waiting to check in, a guy I had never met rolled a very large piece of luggage past us. The well-coached FBI Agent Hilgeman swore that by moving my head after his passing, it was proof positive that I *knew* this man and was in a conspiracy with him to overthrow the government![11]

To this day, I have never met the guy.

When allowed to rebut, Dave Fischer showed the video to the jury again while Sharon was on the witness stand. This time he presented the *entire* hotel security tape, which we designated Caldwell Exhibit 150. Found hidden in a mountain of evidence by Kim, it was the *exact same video,* only beginning ten seconds *earlier*. There I was, making the same head-nodding movement to loosen my deflicted neck vertebrae (they have since been permanently fused together) after an almost two-hour drive from home.

When prompted by Dave about what I was doing in the portion of the video the government refused to show, Sharon's statement was priceless.

"Do you see anything?" Mr. Fischer asked.

"He does that same movement with his neck. Look at that! Isn't that *surprising*! Before the other guy even comes into the hotel, what do you know? He went like that to crack his neck."[12]

Am I the only person who has ever tried to loosen or stretch a stiff neck? I should warn others that they could be prosecuted for it.

This innocent movement was presented by Manzo as proof of a conspiracy to overthrow the government and fully supportive of life in prison for me. The jury *must* have seen that this was yet another phony representation by a phony prosecutor in a phony case.

At least we prayed that they did.

What better way to continue to tear down the government's lies than to use the tools of their own invention?

On the morning of November 3, Dave Fischer turned to *Fraudulent Government Exhibit 1556*. Using columns and rows, it graphically presented all Oath Keeper "Signal Chat" groups, and every defendant's alleged participation in each, around J6. The jury had been told repeatedly that these invitation-only groups were *the* way Oath Keeper "conspirators" communicated. Kate Rakoczy realized, with government witness FBI Special Agent John Moore on the stand, that this exhibit was exculpatory for me. In an instant she decided it must not be shown to the jury. Dave had anticipated the government hijinks and simply renamed the exhibit "Caldwell 126." Dave began his questioning of Agent Moore when Rakoczy surged into opposition in open court to stop him again! [13]

That's because, for each and every one of the over two dozen Oath Keeper Signal chat groups, I was shown to be on *none of them.* Not a single one. I am *not* an Oath Keeper and had no clue what they were talking about prior to J6. Next to my name at the bottom of each column of the prosecution's evidence appeared the entry N/A: "Not applicable."[14]

Rakoczy began a frantic On-the-Sidebar-Phones session with the judge to block the jury from seeing that her own matrix supported my innocence! First she told the judge that FBI Special Agent Moore, pre-briefed on this exhibit by the prosecution, suddenly wasn't familiar with the "exact data" it contained. A few panicky breaths later she told the judge something different:

"This was an exhibit that I put together," Rakoczy said, "and so I think there may be some things that are slightly off. I don't know off the top of my head right now which of them may be slightly off."

She blamed an underling for the non-existent problem, of course, saying someone else "tweaked some of the data." None of this was true, but since she thought she could get away with it, why not try, I suppose.

The judge ruled that *neither* of the exculpatory exhibits—*Government Exhibit 1556* or its identical twin, the renamed Caldwell 126—could be shown to the jury or officially entered into evidence. [15]

The judge's decision hardly slowed Dave Fischer down. He was prepared for anything, be it clown show or collusion. Nothing would keep him from showing the exhibit to the witness only and simply asking him to tell the jury, "Was Mr. Caldwell on what's called the Old Leadership Signal chat?"

"No."

"How about the DC Op Jan 6 21 Signal chat?"

"No."

The witness was asked about one Signal chat at a time. On and on ...

But did the jury actually *get* it?

Fake Government Exhibit 1500 was an animated video intended to deceive the jury about my walk down Constitution Avenue and the journey of Oath Keepers down Pennsylvania Avenue to a non-existent rendezvous with me near the U.S. Capitol grounds. This was to "prove" I had directed the attack on the building.

When questioned about this path of movement by the Oath Keeper group that day, FBI Special Agent Whitney Drew, the government's own witness, confessed to the jury that *Government Exhibit 1500* was wrong. In plain English: prosecutors presented another falsified exhibit which had been sworn to be accurate by a government witness under oath! Special Agent Drew now swore the Oath Keepers never came to the Peace Fountain where Sharon and I had sat the afternoon of January 6. There had been no conspiracy between us to "storm the Capitol." The exhibit was as phony as was the testimony about it, which had been entered only hours previously. [16]

This exhibit also boldly and deceitfully identified the trek of my wife and me toward Capitol Hill as the line of attack of their invented QRF: heavily armed, ultra-trained fighters intent on conquering the Capitol building. The prosecutors wanted the jury to believe that just Sharon and I, flags in hand and bundled against the cold, were the gun-toting assault force.

What did Nestler do after his false "evidence" was exposed? He deliberately showed the discredited animation *again* later in the trial, having never changed it one bit. The judge *never* admonished or cautioned the prosecution about this, and our complaints about it to the judge went nowhere.

History records Adolf Hitler as saying, "If you're going to tell a lie, tell a big one and keep telling it. Sooner or later the weak minded will believe you."

Phony Government Exhibit 1533 was another middle school-type poster board alleged to show a "massive stockpile" of weapons to be used in the alleged "attack on the U.S. Capitol." Granted, it showed several photos from the lobby area of a Virginia motel from which the jury was expected to infer the people shown had scary guns under their arms or in sealed luggage. In fact, the exhibit showed three photos of inoperable hunting rifles allegedly found at the home of at least one person on trial with me. *None* was ever even alleged to have been brought anywhere near the District on January 6. But most telling, *Exhibit 1533* was overflowing with a list of shooting *accessories*, not firearms! All supposedly collected at defendants' homes many miles from DC. [17]

It was incredible to me! The prosecutors terrorized the gullible jurors by reading off a list of pouches, empty magazines, attachment rails and mounts, optics, scope mounts, a light (yes, one light only), two different shoulder slings, an empty rifle case, and two bipods. There was no testimony as to how these accessories posed a threat to anyone. There is no indication that anyone on the jury had a clue that they were being snowed. There was no indication they would have cared.

The list of phony exhibits goes on and on.

The DOJ J6 prosecutors lied the way normal people blink or inhale. It's automatic. It's instinctive.

We couldn't stop them, the judge *wouldn't* stop them. And no U.S. citizen the prosecutors wanted to hurt could have stopped them either.

***

While I suffered through all of this, defense counsel Dave Fischer tackled the falsehoods, driving government witnesses to back-pedal or stumble. Prosecutors were always given the last word to double-speak their way around the truth Dave had extracted. I couldn't be sure in the heat of the moment what registered with jurors and what did not. Likewise, who knew if it even mattered to any jurors who had already made up their minds to convict simply because they were predisposed to do so. Evidence of a prejudicial mindset was clearly provided through the professional Inlux polling survey and two additional surveys.

It didn't help us.

We were prohibited from pursuing questioning of witnesses regarding one of the most egregious lies the government leveled against me since this two-year travesty began. This involved Assistant United States Attorney (AUSA) Christopher Kavanaugh of the DOJ willfully lying in order to have me held in solitary, telling a bail-hearing judge that I was a "fugitive from justice"!

Dave Fischer pushed for the jury to know the details about this lie and how it was used to imprison me and violate my Constitutional rights. The following is the determined give-and-take, which was kept secret from the jury:

"Mr. Fischer," began the Honorable Judge Mehta, "seeks to have admitted a statement pertaining to Mr. Caldwell's 'purported' criminal history. Mr. Fischer, I take it that it is inaccurate, in stating that Mr. Caldwell was on fugitive status?"

"That's correct. He has no criminal history," Dave responded.

The judge rightly put Rakoczy on the spot.

"Okay. Ms. Rakoczy, do you know how this happened?"

In an attempt to save her case and perhaps her career, Rakoczy began, "My recollection—and this is just my recollection, so it could be wrong—is that that information was not on the pretrial report. My recollection—so this detention hearing was in the Western District of Virginia, was handled by an AUSA in that district who was doing the government a favor and *operating solely on the information that we provided.*"[18]

She took a moment and continued, "And my recollection is—and this could be wrong, but *my recollection is that I personally misread the NCIC report.* I either had it for a different Mr. Caldwell or it was—I was misreading what I had for the correct Mr. Caldwell. I can't recall. And I recall giving that fact to the AUSA in the Western District."[19]

"And I think that is what he based that argument on, if that—to the best of my recollection, that is what transpired. And so I think it was an error on the part of government counsel here who was not speaking there. And I can't recall exactly what I was looking at, but that's my recollection."[20]

In her rambling, *Three Stooges* way, did Rakoczy grudgingly admit it was *she* who did it as she plays it off as a simple "mistake," no big deal? Yes, she admitted it, alright! It was *she* who invented the "fugitive from justice" lie that locked me inside a sadistic torture dungeon. It was *she* who told Kavanaugh to lie and do her dirty work at my detention hearing. And he did so with great passion.

If Dave could only have gotten Attorney Christopher Kavanaugh on the witness stand.

"Okay," said the judge. "All right. Well, I'll admit it for the purpose that Mr. Fischer is seeking to admit it, which is *not about the truth of the matter, but about the representation.*"

Huh?

Rakoczy was not satisfied that the judge had saved her and said, "I just think it's a little bit unfair, your honor. I'm not really sure I completely understand the relevance of the government making a mistake."[21]

If only the jury could have heard THAT! AUSA Kathryn Rakoczy, imbued with virtually limitless power to harass and prosecute by the U.S. Attorney General, free of consequence, tells a federal judge that she does not "completely understand the relevance of the government (meaning *her*) making a *mistake*" and falsely accusing and imprisoning someone!

The NCIC thing she referenced is the National Crime Information Center, a criminal files database allowing agencies to enter or search for information including individuals' criminal histories and current criminal status. It links all 50 states, U.S. Territories and possessions, and some foreign countries' criminal databases. It's accessed through a portal by an authorized user, of which the DOJ has an almost limitless number.

Even if we accept the possibility of gross incompetence by the person using the system (no doubt who *that* was), the query protocol and the multiple database entry fields required make it *impossible* to commit the "mistake" Rakoczy is claiming. *Impossible.*

I know all of this because in my various computer systems adventures as an FBI professional, a government job I once held despite the reluctance of the DOJ to acknowledge that fact, I *personally* sat at an NCIC terminal for such queries. It was part of my job. Each data field is another qualifier used to make sure you are homing in on the correct person. I first learned how and made such queries when I worked for the U.S. Drug Enforcement Administration.

Rakoczy, Nestler, Manzo, and their confederates sure are making it hard for me to pray for them and forgive them. They just keep doing more fiendish stuff.

Frankly, I'm getting exhausted!

And the band played on.

***

When Dave, Kim, and I were given lunch breaks or all-too infrequent bathroom respites from the foolishness, we scampered off to make water and stretch our legs. I was fortunate the court allowed me an ergonomic chair brought from our home, one which offered a modicum of support for my multi-fused spine. Still, the waves of electricity rippled up and down back and legs in an agonizing rush much of the time.

Then came the day that I was suddenly aware that another seizure episode was upon me while sitting in the courtroom. Like jolting from a bad dream to a worse reality, I was aware that I was trembling all over: an uncontrollable quivering akin to the dungeon experience in front of the arctic blower.

It was time for a court-ordered recess. With the help of my trusty cane I clumped down the hallway to the restrooms. I reached the handicapped stall and practically ripped my suit jacket away while I felt a great dizziness and a ramping up of the trembling take hold. Get the jacket on the hook, suspenders off your shoulders, and sit down quick!

That's all I can remember before I hit the floor.

Face-down in a courthouse bathroom stall is no place to be. While I was shaking on the floor, it occurred to me that I may have rearranged my facial features through a blunt force trauma face-plant. The real problem now was that I could not get my limbs under control, let alone stand up. I just kept shaking violently in the throes of this new seizure.

It took a while to get my body to obey once the shaking eased. I cleaned up as best I could, dashing my face with sink water and starting back to the show trial room, well aware that I had sweated through both my T-shirt and dress shirt.

Court was back in session as I carefully lowered into my chair and suffered the wrath of Dave Fischer who rolled his seat close to growl at me for not being back on time for my post pee-time psychological punishment session.

There was no time to explain what had happened or make excuses. There was nothing to be done about what I was suffering and thus no reason to waste a single breath. Nothing to do but sit shivering in damp clothes and endeavor to persevere. Physically, I was breaking down.

The bad dream repeats itself because it forgets itself.

***

Sharon had taken a video with her smartphone during our five-minute stay amongst a festive and non-violent crowd on the inaugural balcony January 6. It was self-deprecating humor, actually, which got the recorded laughter reaction I desired from my wife before she concluded the approximately one-minute self-narrated video. The government seized upon this kooky film and designated it *Government Exhibit 22.V.2*. But that's not what they showed the jury! When it was shown in open court, the jury saw only a *segment*, a fraction of the recording. The jury was shown *Government Exhibit 22.V.2.E*, a *shortened* version of the video that was officially entered into evidence! Why? Because to show the full video, with its timestamp, would have destroyed the important falsehood that I had participated in violence that occurred *after* Sharon and I left the vicinity of the Capitol that day.[22]

At the time of its creation, on a video we both thought would be a funny memento, I committed what our persecutors thought was the unpardonable sin: I made a joke about an elected official who was a Democrat! The galloping Nessies of the prosecution showed this video in court multiple times in the "how dare he say something about an elected official" mode, attempting to generate outrage in the courtroom.

What was the thing so horrible that it is still being used as the justification to condemn me to 20 years-plus in a federal lock-up? The haughty prosecution played our Capitol Hill video and my goofy, satirical statement: "Today I wiped my a** on Pelosi's doorknob!"[23]

The packed courtroom *erupted* in laughter just as Sharon had on January 6! The soundtrack of the video had captured my silliness and now it was played to the absolute delight of the assembled.

The mirth echoing off the walls of the courtroom lasted for a long time. It was the bursting of a pressure-filled misery balloon for all at the defendant and defense attorneys' table. Even the prosecutor groupies, the federal agents, and nearly every non-prosecutor in the room laughed uncontrollably, some even to tears. I'm sure it seemed to last for an eternity to the attack lawyers. I never noticed whether the judge himself or his court assistant laughed, but it's possible.

Let's just say this outpouring was *not* the reaction the prosecution expected or wanted.

The courtroom roared again the *next* time they showed the video in court, too.

And the *next* time.

To be clear, no DNA evidence exists to link me to anybody's doorknob.

Patiently, Dave held out for several days until November 20, when government witness FBI Special Agent Whitney Drew was on the stand. What the jury saw and heard for the first time that day was the *entire* video, including Sharon's running recorded commentary stating that "Congress has left," which is what we were told before we approached the Capitol.[24] It is true that Congress *had* departed prior to our entering Capitol grounds, and that fact was supported by government witnesses under oath and by government exhibits.[25, 26, 27]

No violence was captured on that video, and none occurred anywhere around us. The instant Sharon concluded her recording, we walked purposefully to a downward staircase and exited the Capitol grounds. Now the jury had seen the whole thing *with* timestamps.

Sharon has since said that we should have been given a gold medal or perhaps a trophy for being the people who were on the Inaugural Balcony on the west side of the U.S. Capitol for the least amount of time. Maybe she's right, but I don't think there will be any award forthcoming. I am just hoping this whole nightmare doesn't result in the DOJ taking my life.

"If you want to know who controls you,
look at whom you are not allowed to criticize."

— Voltaire, 18th century French satirist and philosopher

The people in the DOJ who are committing these detestable acts are different from most people. I believe it is quite fair and appropriate to refer to them as being culturally bankrupt: as far from the rich traditional and moral development of their targeted American citizens as the east is from the west.

***

At considerable expense, we were obliged to engage our own forensics professional to pull data from extracts of my phone and computers so that we could conduct our own analysis. But only on *redacted* extracts *provided by the DOJ.* There we found important evidence, but maddeningly we were not allowed to extract data *directly* from the devices themselves! Thus, we were searching for crumbs when there may have been entire loaves kept from the defense.

We couldn't stop praising the Lord for bringing Kim Bommersbach to our defense team. She spent hundreds of hours digging through hard-to-identify video evidence on that convoluted and amateurish Deloitte application. One day she found a particular bit of the government's own closed circuit television (CCTV) stuff that the prosecution likely had seen but did not want the jury to see. The government's own video completely demolished their case against me.

Regrettably, proof positive of innocence is not sufficient to save someone from the fury of a witch-hunt, as the harmless, persecuted dead in their graves in Salem, Massachusetts, will attest.

Armed with Kim's government videos of exoneration, we shouldn't have been surprised that the judge would not let the jury see it. We showed it to the judge. We showed it to the prosecutors. Then the prosecutors politicked with the presiding judge to keep this video out of court. And so it was not allowed to be shown. Exculpatory evidence withheld from the defense and the jury. And when the defense found it anyway, a federal judge would not let it be used at trial.[28]

The death of truth, justice, and the American way is a bitter thing to experience in real-time.

***

If you no longer use your social media accounts for some reason, the "content" you have placed there becomes the property of the host or provider. You wouldn't want something personal like your granddaughter's photo floating out there for a pedophile, now would you? As I prepared to move from Facebook to their competitor Parler, I knew inaction meant relinquishing my stuff to the despicable Fakebook, Google, Twitter, Gmail, the Cloud, or a host of e-mail providers. But there was a way in those days called *unsend*, through which you could remove a photo from where it appeared on the web while saving and not destroying it.

I had emailed and texted the same block of about 11 to 16 great pictures from January 6 to friends and family members. Mostly selfies of Sharon and me and nice crowd shots. By sending the same block of joyous, non-threatening pictures to friends and family and then denying perpetual ownership of them to Facebook's Mark Zuckerburg through unsending copies of a few, the DOJ claimed I had "destroyed evidence of his attack on the U.S. Capitol." A felony.

What nonsense!

The government's own witness from Meta, the company that maintains the databases for Facebook, testified that *unsending* content does not make it inaccessible and certainly not to the government. It is standard procedure for the government to issue a Preservation Notice when requesting content, freezing the content at a point in time on the backup servers. We learned that the FBI *did* request and receive my Facebook records from Meta.[29]

In the midst of the squawking about my keeping things from the mythological grand jury, the government already had all the images they were still whining about. Some were included in print as part of the *arrest warrant* and *criminal complaint* documents signed by a misguided judge two days prior to the SWAT attack on our farm. Those and others were reviewed by Agents Palian and Robinson and me on Palian's laptop the day of my arrest.[30]

The charge of tampering with evidence was just another lie.

Innocence didn't matter. Only Rakoczy's "opinion" of the case.

As we readied ourselves to present our Defense case, October had dragged into November. We were so tired, so driven down. But we knew we had strong exculpatory evidence. Our plan to put people on the stand, including FBI personnel, could enable full exposure of that evidence before the jury.

The DOJ made sure that the FBI special agents we wished to call as witnesses could never appear. There would be no repeat of our beneficial cross-examination of Agent Michael Palian. His partner, Agent Steve Robinson was "unavailable" for reasons never made clear. Special Agent Lochner, who misled the grand jury to support my original indictment, had been "removed" from the case and "reassigned"—or so testified the Quarterback under cross-examination by Dave Fischer. Palian's sworn testimony confirmed Special Agent Lochner's deception and perjury before a grand jury that would give rise to my indictment. The DOJ could not afford to have Lochner cross-examined by Dave. They might have claimed he had been reassigned to the moon in order to prohibit his appearance.[31] Other people we wanted to call but over whom the DOJ exercised full control were likewise inaccessible. This witness suppression was disheartening, to say the least.

We were required ahead of our defense case to give the Feds *our* Witness List. This facilitated, of course, the prosecution's intimidation and threatening of any and all witnesses we intended to call to testify. Just another example of how the system is rigged to favor the government.

The testimony guaranteed to clear me, which would have come from former Oath Keepers residing in North Carolina, never got to the jury.

The affable Marine, Paul Stamey, was never a viable option to appear for the defense because, as we expected, Kate Rakoczy told Mr. Stamey's attorney that his client "had not been relieved from focus." Think of that as crooked lawyer-speak for "we still have the ability to charge your guy if he comes to DC to serve as a witness for Caldwell." Stamey and Doug Smith were only two of the people facing consequences if they had chosen to testify on my behalf. Naturally, Stamey's attorney advised him not to testify and spoke to Lawyer Dave about it. Hunkering down was a matter of self-preservation for these Carolina boys, who must have been terrified by the power of the DOJ and their manic attacks against yours truly.[32]

Without their in-person testimony, the task of proving my innocence became harder still. Dave asked that they be granted if not *immunity*, then some kind of protection by the judge to testify about the charges against me, so that the trial might not be distorted through the exclusion of their testimony. The DOJ argued vigorously against it, and the judge sided with them.[33]

But we still had the videotaped and transcribed proffers of both gentlemen, conducted in the presence of their attorneys, as well as the DOJ lawyers and FBI agents. Shutting down Dave's follow-on requests, the judge blocked the entry into trial of the transcripts and videos of their proffers under oath or any excerpts therefrom. This makes no sense if the truth was what was really being sought by the court.[34]

The DOJ knew any portion of such testimony could have been very damaging to their fictitious case. Our defense team knew how damaging the DOJ's long-planned suppression of the truth was to *our* case.

The FBI went about contacting and intimidating other potential defense witnesses with varying degrees of success. Although they had threatened and scared off some, the DOJ was still concerned at the number and variety of those waiting in the wings to support me with testimony, including those appearing solely as character witnesses.

Chapter 11

In Our Lord's Hands

The DOJ scheduling shell-game caused particular problems for defense witnesses traveling from afar to appear in court. Case in point is my Christian brother, Michael, with whom I have had a transcendent kinship spanning four decades. This rawhide-tough Texan and devout gentleman changed his flight arrangements from the Lone Star State multiple times in check-mate response to prosecutorial hijinks. His arrival sent our spirits soaring.

After weeks of constant pressure during trial, a rainy night's dinner at a nearby restaurant was a release and a relief almost indescribable. Sharon and I ached for this tortuous trial to be over. The brief time reunited to reminisce and laugh and talk about trips soon to come to his Texas ranch eased the pressure on us for one blessed evening. Through this renewed brotherhood, we escaped and enjoyed, remembering old acquaintances and old glories. Cocktails and tall tales.

It was this dear brother Michael who, while I was locked in Hell, shared with Sharon from Jeremiah 29:11 "For I know the plans I have for you," declares the LORD, "plans to prosper you and not to harm you, plans to give you hope and a future." We three allowed ourselves to speak hopefully of a bright future yet to come. That night my aching head swirled with the vision of his striding to the witness stand and my impish statement to the Lord: "Wait till they get a load of *this guy*!" I used to tell our co-workers when we served our country in the Navy together that he is so honorable and exemplary that "men want to *be* him and women want to be around him!" His strength and his faith are the first things to enter the room ahead of him. My evaluation has not changed through the years.

***

Sharon's testimony at trial was an absolute game-changer and, for credibility, she was unmatched by anything the prosecution had engineered with their limitless resources and scheming. Cool and forthright, she gave a step-by-step accounting of the run-up to January 6 and our innocent actions of that day and those that followed. During aggressive cross-examination by the DOJ hellhounds, her countering and dismantling of the phony case was a breath of fresh air.

At one point while Sharon was on the stand, *Manzo for the prosecution* displayed for all to see one of the many happy pictures I had taken on January 6. It was a picture of Sharon with a number of strangers in the distance behind her, standing still, while others were either taking photos or looking down at their handheld phones. This photo was christened Government Exhibit 22.P.8.

Sharon was instructed to look at the photo, and she complied.

Louis Manzo blurted accusingly, "Look at that picture! Were you uncomfortable? How did it *feel* to be part of a *riot*?"

"I'm not seeing any violence around me. It looks to me like everybody's just standing around taking pictures," she replied.[1]

Manzo removed the picture from the jury's sight with lightning speed!

"Your honor, if we could take our 3 o'clock break now. We're just having a little technical difficulty," said Manzo.[2]

Manzo was desperate to stop the testimony of my darling Sharon, who was the beautiful, petite "technical difficulty" of his cross-examination. He was no match for her on any level, especially intellectually. She is a very strong, forthright woman of Faith, and he was in my opinion, well, obviously out of his depth.

"Nothing spoils a good lie like the arrival of an eyewitness."
— Mark Twain, author, adventurer and humorist

***

No reference to The Ten Commandments or to God remain in the federal courthouse in Washington, DC. No one is compelled to place a hand upon the Bible or swear "so help me God" when taking the witness stand and, by so saying, declare that they will tell the truth. The leftists have succeeded, to their glee, in removing reference to Him from their *system*, top to bottom.

During the entirety of the ten-week travesty of this so-called Oath Keeper trial, one and *only one* of the nearly 100 witnesses called ever said with hand raised prior to testifying, "so help me God."

Only one.

It is the person who is sharing this true story.

The back pain was burning through, and I endured a long time on the witness stand being berated by the junior legal hack Louis Manzo. His questioning was a sarcastic character assassination, which apparently didn't play well with the jury. Dave never "prepped" Sharon or me or any coming to our defense, which contrasts sharply with the exhaustive rehearsals by the inquisitors and their "witnesses," eager for a slick production. Perhaps Dave just wanted all of us to speak from the heart and tell the truth in a forthright and off-the-cuff way. That's what he got, and it helped.

During the trial, the DOJ prosecutors' hatred for the United States military and for all veterans was revealed to be profound. Couple that with the moral and cultural bankruptcy they displayed and you end up with questioning that makes no sense.

"You testified that you have served at *classified locations* during your military career," stated Manzo.

"I never said that," I responded.

A hush fell over the courtroom as Manzo fumbled for his next scripted question. He thought he had his big moment all worked out. Manzo knows nothing about the military, and he paid not one lick of attention to my actual direct testimony. Military bases, headquarters, and port facilities are funded by the taxpayers and their locations are a matter of public record, not secret.

"You were trained by the CIA, correct?" he accused.

"No."

"And you were taught in the military to hurt and kill people, correct!?!" Manzo demanded.

"No."[3]

It seems these prosecutors live in a fantasy world where all military personnel operate from some secret hollowed-out mountain volcano. There's no James Bond 007 in my background, no imaginary safe houses. I am not aware of a Navy *Hurt and Kill People School*, especially for intelligence analysts who spend most of their time at a desk.

Futile is the attempt to explain to those who don't care to know exactly what the Navy does to protect the sea lanes so that people can continue to receive little plastic trinkets they don't need from China via cargo ships. The misguided vision of me as someone along the lines of our SEAL Team heroes, rather than an analyst at a console, would be comical if it were not so pitifully sad.

No one engaged in my prosecution had any familiarity with the military, but they themselves had coalesced into a formidable destructive force. They (the DOJ) had accepted that their commitment to the ideal of justice was dead. That in turn made them capable of literally anything in an attempt to crush me without mercy, without compassion, and without remorse. All political theatre and the persecution of innocents depends upon it.

You can quote me.

It was always the determined and faithful Dave Fischer who was at the vanguard in directly challenging the prosecution. Inevitably, Manzo's folly in belittling witnesses had become so disagreeable that the following exchange took place in the stifling courtroom:

Manzo sneered, "What did you *feel* when you heard that the riots were surging forward and the doors of the Capitol had been breached?"

"Your honor, I object," Dave said.

"*Why?*" Manzo whimpered.

"Because it's *stupid*."

The court room burst into laughter! I guess no one could believe that Lou Manzo actually blurted out "Why?" like a little girl not allowed to have a sleep-over. Dave's quip caused everybody *not* at the prosecutors' table to simply lose it! Even the media reps joined in with thunderous guffaws—a spontaneous release in a trial most foul.[4]

Manzo's blush was a completely unique color that a home improvement store might adopt as *Humiliation Red*. This moment is the stuff of courtroom legend, and the unbridled mirth among the defendants was an all-too-brief respite from the inquisitors' rack.

In retrospect it looks to be one of many blessings that Manzo was the one who was selected to interrogate first Sharon and then me. The legal community's own gossipy opinion, also whispered amongst the media in and near the courtroom, was that Lou Manzo was one of the most effective members of the Caldwell defense team.

The same tired talking points, the same practiced theatrics by the DOJ lawyers, were wearing thin on the jurors as the trial plodded along. Could the badgering and reliance on demonizing my Constitutionally protected free expressions and my life in service to our Nation ultimately backfire on the DOJ?

***

During my three-hour interrogation on that cold January morning nearly two years ago, FBI Special Agent Michael Palian was often texting on his cellphone, messaging Kathryn Rakoczy and other DOJ lawyers.[5] Palian's laptop was on and open, displaying a large collection of thumbnails, smallish versions of digital pictures. I recognized many photos as ones snapped by me on January 6. Though the government would later charge me with deleting these exculpatory photos from the date in question, here they were on full display, row upon row.

"Would you show us the pictures that you took that day?" Palian asked.

"I think you've already got 'em," I replied casually.

"Well, no, I don't have them all."

"Ha ha ... what a joke! You don't have them all!" I mocked.

"I clearly don't," Palian lied.[6]

That's when I am visible on the interrogation video you will never see, pointing to these images on Palian's computer.

"You have the pictures right there. Right there! You've seen them and they're great pictures."

"Ha ha!" Special Agent Robinson laughed at my busting of his boss.

"Okay. Not bad," Palian conceded.

"I see the closest you got to the interior of the Capitol was on the, up on the porch?" Robinson asked, trying to take over the questioning.

"Yes, the balcony."

"Okay. Umm, if anybody said they had a picture of you in the Capitol, are they mistaken?" he continued.

"Absolutely."

"We'll go through this again ..." Robinson began.

I cut him off. "Look, man, you guys, you woke me up at 6:00 when I went to bed at 2:30, and my back is hurting. I'm chained up and I haven't done a thing wrong and I think I'm being damn friendly ..."

"I got no problem with that, yes you are," he butted in.

Now Agent Robinson puffed up and said, "So, my goal ... I ... I am an independent arbiter of the facts. That's all I am. I got no ax to grind with you, I got no ax to grind with anybody. All I am trying to do is I'm trying to get your story with as much accuracy as I can."

"Uh huh. Right. Sure," I replied, rolling my eyes.

Robinson continued: "... to corroborate what other people are telling us, what ... what, you know, what the media says, that is."[7]

They came in the dark on January 19, 2021, not only to terrify my wife but to corroborate what the *media* says? Nice to know, Special Agent Robinson. Thanks so much for clearing that up.

Is it any wonder that neither the video nor the transcript of my interrogation would ever be seen by the jury? Any wonder why I was blocked from testifying about what was said by the FBI during this interrogation? Of course, it didn't stop the government from lying about the interrogation, with us unable to refute.

That whole "corroborate what you know, what the media says, that is" would have been fun for Dave to confront Special Agent Robinson with.

> *"The greatest evils in the world are not carried out by men with guns, but by men in suits sitting behind desks"*
>
> — C.S. Lewis, writer, lay theologian, and scholar

After two months of wrongful criminal trial I had seen every piece of discovery evidence provided by the government to not only our little defense team but to the attorneys for all of us caught in this J6 web of government lies. I knew the so-called "evidence" against some of the accused better than either they or their attorneys. My beleaguered co-defendants had been locked up and given only an hour here and an hour there to view the stuff on buggy prison-housed computers, doubtless with each keystroke monitored by the government. I could scour it 24/7 if only I could stay upright for that long.

I was paying close attention during trial. I saw not one scintilla, not one scrap of evidence supporting a guilty verdict of a felony against anyone! Maybe a couple of these hardy few had walked through an open door into the Capitol, but they weren't charged with that. That's simple trespassing—not a felony! That's a ticket and a fine, not years in confinement.

These people are all innocent!

It might be hard to believe, especially in light of my detailed descriptions of the meanies in this Shakespearean tragedy, but I always look to find the good in people. Sometimes it's easy and sometimes it's hard. I have had a lot of time to study the cruel and misguided ones who have played such a large role in this saga. I guess it's the same as it ever was. Light versus darkness. Good versus bad. There's no sense trying to sugarcoat what they're doing; no sense trying to put lip gloss on a pig. Things are what they are, and some individuals are simply *who* they are.

For the DOJ lawyers of the J6 prosecutions, I submit: Their every accusation is their own *confession*.

When people tell a truth that these DOJ leftist lawyers don't like, those people are decried again and again as liars. When the DOJ lawyers themselves withhold, hide, forge, and even delete evidence, they accuse the targets of their wrath of having *destroyed* evidence. Each time they accused the defendants of actions which "struck at the foundation of our democracy," it was their dishonest chess-moves that shattered the justice system upon which our Republic is built.

As they operated unchecked with ill intent, the DOJ lawyers called their enemies evil. I cannot count the number of times I was slandered with the term *evil*. This from those caught so many times in their dirty tricks while violating their oath of duty to the court and our Constitution. I'd call doing such things to hurt people with the hopes of personal, professional, and financial advancement the *epitome* of evil. I doubt they will ever be held to account. That is because they operate beneath the cover of *absolute immunity* even while they harm others.[8]

They couldn't possibly be doing the things they do with such apparent delight without knowing it's wrong. Subconsciously, then, perhaps every time they've opened their mouths they were indeed confessing to their own sins. Although I can hear and register their confessions, it is not for me to provide their absolution.

***

When at last we reached the time called closing arguments, mysterious technical glitches and gremlins arose within the court-provided video and audio hookups. It deprived us of showing key evidence to the jury in the most impactful way. This was maddening, but in spite of these problems, Dave's remarks were powerful.

It mattered not what evidence we presented or how clearly Dave had exposed the fabrications of the DOJ. The tormentors went back to regurgitating the same muck they had chucked all along like a momma bird puking worms to feed her hungry jury box chicks with mouths agape. It was another indignity to be endured.

A long-time friend and mentor of mine who I will call Allan was present in the courtroom for the closing diatribe from Jeffrey Nestler. Afterward, Allan was visibly shell-shocked and commented that the government's posturing was "disgusting and totally deceptive." He also offered up something which I have never forgotten, saying in essence, "He [Nestler] *threatened* the jury if they didn't produce a guilty verdict! I'd be terrified if I was one of them! The government knows where those people *live*!"

***

No discussion of the so-called Oath Keeper trial would be complete without the civilian star witness for the prosecution whose name in the courtroom was presented as Abdullah Rasheed.[9]

There was no delicate way to put it. To me, this guy was a dead-ringer for the Crypt Keeper from the old HBO program *Tales from the Crypt.* Go online to find the image. Well, Rasheed might have had a *little* more flesh on his bones. Emaciated, with sunken eyes and cheeks, a longish wisp of pale hair, and a death-warmed-over look, *this* was the government's ultimate civilian star witness.

Rasheed crept more than walked into the courtroom on day 635 of our abuse. His head was covered by a knit cap and a hoodie, drawstring-pulled tight around his face. He wore a solid mask in honor of the Covid mandate and dark, mirrored sunglasses. To the judge's credit, he wasn't having it and instructed Rasheed to make more of his face visible.

Everyone smelled a rat.

The prosecution contended that this guy unilaterally recorded a GoToMeeting online event and was so *outraged* by the Oath Keepers' discussions that he, being a good and upright citizen, was compelled to give the tape to the FBI. Kate Rakoczy's scripted and well-rehearsed Q&A with the Crypt Keeper crumbled first under the onslaught of a ramrod-straight Texan named Lee Bright from Mr. Rhodes' defense team.

Under cross from multiple defense counsel, it was revealed that Rasheed knew no particulars of the recording he supposedly made of the Oath Keepers, nor could he explain how the recording was done.

He couldn't explain the source of the recording equipment or how he knew about the invitation-only online meeting. Rasheed had never met nor communicated with a single member. He demonstrated only a vague idea about anything the Oath Keeper group stood for, despite professing to be their West Virginia state Commander.

Rasheed, celebrated in the fawning press, nevertheless was not even eligible to be a member of the Oath Keepers by virtue of his disturbing criminal history.

Lee Bright's defense question: "Are you a convicted felon?"

"Yeah," Rasheed answered.

"Sir, why have you changed your name six times in the past 20 years?"

"I don't ... I don't know that I have, but you're saying so, so ..." Rasheed responded nervously.

"You'll forgive me, sir," Lee continued, "but according to documentation that's been given to me by the government, you've gone by the name Sergei Neklovech ...?"

Rakoczy blurted, "Objection!"

"On the phone, please," said the judge, telling counsel to pick up the telephone handsets that the ensuing conversation might be kept from the jurors who were straining to know what was up.

Could Rasheed be what defense counsel nationwide refer to as a "professional snitch?" Rakoczy seemed desperate to ensure no further alias for Rasheed be entered into the official record of trial. The judge allowed defense counsel questioning to proceed within strict limitations.

Lee continued, "I would simply ask if you would agree with me that since, really, closer to 2007, you have gone by six different names and personas. Is that correct?"

Rasheed answered thoughtfully, "Probably more like 30 or 40."[10]

What? He volunteered that he has used between *30 and 40* different fake names!

"Thank you for sharing that," was defense counsel reply without missing a beat. "You state that you were concerned by the things that you heard being discussed on the GoToMeeting chat, correct?"

"Yes, sir," the witness responded.

"[You said] you would not agree that that meeting was online for two hours? How long would you say it went on?"

Rasheed stammered. "I—I need more information to answer that question. I mean, I could answer it if you tell me how long the government's exhibit is."

Going back to Rasheed's earlier testimony, he was asked, "And you're aware that no part of that meeting or transcript says it was okay to bring guns into the Capital [city], correct?"

"I didn't say that it was."

"You just a moment ago did, sir, on direct examination with Ms. Rakoczy."

"I think you're misquoting me—or at least—misspoke," was Rasheed's shaky reply.

"—and you also said a moment ago the plan was to, quote, 'take over the White House'?"

Rasheed answered, "Yeah."

Rasheed clearly forgot that he was supposed to testify that the Oath Keepers were going to the *U.S. Capitol, <u>not</u> the White House.* Oops!

There is so much more nonsense in this person's testimony, but some really stood out. Like that elicited by defense counsel Jonathan Crisp.

"Sir, to be clear, your prior conviction is for *aggravated sexual assault of a child?*"

"Uh-huh," muttered Rasheed.

"Is that correct?" Jonathan Crisp asked.

"Yes."

"Okay," Jonathan continued: "One of the things you asked the government for in compensation for your testimony today was a new identity; is that fair to say?"

"Some kind of protection, yes."

"You wanted a new identity?"

Rasheed confirmed, "It was an option, yes."[11]

I was still shaking my head minutes later as Dave Fischer took his turn eliciting revealing testimony from this witness, including:

"Sir, the recording that you made, did anybody in federal or state law enforcement or any federal or state agency encourage you in any way to make that recording?"

Rasheed responded defensively, "I'd never talked to one in this—I'm sorry. I'm looking for words. I've never—prior to that recorder, I haven't spoken to any federal, state, or local agency considering anything to do with any Oath Keepers or January 6th or November 9th or anything."

"You didn't have a handler?" Dave asked.

"Huh?"

"You didn't have a *handler*?"

"You mean like a Russian spy?" Rasheed responded.

"No. I mean like federal *law enforcement,*" Dave clarified.

"I don't even know what that is."

"Okay," Dave said, as puzzled as the jury seemed to be.

Rasheed blurted out, "So if you would like my bank accounts to see my—I don't have a federal income."

"You don't have any *federal income*?"

"No. I mean, if you're accusing me of being a government agent!" said Rasheed.

"Sir, no, I'm just asking. So you *just happen* to decide that day you wanted to videotape a GoToMeeting with the Oath Keepers?"

Rasheed's nervous response as he looked to the prosecutors' table for support: "I think it's been—yes." [12]

The questioning of this guy went on for a long time with more revelations suggesting the Oath Keepers had been the target of a set-up since at least around election time in November 2020. As a former Intelligence analyst, my conclusion is that a lot of planning had gone into this convoluted January 6 deception and the targeting of American citizens for phony prosecution. The Oath Keepers were nothing but patsies. I was roadkill because I had met a couple of their law-abiding membership.

A person convicted of felony aggravated sexual assault of a child. A person who might logically be expected to say anything to avoid prison time and instead obtain a new identity while avoiding registering as a sex offender was a key witness in the prosecution of the Oath Keepers! I bet that will never get into the media.

Like they told me in prison: *a creeper.*

Don't ask me where Rasheed is today with the freedom facilitated by Merrick Garland's DOJ in trade for his ridiculous testimony. Maybe he's lurking in your neighborhood. Maybe he's using fake identity number 41.

Maybe he's changed his name to Nestler.

***

Anxious uncertainty is the best descriptor for those days that followed the commencement of jury deliberations about the rest of my life. When not involved in idle chatter or wondering aloud how this exhibit or that answer to a question might have resonated with the jury, our four-person team put a good face on our dire circumstance.

My chief distraction was handcrafting personal messages to many of our supporters. Reading their heartfelt messages from across the country propped up our sagging spirits and distracted us from our troubles with images of towns and communities, homes and ranches, and new family members we might be able to see in the flesh when my hoped-for vindication had come. For truly they had become our family, risen from every state in the Union and moved by their compassion and genuine concern for a creaky old veteran and his wife.

During this Oath Keepers Trial, the Department of Justice solidified its place in the pantheon of corrupt institutions. Absolute power does in fact corrupt absolutely.

It's not that they're simply misguided; they're shockingly so very full of themselves. I have had many hours to reflect upon this good fight that we have fought and have formed some conclusions:

It's easier to destroy than it is to create.

- That's why terrorists demolish antiquities.
- That's why socialists denigrate our history and our heroes.

It's easier to pervert than uphold and cherish.

- That's why the twisted revile a child's innocence.
- That's why ugliness strives to disfigure the beautiful.

It's easier to mock than to understand.

- That's why insults fly more often than compassion.
- That's why the dishonest accuse others of insincerity.

Persecution is easier than introspection.

- That's why bullies use power to hurt the innocent.
- That's why pain is so often paid forward.

It's easier to lie to support your opinion than to consider the truth of someone else's.

- That's why the compulsive liar cannot conceive that any belief but theirs is true.
- That's why the dishonest shout deception and insults lest their true nature be exposed.

***

Tuesday, November 29, 2022, found us still waiting for the jury. Sharon was sometimes on her phone with friends and family, working around the issues which foiled most electronic contact with the outside world. I had no such problems, since my cell had been committed to the innards of some FBI storage locker. Along with my Constitutional rights.

We had just prepared to leave for the day, evening's rapid approach shown only on our watch faces in the windowless and dreary defense workroom. We planned tomorrow's rendezvous in quiet acceptance that days like this were to be the norm for the time being. What we previously knew as "normal life" with its comfort and peace might never return.

Dave entered, and his voice jerked us from our preparations.

The verdict was in.

I tightened my necktie and snatched my suit jacket from the teetering coat rack. I stuffed cards and computer into my worn shoulder bag as my heart began to race with a flood of adrenaline dumped into a worn-out body. I realized that in a few minutes it wouldn't matter what I stuffed into my bag. Computer, legal pad, letters unsealed but already franked ... might soon have no meaning whatsoever in my life.

There was a small crowd milling about outside the courtroom. Sharon and I moved to the right side of the hallway and waited, hand in hand, along with Kim, who seemed in many ways to be nearly as nervous as we two. Dave soon joined us, facing the slow procession of people queuing up for the show.

I went silently into a most urgent moment of private prayer to the Lord for His protection and, yes, His deliverance from the hands of the satanists who had schemed against Sharon and me for nearly two years. I don't remember all of the deepest feelings I shared with Him, though He knew my heart as well as I did. Sharon and I were positive that it was He who had led us through this time of tribulation and vilification. Led us to this moment.

Romans 10:13 (NKJV)
"For whoever calls on the name of the Lord shall be saved."

Then the doors were opened and we waddled in amongst the pressing throng eager to get their seats for the big reveal before happy-hour time. Attorneys for Lucifer and for the Lord of Creation assumed positions at their respective tables while the gallery pews filled up with all sorts, including the rabid media, foaming for the executioner's headlines sure to come. The only thing missing on the left side of the aisle was a popcorn vendor or perhaps cotton candy to complete the accompaniment for this freak show and carnival.

I was joined by my fellow defendants, who had been rushed to the sacrifice by the U.S. Marshals Service. With grim visages all, they plopped into the same bargain basement chairs. I met eyes with the only defendant I knew even a bit, Jessica Watkins, who winked and nodded in acknowledgment of what might come next in this frightful place.

In a flash, the foreperson had arisen and, as instructed by the court, read out the verdicts. It was all a bit of a blur as my prayers were interrupted by my name bouncing off the walls of that godless place and then the words, "Seditious Conspiracy: NOT GUILTY!" My heart leaped to my throat! Thank you, Father God! More chattering, then my name echoing once more followed by the "Conspiracy to Obstruct an Official Proceeding: NOT GUILTY" I had longed for! "Conspiracy to Prevent an Officer from Discharging Duties: NOT GUILTY."

Dear Jesus, could it be true that You have saved Your servant once again? Each charge alleged in the indictment was announced during this process, followed by each defendant's name and then the verdict. As the last defendant, I enjoyed the briefest moment of heart-pounding elation at being found not guilty, as I knew I truly was.

Then the bottom fell out.

Obstruction of an official proceeding. Thomas Edward Caldwell. "GUILTY."

How could this happen?

It was a blur after that. I vaguely was aware of my name being spoken again followed by another "Guilty" pronouncement for something. It didn't matter. I was innocent and yet these people had been conned into believing lies. Then again, perhaps the fix had been in all along.

All of my fellow defendants would remain in the infamous DC Gulag, but I was spared that fate by Judge Mehta. Nestler was incensed. He was fuming like a spoiled brat who had received a Malibu Barbie rather than a Ballerina Barbie at her birthday party. He dashed to the lectern to demand the judge throw me into prison on the spot. The judge would not be moved, as Dave Fischer's argument against such nonsense reinforced the pronouncement.

I was wrongly convicted, but I would go home for now to sleep in my own bed. I had fared better than any of the other defendants. Praise be to God.

The insanity was still ringing inside my head. Kim, tears welling up, made a beeline to me and clasped me tightly as the emotion took command of her. She had been with Sharon and me and Dave through the tempest times. As we hugged, I understood that she cried not only because of the wrongfulness of it all, but *for* me. She cried because she knew I would *not* cry or act out at the injustice. Easing from her trembling embrace, our eyes shared disappointment, making words unnecessary.

Sharon was stuck on the other side of the swinging gate, trying to gain my attention. Dave told me that we should go to the workroom as I, with jaw set, revealed nothing to gawkers of any stripe.

Sharon scooped up my eyes in hers, drawing me past the gleeful prosecutors and their FBI accomplices. Nestler and Rakoczy were in their glory as Manzo worked his way through the throng toward the gates. In their sputtering orgasm of triumph, I am supposing that FBI Special Agent Michael Palian, among others, understood his career might have been saved by an intimidated jury.

Sharon hugged me, and before we began our exit from the abattoir where dreams of justice go to die, I turned to locate Dave and Kim.

That's when I saw them. Dave and Manzo.

I didn't ask Dave Fischer exactly what snide comment Manzo had made to him in his moment of deluded self-importance. Possibly he just sneered at Dave as he had often sneered at me. In the briefest of moments while Sharon and I embraced, *something* had happened.

In prison parlance, Dave had now *stepped to him.*

Mr. David Fischer is the consummate professional with an easy-going manner that makes him immediately likable. That having been said, he was a highly decorated scholar-athlete in college and his still-muscular power-forward build and 6'6" All-Star frame can be very imposing. He is not the dude I would want to have even slightly perturbed at me. Louie Manzo was learning something from a better man that evening.

I couldn't make out what Dave was saying, but he was clearly laying out a bit of country wisdom in small, well-chosen words so they would be understood. As I watched, Manzo yelped like a little girl and lurched back in shock and perhaps terror. That's right: yelped out loud.

Curious how bullies can turn to butter before your eyes.

No physical contact was ever contemplated by Mr. Fischer. The squeaking was just overreaction by a junior prosecutor, who luckily was wearing a dark suit. Dave turned away, in essence dismissing the person and the moment as if discarding belly button lint. Manzo scampered to report to his mentor, Nestler, only to be ignored in a most obvious and, in my opinion, highly amusing way.

In our workroom, I slammed my bag onto the table in disgust and frustration. I dropped my cane and plopped into an unsteady government chair. I had been lied about for nearly two years and my wife and I had been subjected to all manner of mistreatment by the people *absolutely* guilty of a true conspiracy in this case: Joe Biden's Federal Government.

I was inconsolable. I had no words to share as our little team sat on all sides of the worktable as if arranged for a light-hearted board game. In low tones, discussion went on amongst the would-be players while I sat and said nothing. There were sounds outside our closed door: media vultures sidling close to gain a quote before filing their stories. Kim rose and with dagger-looks scattered any who lingered there.

I have no idea how long we sat, but there was no need to rush outside the building to endure the bright lights and cameras doubtless hovering on the sidewalk. After some measure of time had passed, and with the consensus declaration that we would "appeal," our tattered little team plodded to the elevators and an exodus.

Focused on the red taillights of a darkened city, I began to verbalize my dismay, asking rhetorically how such a total injustice could have happened. My beautiful Sharon had suffered right along with me every step of the way. Now in my despondence, it was Sharon alone who had the big picture of these unjust results.

"Don't you *get* it?" she asked. "We *won*. *You* won!"

"Are you nuts?" I'm thinking. Spitting my words into the night through clenched teeth I retorted, "They found me guilty of two things that I DIDN'T DO!"

"We'll beat those on appeal!" she exclaimed. "Even in a city where we *knew* we'd never get a fair trial, the jury didn't buy the prosecution's nonsense! If you'd been found guilty of even *one* of those conspiracies, they would've dragged you off. We *won*! We beat the worst they could dish out! Praise the Lord!"

As we wound our way through the clog of cars and buses, though I couldn't flush away my hurt, I had to admit Sharon was absolutely correct. It was far from over for us. Even as stressed and worried as she was, she still had focus. She understood that the fictional conspiracy was invented precisely for the purpose of putting people away for a long time. God had indeed delivered a huge victory for Him and for us this day. I had been squeezed so hard for so long, I couldn't see it. Not until Sharon made it clear to me!

This was an epic moment in my life and in our lives together. Another miracle against overwhelming odds. The Lord had saved our lives when the FBI attacked and He saved them again now. In between He had sent a defender. He raised me from a death pit in Virginia and now from a pit of despair in a filthy American city.

Through the oily black night we inched with traffic toward the familiar 14th Street Bridge. Bathed in the uneven glare of white lights and reds, I pulled from my pocket the encouraging letter written by our dear Christian sister Eileen from South Carolina way back on September 21. At a full stop in traffic, my eyes strained to read the prophetic words once more.

- God is able to do exceedingly more than we ask or imagine.
- God always causes you to triumph in Christ Jesus.
- For the Lord your God is going with you. He will fight for you against your enemies and He will give you the victory.
- In all things we are more than conquerors through Him who loves us.
- In case I have not told you: you have the victory.
- *Please don't be disappointed if the victory isn't immediate.*

I refolded the note and pocketed it once more near my heart.

Holding Sharon's gentle hand, I thought, "Absolutely right, Eileen." It's not the *total* victory we were hoping for, but it is *A* victory. The Lord's Victory. God's timing is always perfect. Praise the Lord.

Three wins in a DC court.

And that's enough for tonight.

Chapter 12

Manic Persecution

We awoke in our bed exhausted, but the next few days were ones of praise, prayer, and gratitude that the Lord had delivered us from the worst of the false charges. Phone calls, emails, letters, and visits churned locally and across the nation with the good news. No matter how the propagandists tried to spin it, our verdicts were anything but the slam-dunk my persecutors desperately craved.

There I was, the guy who for two years had been accused as the principal figure in the January 6 *insurrection*, acquitted of all three conspiracy charges. Uneasiness still hung over Sharon and me, our future in jeopardy because of the mystifying guilty verdicts. In the aftermath, mention of me was usually relegated in print media to a one liner saying that I was convicted of two felonies. I would have been front and center if we had not achieved such a great win.

How to pick up the pieces of our lives while knowing that this American horror story was not over?

We wouldn't have been able to handle the financial crush of existing in temporary quarters inside the Beltway without each and every member of our nationwide support family. How incredibly blessed we are that our amazing new family of angels had kept our noses above water and kept us fighting. This was *their* victory, too.

When I was alone, sometimes the effects of the prison were visited upon me again. I could hear the screams and slams of the satanic cacophony of that place. I could smell the stale pee and filthy concrete. I wondered at questions with no answer. How could people supposedly sworn to uphold the law purposely break it over and over with such determination and commitment? How were they brainwashed to hate with such passion, to condemn someone they had never met and whom the evidence they suppressed so thoroughly would have cleared?

I couldn't help but think of how many citizens they were still doing this to.

***

A dire financial state had little impact on a joyous second Christmas celebration together since this manic persecution began. Although we always liked to surprise each other with some special gift at Christmastime, Sharon and I could no longer afford such luxuries. We had lost so many of the material possessions and, of course, the nest egg which we had felt would carry us through medical bills, and similar cash-devouring catastrophes in our old age. Now we were happy, yes happy, with the things that truly matter. Things that cannot be purchased in a store, ordered from a catalog, or discovered on the internet.

Sharon and I wanted so much to have our quiet lives back and, with vulnerability, I shared some of our hopes and dreams, Christmastime experiences, and reflections of our shared faith with our nationwide family. Still dealing with the disappointment of not being fully exonerated, we found solace in crafting cards and letters by the score to be sent to many of the people we love all across the Nation. There was no other way to explain the fact that a victory had been won than to give all credit and glory to the Lord Who had held us in the palm of His hand all this time.

Dave Fischer had a plan and had been working on it for quite some time. It's called a Motion for Judgement of Acquittal, also referred to as a *Rule 29* motion, and a legal process which is a petition to the presiding judge to set aside the guilty verdicts rendered by a jury.[1]

Dave's arguments included his contention that the DOJ had misused a statute called 1512(c)(2) to charge me with Obstruction of an Official Proceeding. This had been written into law in 2002 as a knee-jerk reaction to the Enron Scandal and specifically addressed the destruction of evidence such as official documents and the like. Clearly this had nothing to do with what I did standing outside the Capitol and practicing my right of free assembly.

By the numbers, Dave laid out the fact there was no actual evidence against me whatsoever to support the guilty renderings—verdicts that seemed nothing more than an afterthought. Especially in light of my outright acquittal on three conspiracy charges! One thing was irrefutable: character assassination should never be sufficient to support guilty verdicts and definitely not under *this* statute.

Dave Fischer reassured us that the judge had, through the detailed Rule 29 motion, all the justification needed at his fingertips to throw out the fraudulent verdicts.[2]

If he actually wanted to.

***

Anyone found guilty of something in the federal system is subject to atrocities galore, as is their family. This brings us to the next plague: the Pre-Sentencing Report (PSR).

This is a multi-stage process in which the government forced me to compile and submit the data-history of my life. Phase one was a telephone interview with a representative of the DC Parole Office who asked psychiatrist stuff such as if you hated your parents growing up, do you like girls, etc. Phase two was a requirement to research and build, with the complexity and thoroughness of a master's thesis, a sterile history of every detail of my life and Sharon's life and then submit it to the DOJ so that it could be shared with anyone as they saw fit.

Our part would end up being a stack of laboriously researched and completed forms many inches tall. The demanded materials included every kind of personal information imaginable on my entire family living and dead, every address at which they and I (even as an infant) had ever lived, and the dates of residence. Not to mention all schools attended, all jobs ever held, to include dates, addresses, and names and phone numbers of supervisors or co-workers who could be reached and then badgered by the government. How do I know the location of a guy I worked for 50 years ago when I was eighteen? How many places at which I worked still exist?

No backtalk, you filthy country boy, disabled veteran Trump criminal! Get busy!

The DOJ demanded information for all of our bank accounts. If I'd had a small IRA, they wanted to know. They demanded our tax returns for the previous five years, a monthly expenditures and income report—what?—copies of all of our bills for the past six months, and the deed to the farm (of course, so they can seize it at any time). On and on went the outrages. All of this information was disseminated throughout the DOJ and who knows where else (either legally or illegally)? Rather than fill out their fool forms, it would have been simpler to tell them that in order to fight their malicious prosecution, we were now broke. Easy. Done.

It struck me like a lightning bolt! Is *this* how they developed the database they used to torment Jones in the Terror Tower in Harrisonburg, Virginia? I thought of Jones' sorrowful expression. The recounting of the detailed and *mocking* examination of his family's history all offered up with sneering recriminations and outright threats against what he held dear. In his own legal battle, he was forced to give what was being extracted from us now. Now it's our turn to supplement their records and expand a new database table in the Colorado Data Center and at People's Computer Headquarters Number 4 in Wuhan, China.

The record of my life has since been transferred to Artificial Intelligence and dissected by the government just as it was for Jones and how many thousands, even scores of millions, of other Americans.[3]

When the DOJ had completed its part, the report was ready for the judge. Using some of the information in the PSR, the prosecutors demanded that he sentence me to 14 years in federal prison! After all of the shameful and deceitful things that Rakoczy and Nestler and Manzo *et al* had done, their 44-page heap filled with scurrilous lies demanded that the judge sentence me even for things of which I had been found *not guilty*.[4]

The Offense Conduct portion of my Pre-Sentence Report reads: "The information contained in this section was obtained from the various indictments filed in this case, the government's *opposition* to defendants' motions for judgement of acquittal, and additional information provided by the government." What? *Not guilty* verdicts as a result of trial were *not* taken into account in this PSR![5]

The Bureau of Prisons (BOP), an integral part of the DOJ lawfare apparatus, refers to the Pre-Sentence Report as *The Bible*. I guess this is appropriate for them in their secular, even blasphemous existence. The point is that the BOP bureaucrats, some would say sadists, take their direction from this inches-high pile of paper, however ridiculous or false its contents are. I had been found not guilty of the three most serious charges, never went into the Capitol, and was totally non-violent, yet the completed document never mentioned those facts. Instead, it read as though I were some kind of monster.

Only false accusations and stacked charges were included, and whatever the sentence handed down by the judge, all of the same old lies would serve as the road map of my mistreatment for the prison authorities. Accordingly, our prison consultant, who had worked many years for the BOP, made it crystal clear that I would be placed in a harsh prison environment, possibly even a maximum security facility, where the violence of both the population and the guards was unmatched. There would be no prison "camp," no white-collar resort for me. I would be housed with hardened criminals and resume the same dismissive medical care I had endured in a decaying Virginia jail. It was plain to everyone with knowledge of these developments that my silence—*permanent* silence—was what the DOJ prosecutors of the *Capitol Siege Section* were counting on.

For Sharon and me, dismay was replaced by sheer astonishment when Dave Fischer informed us matter-of-factly that the judge can choose to *ignore* all of the jury's not guilty verdicts if he wants to. Why the heck did we have to endure a trial and be plunged forever into debt just to go through that? I guarantee most Americans don't know it's even possible. Most Americans would probably argue that it couldn't happen in this country even if I told them it happened to me.

There is a name in professional shrink-lingo for people who cannot conceive that they might be incorrect about anything. Someone with *anosognosia* isn't simply in denial or stubborn. Their brains can't process the fact that their thoughts and moods don't reflect reality.

That in turn helps them to justify their actions. So, in my opinion, it's clear that the prosecutors' behavior has a name.[6]

And the judicial system not only has no intervention plan, it serves as an enabler.

Mentally, we dug in, knowing that the judge could take weeks and even months to render a decision.

I contemplated our daily devotional written by Jennifer E. Jones, who opined that God's miracles were on a slow burn and how the Bible is filled with stories of how people had to be patient and wait for the Lord to do His thing. While we waited, I had to do *my* thing, too. Exactly *what* He wanted me to do was mine alone to figure out.

Sharon and I were still a great team. When one of us was driven down by physical weakness and emotional exhaustion, the other seemed to have more optimism than ever. I was reminded by our readings that as we seek more Grace from Him, the Lord writes emotion-filled epics of our lives, not comic books. It takes time to craft such detailed works in us. The significance of each plot twist and outrage has been hard to see in the moment. Sharon and I have had so many of the lessons of the Bible proved to us in our own undeniable experiences that it is almost overwhelming. But how and when will the torment end, Lord?

Sometimes the only nugget I could focus on is that God doesn't always just snatch us out of our troubles, even though He hears each of our requests. The forces of darkness which hold us tightly seem to revel in our torture. But we know that God has good plans, and part of the story He is writing in us involves the incredible people He has brought into our lives along the way. Each victory which has been and will be is theirs as well. We want only to be free and perhaps comfortable again, but maybe The Father is interested to see how much I can develop and mature in this incredible mess.

Comfortable is a much nicer place to be, but nothing grows there.

***

We used to say in the Navy that the final act in any evolution was awards and accolades for the non-participants. This was our tongue-in-cheek acknowledgment of there being no limit to what a person could accomplish if they didn't care to get credit for it. Military history is rife with examples of mid-grade and senior officers giving each other medals, promotions, and the like for successes in which they played little or no role. Those actually responsible for success usually get the short end of the stick.

At the *71st Annual Attorney General's Awards* extravaganza in early 2023, it was clear that the weaponized Department of Justice was very up-front in acknowledging loyal minions who followed the direction of their puppet-masters while ignoring the charge to support the rule of law and the United States Constitution.

Case in point is that year's *10th Distinguished Service Award* recognition for all of the major players in the totally phony "Oath Keepers" trial conducted in calendar year 2022. Posted for all the world to see but purposefully not identified as having participated in the dreaded *Complex Conspiracy Unit, Capitol Siege Section* prosecutions were the names of all the major players in our three-ring J6 Circus of the Insane. First on the list, even though they mispronounced her name through the loudspeakers at the awards ceremony, Rakoczy had finally achieved number-one status over her bitter rival, the diminutive Jeffrey Nestler. Heck, she even got to hold a little trophy while on stage.[7]

Troy Edwards and Alexandra Hughes, as well as FBI co-conspirators Michael Palian, Sylvia Hilgeman, John Moore, Joanna Abrams, Byron Cody, and others were listed prominently. All were rewarded through official government channels for fealty to the cause of assigning blame and securing convictions through whatever means the taxpayers' deep pockets could facilitate.[8]

I have no idea if cash bonuses to the DOJ lawyers and such were paid in connection with *these* awards or whether the big bucks were ponied up under some other guise by Matthew Graves, the U.S. Attorney for the District of Columbia. After all, each senior U.S. Attorney in the various regions or districts across the country has a special slush fund from which he or she can hand out bonuses to underlings in amounts up to and including one million dollars *per person*.[9] I know this because I used to work for them. Heck, they don't even hide it by washing it though another agency, such as USAID.

Those being recognized for framing and incarcerating people tied to the "worst attack on our democracy since the War of 1812" should certainly expect more than a hearty handshake and a plaque. Think of the hours they invested! All that fake evidence, those phony exhibits and falsified time sheets don't create *themselves*, you know.

A financial incentive works wonders for prosecutorial motivation and focus.

I suppose in addition to praying for the FBI people I should also have felt sorry for them. I have no idea how they might receive *their* graft, if any. It probably wouldn't come from the same pot o' gold held by Washington Field Office Chief David Sundberg unless there have been some major changes since *I* worked for the FBI.

***

Hard-working reporter Steve Baker exposed through an article and a podcast that at least one U.S. Capitol Police Officer testifying in the trial of which I was a part knowingly perjured himself in providing damning evidence against my co-defendants. No great revelation to me. Mr. Baker used Capitol Police CCTV security video that had been withheld by the government to shatter the DOJ's case and claims.[10] Soon a consortium of media companies were suing over the FBI's refusal to honor a Freedom of Information Act request to release thousands of hours of video in its possession, most of which was exculpatory for hundreds of J6 defendants. But the FBI and the DOJ would not be compelled, safe beneath the leathery wings of the Biden Administration. And no one could do anything about it.

In another high-profile J6 case, an FBI special agent under cross-examination was presented with emails which led to her "admitting fabricating evidence and following orders to destroy hundreds of items (338) of evidence." In the same case, the government had withheld recently surfaced video footage from January 6 that was exculpatory. Evidence the government knowingly withheld—another perversion of the *Brady* rule that violated the Constitutional rights of an American citizen.[11]

Every single one of these outrages was completely preventable. They didn't happen by accident. These desecrations of the rule of law and of individual Constitutional rights were directed and executed with malice aforethought, as were the abominable attacks against me.

There were lots of people working to expose the offenses of the DOJ and calling for reversals of convictions and outright dismissals of the cases where the appearance of prosecutorial impropriety was glaring. The federal judges in DC, acting as one, would have none of it. The die had been cast long ago and fates sealed. It was discouraging, rotten, and smelled of conspiracy.

My battered old psyche and body, having endured ever-increasing levels of stress, was betraying me. The tremors and the prolonged episodes of chest-pounding exhaustion from the worst days in the dungeons were upon me again. Often the unfathomable pain would switch suddenly into that frightening yellow-orange view of the world which was all my eyes could register. I still can't understand how pain can manifest itself visually like that. There must be a name for it. Maybe the word is nuts.

I was perpetually on edge after over two years of relentless attack. I dreaded phone calls, my mind immediately springing to an expectation of bad news, perhaps another unwarranted attack by the DOJ hate-mongers. Not a normal response for a normal guy under normal circumstances. There was *nothing* normal about our situation now. What the heck would these godless you-know-whats invent in order to mess with us next? Bless their hearts.

We hadn't long to wait for an answer.

***

In March 2023, the Department of Justice prosecutors' offices contacted a little-known federal bureaucratic backwater called the Department of Veterans Affairs Health Eligibility Center in Georgia. The faithful worker bees there complied with the Main Justice directive to illegally terminate my access to the medical care I honorably earned through nearly 20 years of active-duty Navy service. This move also cancelled all medical care benefits for Sharon, stopped our access to the Veterans Administration Hospitals and Clinics, and ended prescription drug coverage for us both. The DOJ was at it again.[12]

I did not react well to the form letter from Georgia informing us of their decision that I "no longer met eligibility requirements."[13]

Once more, thanks to God for Dave Fischer, who had started taking the malignancy of the DOJ personally. He rushed into a fight with no clear end. To me, it felt like the DOJ was inflicting pain simply because they could. Perhaps they were "getting even" for their losses in federal court. Dave would later say they had become so crazed because we had fought them so hard. Whatever motivated them, they were relentless. He just *had* to stop them somehow.

Remember good ol' United Services Automobile Association and how they cancelled our credit card? They showed their love for this veteran with a form letter to tell us that after faithfully paying premiums for over 46 years, our auto insurance would "not be renewed." I smelled the wokeness clear to our tumble-down farm and pictured their eager responsiveness to the request from what the DOJ department called the Capitol Siege Section. Our phone and written inquiries to dear USAA regarding their action came to nothing. Thanks for your sacrifice, veteran. We told you two years ago to drop dead, so *do it* already![14]

***

Chinatown

I was summoned by the DOJ once again to the DC courthouse. Just to keep me fully aware that life and freedom were not my own, I was ordered to appear to be booked and processed by the U.S. Marshals Service on April 6, 2023.

Over and above the opportunity to make me come running at their whim, the stated purpose, immortalized forever in an FBI report written by the designated bully of the day, was a bit of housekeeping the FBI was keen to complete. In all of my time locked away within the prison/industrial complex, it turned out I had technically never *really* been a federal inmate at all![15]

It follows that the Feds had built-in deniability for any mistreatment I received in lockup. They had an Intergovernmental Services Agreement (ISA) to house detainees for a fixed cost per day, an indefinite contract officially extended beginning in 2018. They had subcontracted the responsibility for care and feeding, housing, medical, and maybe *abuse*, too, to the CVRJ, Orange, Virginia.

This built in cover for them is why they tried to avoid a paper trail at the Terror Tower in Harrisonburg, Virginia. The most important thing was to injure and demoralize me on the roadside, not go through another administrative police action song-and-dance at a federal building with unavoidable computer entries. They could fingerprint me when I was dead or when I was inevitably convicted and thrown into a super-max prison for life.

Now they had to do some cleanup, and quickly.

Sharon and I were met by two wet-behind-the-ears FBI representatives who were literally incapable of meeting my blistering gaze. After we cleared the metal detector station, they led us down the hall to the double banks of elevators and a trip below the courthouse.

On the appropriate level we disembarked. Entering through a door into a waiting room filthy as any back alley in Mumbai, my eyes beheld a stack of black gym-locker style boxes row upon row. Most were festooned with temporary tape markers displaying the names of the current batch of show-trial unfortunates being abused upstairs on the fourth floor.

Sharon waited while I followed the Feds through the only other door in the room. Echoes marked our steps past dreary holding cells with iron bars like you see in movies about East German Stasi Secret Police headquarters. This must have been where the Oath Keepers had been kept during those pauses during trial. I was told to take a seat to the right of a giant taxpayer-funded console.

Today's events were to revolve around fingerprints and a DNA mouth swab, which would doubtless be in Beijing on tomorrow's DHL flight. As the twins fumbled and chattered in low tones between themselves, I thought of any number of witty things to say to exacerbate their feelings of discomfort and inadequacy. But being a grownup and a nice fellow, I held my tongue.

A man with an official identification badge, in obvious disgust at the ineptitude on display, took charge. The scans of my fingertips completed, he asked where I was born, and I told him. With oozing condescension he asked again louder and more forcefully, as if I were an unruly child. I was put out at having to be there in the first place. I repeated the name of the city of my birth slowly:

"Waaashingggtuuun Deee Ceee," said I, burning his eyes with my own.

Properly refocused, he then asked me, "date of arrest?"

"I was falsely arrested on January nineteenth, twenty twenty-one."

The FBI people didn't like me saying *that*. Oh, not one bit. I guess the truth hit a little too close to home.[16]

The curious implications of the long period of time between my false arrest and today's date of basic "intake" functions were obvious to the machine operator, who I think was an okay guy, all things considered. He was just doing a job. His follow-on question was something more of an indictment of the FBI people and rhetorical, rather than a true inquiry of me.

"Why are you here *now* for booking if you were arrested that long ago?" he asked.

"Some dirtbag prosecutor ordered me to be here," is all I said. I then made a snort-sound of disgust at the entire episode.

Next came the whole DNA mouth swab evolution, which began with one Hoover-ite trying to tear open a hermetically sealed package with the long Q-tip swab inside, and the other fumbling with papers. To be fair, they did finally manage to open the plastic package all by themselves but looked as though they had never seen a cotton swab before. Console man was not amused as we both waited for them to get on with it. And waited some more.

He began to explain to the children how the process worked as he took hold of the swab. Then I politely interrupted and asked if he just wanted me to do this so we two could get on with our lives. Zip, zap I was done and handed back the stick containing the necessary information for the Chinese Commies to develop either my clone or a weaponized designer virus to modify my genetic code.

Just around the corner, several people, including at least one Asian dude who was the alpha, were congregated. The words drifting my way from the Asian man sounded a lot like some guttural grunt-speak developed in the underworld. Maybe he just gargles his Chinese rather than speaks it.

Shortly after my leaving her, Sharon had been witness to the rush past of three guys whose commotion I was hearing now. In the lead she saw a male apparently of Chinese ancestry who carried in his hands a laptop computer, held before him, not in a shoulder bag, as if using it as an interface with something in our planet's atmosphere. With this man in charge were two Anglo-types in cheap suits with the look of gangland knuckle-breakers. These guys, jaws set, projected malice though they followed behind bossman with obvious deference.

Sharon was struck by this whole scene, and her impression was that Chinese guy was some big shot. Perhaps even in charge of this entire area of the transverse colon of the Prettyman Courthouse. He barged through the door and launched a word tsunami, which is what first distracted my attention from the soap opera of ineptitude I was involved in.

Was I actually witnessing full access to the legal/persecution operation against political enemies given over to a foreign government? There's enough evidence of corrupt ties between ours and that of the rotten Chicoms—and, yes, I do understand that not *all* people of Chinese descent are commies bent on world domination. Still, this guy didn't look like your run-of-the-mill government employee, nor did he carry himself as an American. He was *different*. When you *see*, you *know*.

For her part, Sharon was shocked and worried because they had followed me into the crypt. What the heck was going on?

With their backs turned to me, it took a few minutes for the FBI to do something. Precisely *what* I cannot say. Soon they were solving the riddle of a mailer envelope and its self-sticking adhesive. I was not happy that they had my unique genetic code and seemed to be prepping it for shipment with an *international* mailer.

The Chinese accent echo-speak from the other side of the wall had stopped, and with a nod between me and the man at the console, I rose. Turns out those three mystery men were already exiting when I made my move. Possibly with the *electronic* version of my intake and my fingerprints.

"We're done here," I stated matter-of-factly. I walked out, leaving the FBI people and console man behind. I never looked back. I just wanted to leave that place and spit the taste of it from my mouth into the gutter of a once beautiful city. I couldn't wait to scrape the DOJ muck from my body again.

***

One day Sharon and I came home with a meager forage of groceries to find a red message light blinking on the ancient wall-mounted phone in our kitchen. A verbatim rendering of this message identified as *Recorded 9:34 a.m. Tuesday May 2, 2023* follows:

> *"Good morning. This message is for Mr. Thomas Caldwell. My name is Roderick Smith, I'm calling from the Department of Veterans Affairs Health Eligibility Center in Atlanta. Reason for my call today, Mr. Caldwell is uh callin' to uh um reinstate you. Um basically your um health care was uh denied um due to proceedings. Uh we were told to do that by the Department of Justice. Uh callin' to let you know that you have been reinstated into your um healthcare "priority group 1." Um you can start utilizin' the VA healthcare as soon as possible. Um if you have any questions or concerns you can call me back at 404-828-5858. My name is Roderick Smith. My telephone again is 404-828-5858 and this call is to inform you that your healthcare benefits HAVE been reinstated and if you would like to call me back please do so I can uh provide any questions or answers to any of your concerns. Thank you."*[17]

Praise the Lord. God had thrown back the demons once again. With some help from Archangel Dave in Glen Burnie, Maryland.

The psychology of hate is beyond my ability to codify, let alone explain, although I am witness to its psychotic manifestation churning within a federal stronghold in Washington, DC. It has swept across the lives of Sharon and me in a turgid discharge at the spigot end of the January 6 political honey wagon. The Healthcare Benefits attack had been only the beginning of this new twisted campaign of revenge against Sharon and me. I had to ask myself over and over: revenge for *what*? For being *innocent*? Or for having the guts to stand up to them and fight? Sharon and I knew we never had a choice in the matter.

There was much more outrage to come.

***

This should have been such a happy time on the farm, but the cloud of despotism hung over us. The barns and fences were falling into disrepair, the fields and ponds were overgrown and choked. Weeds ruled where crops once flourished. We were still surrounded, watched, and threatened by the DOJ cabal: locked in a type of prison without walls and bars but which retained all of the hope-crushing attributes of the Virginia jailhouse only a few hours away.

Sharon and I could only avert our eyes from the decay and trust in the Lord our God that one day we would be free. If not exonerated, at least free from the penal cloister to shoulder some court-ordered house-arrest yoke of shame and begin to rebuild our lives, our property, and our way of life in the few years we might have left together.

There was no relaxation, no tension-releasing come-down for us during this period. Quite the opposite. The date had been set, May 24, 2023, for my *sentencing*, a public pronouncement of governmental punishment for crimes I did not commit. This after suffering a multi-hour verbal harangue, which would presage my condemnation. Dave Fischer told us he felt there might be no further jail time for me whatsoever, but Sharon and I were not convinced, having experienced first-hand the government's unhinged cruelty.

And so, my wife and I prayed about it. We prayed without ceasing. We thought of how far we'd come with the Lord. How many times we'd been snatched from disaster by His Mercy. We thought of how many people were praying daily for us and how many blessings and miracles we had seen and still experienced regularly.

Look what He has done *for* me personally and *in* me. Did I ever think I could have this kind of a relationship with God?

The Lord can do anything.

***

How could the DOJ machine invent even *more pressure and* lies to hurl at us?

Cue FBI Special Agent Palian, the publicly embarrassed lead *law enforcement* witness for the prosecution, to go to work. He conducted a phone interview with a guy named Jonathan Hoffman, the man in charge at the wretched Central Virginia Regional Jail, Orange, Virginia. His facility's rough treatment of me had been followed by Hoffman's promotion from Lieutenant to Captain to *Major* in less than two years.

The DOJ lawyers had tried to convince anyone who would listen that my statements about my original incarceration were untrue. That I in fact had been held in a virtual country club. In a twisted effort to convince the judge of my "untruthfulness," Hoffman denied I had been held in solitary, denied I had been handcuffed and denied other things wrongfully done under his direction and supervision! All of this was sworn to an FBI Special Agent, who documented same in an official FBI report called a "302." This was another gambit by the prosecution to lead the judge toward a long prison sentence for me as a bad person.[18]

Dave Fischer said he had never seen anything like this in his entire legal career, nor had he seen anything similar actually *solicited* by an FBI special agent. Someday, Palian and Hoffman's actions will be fully exposed, as will they, if not by this court, perhaps in another one. Especially since we are fully armed with complete copies of the Central Virginia Regional Jail's very own documentation of my term of internment and, thus, proof of Hoffman's lies and my actual mistreatment.[19]

I suspected Herr Hoffman was terrified of the FBI, and why wouldn't he be? Fear can make someone do things of which they are not proud. It's no surprise that in our society, here is a guy in charge of a Hell on earth who may be more concerned about saving his own hide than anything else. Even more concerned than he should be about breaking the Ninth Commandment: "*Thou shalt not bear false witness.*"

Someone else I have to forgive and pray for.

***

The appointed day of my sentencing was speeding toward us. I spoke frankly with those closest to us, telling them I did not feel I would be allowed to survive another stint in a federal prison. It would be far more beneficial to the DOJ in every way if I got *Epsteined*. Most people understand the reference to the supposed suicide while in custody of a man with hundreds of verifiable secrets highly embarrassing to our nation's ruling caste. Another one bites the dust.

These thoughts are just the serpent of old pounding on me again. What else is new?

On a beautiful early May evening, Sharon and I began the drive to Wednesday Bible Study at our church. The 600-pound beast in the backseat was the knowledge that this might be the last time we would ever attend such a Wednesday service together. As we rode our aging four-door across the familiar Shenandoah River bridge, Sharon's smartphone chimed with an incoming call from our favorite lawyer and now dear friend Dave Fischer.

For some reason, I did not feel the dreadful oh-what-now feeling.

On the speaker-call, Dave informed us that the presiding judge in our case had called for a special hearing to be held in a DC courtroom the following Monday, May 22, at 10 a.m. This date was two days before my scheduled sentencing. Why would the guy in the black robes order such a thing? Dave was keen to my now normal knee-jerk response to any mention of "court-related"—a reaction not dissimilar to the cringing and jerking away of a battered spouse who has come to expect being backhanded by a loutish abuser. Consequently, Dave was quick to add:

"I think this is a *good* thing."

I have no recollection at this writing of anything he said after that. My only memory of the remainder of our trip and that evening is a feeling of anxiousness and hopeful gratitude while worshipping in the Lord's House.

***

May 22, 2023, was day 854 of our ordeal. Only a very few were in the gallery in the courtroom, with Sharon sitting on a wooden bench at the other side of the saloon doors. Present was an entire J6 outlaw posse assembled against lonely Dave Fischer and me. What was about to happen we could not know. For us, this hearing was allegedly for the judge to pose specific questions and hear answers from both the defense and the prosecution about the Judgment for Acquittal motion authored by Dave months earlier.

For Nestler and Rakoczy, it was an important tag-team opportunity to cement their Ivy league legal reputations. What a way to tie a bow around the *J6 Conspiracy* package served drippy hot to their benefactors! They had long since abandoned any adherence to an oath as officers of the court with their mountains of lies. They rode the prevarication truck toward Sharon and me in wicked overdrive.[20]

The best possible outcome for us was the only just and correct one: The judge would grant the motion in its entirety, throwing out the unsupportable verdicts. I would be a free man at last, and there would be no sentencing for me at all.

Jeffrey Nestler, perhaps itching to move on to the judgeship he may have believed was certain to come from leftist DC Mayor Bowser, commenced a tidal wave of insulting conjuring, overflowing with statements shrouded in "it is reasonable to *infer* that Caldwell *intended* ..." No evidence of crimes, of course. He was simply preaching hard to what he felt were the biases of the judge himself. Inference by the prosecution is not evidence. I don't think Nessie or the judge had the ability to read minds, so the suggestion and their repeated statements in the affirmative that they knew what anyone intended in any circumstance, let alone *me,* was foolishness personified.[21]

My blood was nearly boiling in my veins as the insanely fast heartbeat condition rose and remained. All of this at the spouting of a master charlatan who I think could serve as an adjunct professor teaching *Prevarication 301: Strategies to Avoid the Truth in Court"* and the student favorite: *Advanced Collusion 402: Effectively Conspire to Convict Undesirables Without Evidence.*

> *"Those who can make you believe absurdities*
> *can make you commit atrocities."*
>
> — Voltaire, 18th century French satirist and philosopher

The gallant David Fischer fought each new fiction lobbed our way. He was afforded the briefest opportunity to address the most preposterous new claims. Once more I began to pray in my agony. There's nothing quite like a crisis to develop your prayer life! It doesn't even need to be life-or-death.

Dave Fischer began: "Just a couple points, Your Honor. Respectfully, I disagree with Mr. Nestler. There was no evidence that Mr. Caldwell 'pushed everyone out of the way.' There's no evidence of that. The government claims that Mr. Caldwell drove Congress out of the building. Congress was evacuated and Mr. Caldwell was at the Peace Fountain with his wife. The government's own exhibit proves this. He didn't cause Congress to be evacuated. He's not at the front of the crowd. In fact, the government's own exhibit showed he wasn't."[22]

Yeah, Nestler was lying again, your honor. It's all more Nestler bull feces.

Nestler sat and steamed.

Dave continued: "From the government, every inference goes towards Caldwell's guilt, not the *truth*. But Capitol Hill was saturated with video and there were cell phone videos, too, yet, we *don't have any* video that the government presented showing Mr. Caldwell doing *any* of those things. So, Your Honor, we ask you to grant the motion. Thank you."[23]

It's not that the DOJ prosecutors *can't* tell the truth. It's that they *haven't.*

"I'm going to vacate Mr. Caldwell's sentencing on Wednesday" said the judge at last. "There's a lot to think about. This has been very helpful."[24]

We were dismissed. The sentencing would occur on another day. But not until after the judge could consider what he had heard today, and, of course, Nestler and Rakoczy could lobby him hard to throw out our request. For now, there was nothing to do but go home and wait.

So we did.

Nestler and the other prosecutors immediately energized a legion of liars for a fresh, two-pronged attack. Their first task was to produce a *new* sentencing recommendation filled with more folly and foolishness. No judge bothers to go back and check the record for accuracy, so the second task was to provide a summary of false information about trial testimony to the judge that he might reject our motion. Nestler was free to write and say anything at all. Not facts, but only untruths once again.

Theirs was not a static attack plan; it was dynamic, evolving. Like an anti-justice virus.

Chapter 13

The Long March

2 Chronicles 20:17
"You will not need to fight in this battle. Position yourselves, stand still and see the salvation of the Lord, who is with you."

Since first confronted in court by the DOJ lawyers, I have been keenly aware that my very existence triggers in them an almost rabid compulsion to persecute me. That might seem to be a paranoid, "over-the-top" statement to some, but I don't say it lightly. For having the temerity to actually speak out against their phony prosecution, I have become the focus of their ire. For the heresy of exposing their lies fed to the fawning media whose adoration they cultivate, I must be finished off.

Persecution by definition involves efforts to torment, harass, demoralize, and punish, especially for one's beliefs. This is what they desire to do to all people who do not think or act or vote or live as they themselves do. They have the potential to *get to you* with their callous viciousness. If you don't think so, try voicing your opinions in a public forum such as social media.

Any thought that we had turned back the DOJ in court that day in May and that they would slink back to whence they came was woefully wrong. Soon after our temporary confounding of their fever dream before the court, we were presented with the insane *addendum* to their demands for my confinement, begun when the judge vacated my sentencing. Another raft of slander to worry over and more hours required to rebut these mendacities in writing.

Dave Fischer was in his element. He had been preparing to combat the whoppers presented, and over the next few weeks he constructed multiple supplemental motions to the judge on our behalf. His arguments should be an effective counter to the inane legal doublespeak writings of the bad guys, but who knew which way the judge would go?

Amidst all of this, the eyes of legal scholars turned to what is called the *Fischer case*. Not a reference to Dave Fischer, our lawyer, it was instead the name of a J6 defendant whose own battle for justice had brought his case to the DC Court of Appeals. The case in question involved one of the same charges I was falsely found guilty of and which his counsel argued was misapplied. A win for him represented a potential win for us and many other unfortunates wrongly found guilty of the same alleged offense. Would the judge in our case wait to move forward until this Appellate Court handed down an opinion? Might he also slavishly go along with said decision even if it were wrong?

Or would he rely on the absence of evidence presented in court over nearly ten weeks and take a courageous stand for truth and justice, as is his duty as a federal judge?

***

We found ourselves in a *third* summer of oppression, with farming in the classic sense an impossibility. It hurt us deeply to look at this once happy little cattle operation, now so long devoid of barnyard animals and equipment or much else that would have made it look like an active farm. The tractor, the centerpiece of our equipment group, and its tow-behind brush hog attachment that acted as a mower on steroids had long since been sold to a kindly farmer down the road. Sold when Sharon needed the money desperately to pay for our very first attorney. Without the long-gone sicklebar mower attachment, hay rake, and baler there was no way to cut and bale the hay that we used to grow on a rotational basis in our rolling fields. We managed some stewardship of the land all this time through the good graces of a friend from a neighboring farm who gladly took the hay for his own cattle. But the tractor, the hay machinery, and so many cow-specifics such as head gates would all need to be saved for and replaced before we could even imagine reconstituting a herd of our very own again.

Many basic chores still needed to be addressed, including simple maintenance of the house, ponds, road, barns, outbuildings, and fences, especially in light of their *modification* through the ravages of weather and time. Ultimately some chores, including the ongoing battle with weeds, were attacked with the enthusiastic participation of dear brothers and sisters here in our local community. They gave generously of their time, sweat, and encouragement to help us just barely maintain the farm enough to ensure future viability. Physically I was so beaten down that I frequently felt I added nothing to the efforts. I had still not recovered even a fraction of my pre-incarceration vitality. Maybe I never will.

Through the blessed goodness of hundreds of people, most still strangers, we continued to avoid the unthinkable sale of our tranquil little refuge in order to fund a legal defense. Of the hundreds of millions of American citizens, these precious few kept the fires of justice stoked and burning hot. Perhaps with the secondary benefit of confounding the DOJ endlessly. Only the Lord, the One we all need to trust in all things anyway, could provide such a miracle for us. And those miracles kept coming. In Praise, we kept hanging on.

Some days were better than others.

I was still not permitted to use the internet, a primary way those with discernment could, with a bit of effort, find actual reporting of newsworthy events. My information normally arrived via Sharon, who was under no such restrictions, and it was she who shared what details there were of an FBI SWAT raid that killed a 75-year-old disabled gentleman in Provo, Utah. In a classic shoot first, ask questions later scenario, he was murdered in his home by the FBI as he leaned on his cane. All this as his home was invaded in the dark by dozens of heavily armed people who did not identify themselves before breaking in. We prayed for this murdered man and his family.[1]

Not surprisingly, his neighbors' versions of the episode were diametrically opposed to those of the FBI. The assembling of vehicles and predators in the darkness, the screaming to disorient the peaceful resident on a quiet cul-de-sac, those sights and sounds conjured painful images for me. A military-style vehicle with a battering ram smashing into his home. Overwhelming deadly force in this land of liberty. To think that the assault on *our* farm could have been a dry-run for the actions of the death dealers that day in Provo was an emotional stab to the heart for both Sharon and me.[2]

The voice whispering that I should *not* open the door with cane in hand in the pre-dawn darkness of January 19, 2021, likely staved off a kill-shot by the FBI. Why had I set my cane aside? Was this the Holy Spirit Himself?

When I was trussed up by our attackers and called out to save Sharon from death at the hands of the government hit squad, it was our Heavenly Father who stayed their hands.

Otherwise, she would have become soon-forgotten news copy.

***

The large package arrived in the mail from Dave Fischer's office without fanfare or a prior phone call. Inside were 52 unsorted pages which I recognized right away as shabby copies of official pages from my official Military Service Record. There was little rhyme or reason to these double-sided reproductions, which spoke to the latest disdainful handwave to the legal requirement for the DOJ to provide what might be considered discovery exhibits to their target.[3]

During my time on active duty, military service records accompanied officer and enlisted personnel throughout their careers, to all training schools and duty stations assigned. Nearly one year after the Justice Department's embarrassing defeat in a federal court, prosecutors were still intruding upon my life and my reputation. They were *still* investigating me. Still harassing *us*. Why? This was beyond simple manic obsession on their part.

Like the record of nearly all veterans, mine is now part of the National Archives. It resides at the National Military Records Section in Saint Louis, Missouri, which is not a public library where things are readily available for checkout. I think the information in such records was presumed by vets and their families to enjoy some level of privacy and control. Clearly that had been circumvented in my case and likely for others.

What were they up to now?

It had been years since I had looked at this documentation, including the periodic evaluations of my performance as an officer, created and signed for posterity by a score of senior officers during my career. These are called officer fitness reports, or *fitreps,* in the Navy. Despite the fact that my career had ended in the previous *century,* in this fetid fervor of fanaticism the prosecutors were still trying to create a nexus between imagined events and keep our wounds from a wrongful prosecution open and weeping. This wouldn't do it.

I looked at a particular fitrep report and noticed these words written of me by a Navy Captain: "Faithful, responsible and completely trustworthy."

How would you like to have *that* on a job performance evaluation completed by your employer? I guess the DOJ will have to hide that little tidbit.

Heavenly Father, I am so beaten down ... does any remnant of that former man still exist within me?

***

Word came to us that the Fischer Case had received a split decision by the three judges on the Court of Appeals. How does *that* happen? One agreed that the statute in question, 1512 (c)2, does not apply to political protest. One said it does, and one said in essence uh ... I'll just take the middle-of-the-road position because I don't want to make a decision. The Appellate Court's non-ruling was painful from a justice and judicial integrity standpoint. It appeared to be a blow to our Rule 29 Motion for Judgement of Acquittal and restoration of freedom and citizenship. We were not surprised that a DC Appeals Court would not render a decision favorable to any January 6 defendant.

With September came not only the commencement of the labor-intensive paw paw harvest here at the farm, but also the big countdown to what we anticipated would be the judge's decision regarding those two bogus guilty verdicts hung on me. The Oath Keepers with whom I had been tried had already been sentenced. Other Oath Keepers in later trials, too. It looks like I am the last holdover, perhaps an afterthought.

September 19, 2023, found Dave Fischer projecting hopeful optimism that the judge would throw out at least one of the wrongful verdicts this day. I felt at the time that Dave was just trying to lift our spirits. We were instructed to participate in a teleconference to hear the judge's oral rendering of his decision.

What followed was shattering in every way. All that needs to be said is that it was a verbal bloodbath, and the judge seemed to be following once again a script written by the prosecution lawyers themselves. No phony verdict would be tossed. The judge's pronouncement put the prosecutors over the finish line in a sickening J6 homage to the age-old Malleus Maleficarum, the witch-hunter's guide for persecution, torture, and ritualistic murder of undesirables. It also includes directions for burning at the stake.

I couldn't shake the feeling that we had been *played*.

The prosecutors at the DOJ, architects of the only conspiracy yet proved regarding January 6, would soon have their bonuses. Now their professional standing among peers and patrons would be secure. Heck, if they could convict me, a guy who did absolutely nothing, they could convict *anyone,* and the legal world would know it. The sky was the limit.

The judge had the justification to dismiss the phony verdicts in his hands. If he had wanted to. But he didn't want to, probably never did. In his decision, he made completely false statements as justification for turning down my acquittal.[4] Perhaps they had indeed been provided to him by the prosecutors, knowingly misleading this judge. How could we be certain? Is mine to be, then, a death sentence for independent thought? The ability to conduct this kind of unbridled lawfare *must* be changed somehow! But how could things ever change with the current people in power? How could anything change in time to save me?

Wasn't it the honorable Senator John Kennedy who told us, "You are not truly free if you can't say what you think"?

As one conservative writer put it, "the process is part of the punishment." Punishment of those chosen to serve as the wretched warning to all Americans that anyone, even the truly innocent, will be targeted by those endowed with unchecked life-and-death government power. I am here to say that the American people are *not* terrorists. But I am resigned to the fact that the Constitution's protections are no longer guaranteed for any of us. Now *that's* truly terrifying!

"Terror is an instrument of social hygiene."
— Vladimir Lenin, 1917

Sharon and I were heartbroken and angered by the judge's decision, especially considering his *stated* reasoning for denial was totally bogus and based upon statements disproved in court.[5] The undeniable fact is that there are those who have the ability to end the love story that Sharon and I share, all for their own personal gain and, who knows, perhaps the modern-day equivalent of a pocketful of silver.

What is referred to in legal circles as the federal *system* is hopelessly skewed in favor of Uncle Sam. I'd wager 99 percent of Americans have no idea how bad it is and how little justice actually exists there for the common man or woman.

The truth is that an indictment is nearly always the same as a conviction, and never more so than in this political sideshow unfolding a new twist seemingly every day. Let's not forget the sentencing guidelines used in January 6 cases, which established the most incredibly cruel and barbarous sentences for convictions—convictions achieved with the flimsiest or totally invented evidence imaginable and guaranteed to destroy or end lives. This is what we were up against.

Perhaps I am indeed fated to *EXpire* rather than to *INspire*!

The next date established by the court for my sentencing was December 20, 2023. What a rotten impostor of a Christmas present.

We were back to being road warriors once more, making the nearly two-hour trek in our sputtery old SUV to Dave's office in the Crab

State. There to powwow and dig out a working session with Dave as he juggled responsibilities to other clients desperately in need of the best criminal defense possible. Since taking up our standard, he had dramatically cut back on other cases so as to fully immerse himself in the battle to defend us. No one save we, Dave's family, and the Lord Himself knows that Dave is spending nearly every hour battling the principality of darkness in the DC swamp.

***

We tried to focus on the many blessings from the Lord we have received. Among these was the wonderfully compassionate outreach of thousands of average citizens just like us. Former strangers who were now friends and family. Though it had been difficult to overcome the disinformation machine spewing accusations about Sharon and me, the cards and letters and phone calls continued to pour in from people who believed in us and cared for us.

For well over two years we'd had multiple prayer groups doing the loving work of intercession on our behalf, lifting us up to the Lord. During this tribulation we continued to receive blessed encouragement from hundreds of Americans around the country, many of them Christian believers. There have never been enough hours to write the letters I wanted to write to tell them how much they mean to us. The prohibition of my ability to use something as simple as email meant that "snail mail" was all that was left to me, and that with a mangled hand and broken wrist on top of everything else.

I often worked long into the night, striving to answer the joyful support from this wellspring of correspondence. My handwritten ramblings in shaky granddaddy print looked more like undecipherable Picasso-esque scribble than true written communication. I could barely keep up, though I wanted so much to say, from the heart, what their messages meant to Sharon and me. How very inadequate I was at being able to make these amazing heroes feel the tenderness we tried to send in return for all they gave us.

Sharon and I had survived not because we were tougher or stronger or more resolute than any other person wrongfully targeted in America. We'd survived simply because maybe the Lord, inexplicably, is not finished with us yet. That is humbling beyond measure.

Joshua 1:9
"Have I not commanded you? Be strong and courageous. Do not tremble or be dismayed, for the Lord your God is with you wherever you go."

***

As the days got fewer until the appointed sentencing date, Rakoczy and her co-workers continued to slander me in their written arguments before the court. They brought more falsified exhibits to the judge in an effort to fool him once again. Woven into their demands for years of incarceration was a particular bit of so-called evidence called *Government's sentencing Exhibit-9*.[6]

Sentencing Exhibit-9 was an allegedly 304-page pile of paperwork provided under signature of the reliable prosecutorial tool Jonathan Hoffman, Commandant of the prison which had held me. Responding to a grand jury subpoena issued in August 2022 and signed by AUSA Kathryn Rakoczy, Hoffman affixed his signature to the transmittal letter and provided the requested information, along with a "summary" of events for my 53 days of incarceration. However, we soon discovered there was much more significance to this Exhibit-9 than Hoffman's personal false declarations or even the fact that Rakoczy had held these printed pages for a *year* before sharing them with our defense team.[7] We also noted that she had given us only *302* pages of the document, not the full *304*, which turned out to be a significant omission.

Now came the payoff for my responding to the guidance of the Holy Spirit way back in March of 2021 and contacting prison staff directly to obtain my own *complete* copies of official jail records. This before any could be altered or destroyed by the facility or the Feds.

Dave Fischer filed a Supplemental Sentencing Memo, which, among other things, called out Rakoczy and her teammates in a very public way.

> "The government's sentencing Exhibit-9 purports to be a complete copy of Caldwell's medical records from CVRJ. These medical records, according to the government, "cast doubt upon [Caldwell's] current claims" regarding his disabilities. ECF 580 at 20. Fortunately, the undersigned

previously obtained a full copy of Caldwell's CVRJ medical records in 2021, directly from CVRJ. Interestingly, the undersigned's copy and the government's copy of the CVRJ records are identical with one notable exception: the government's copy, i.e., Government Exhibit-9, is missing one [critical] page—a page that sets forth in detail which medications Caldwell received (and the dates they were administered) while at CVRJ. This missing page proves that Caldwell was not provided with six of his seven prescribed medications while at CVRJ. See Exhibit A (attached) (missing page of Caldwell's CVRJ medical records). Respectfully, the government should retract its claim that Caldwell misled the public vis-a'-vis not receiving his prescribed medications."[8]

The government never retracted its latest phony claims about me, these regarding my brutal incarceration. They just don't do such things. Nor did Judge Amit Mehta ever admonish a single government lawyer for falsifying yet another submission before the court.

Why did AUSA Kathryn Rakoczy or someone at her command feel it necessary to remove some of the prison documentation before handing it over to the Defense? Could it be that she or other members of the prosecution team were destroying yet another example of indisputable proof of malicious prosecution and their own criminal culpability?

***

"A RED FLAG": IS SCOTUS POISED TO OVERTURN KEY J6 FELONY COUNT?

If the highest court determines the Department of Justice and judges misapplied a corporate fraud statute against hundreds of January 6 defendants, the repercussions will be felt for years to come.

Julie Kelly DEC 16, 2023

An order published by the Supreme Court on December 13 represented a moment hundreds of January 6 defendants and their loved ones had been waiting for: the highest court

> granted a writ of certiorari petition in the case of Fischer v. USA.
>
> In a nutshell, after more than two years of litigation before federal judges in Washington, SCOTUS will review the Department of Justice's use of 1512(c)(2), obstruction of an official proceeding, in January 6 cases.
>
> The political world now waits with bated breath for the outcome.
>
> If a majority of the justices conclude **the DOJ misused the law**, the Biden regime's ongoing prosecution of January 6 will suffer a death blow. And federal judges in Washington who willfully endorsed such intentional prosecutorial abuse will suffer a collective black eye, justifying calls for mass resignations and retirements.

***

Emotionally battered as we were, Sharon and I could draw only one conclusion from the Supreme Court's decision to consider the applicability of the whole 1512(c)(2) nonsense: that it was a *good* thing.

This 1512(c)(2) charge, also called "Obstruction of an Official Proceeding," represented one of the phony guilty verdicts I was still saddled with. It was the main charge the prosecution was using to try to imprison me for fourteen years (likely the rest of my life). This Enron-era statute was crafted to be all about preserving evidence for Congressional inquiry into financial crimes. The Supremes would at long last consider whether it was a statute applicable to political protest, or in my case, the simple act of visiting the exterior of the U.S. Capitol on January 6, 2021, *after* all of Congress had left. The Lord Himself must be moving behind the scenes once again just as things seemed to be so dire for us. Once again our spirits took flight.

Against this backdrop, we received the news that the judge had vacated my sentencing scheduled for December 20, 2023! Instead, he would have a "status conference" on the same date via teleconference. Surely the judge, political animal that he was, knew all about what the Supreme Court was doing. He himself would delay sentencing until mid-to-late summer, giving the High Court ample time to hear arguments on the ridiculously misapplied 1512(c)(2) charge. A charge he had failed to throw out.

We had been pressed down for so long, it was amazing that we could actually feel more than a bit of happiness once again. Soon, Sharon and I even spoke excitedly about how we might petition the court to return our lives to some level of normalcy. I was still limping around with the clunky electronic tracking device on my ankle. The DOJ's heavy-handed restrictions continued to block my attendance at weddings, graduations, confirmations, funerals, and even participation in health-care and loving-friendship visits to friends and family struggling with cancer or the ravages of other medical conditions. A lessening of my isolation from community and family seemed almost dreamlike: a fantasy just beyond reach.

Once again, the sickness of the so-called legal system in our land reared its repugnant head.

Day 1,066 of our battle for justice was marked on the calendar as December 20, 2023. On the Zoom call that day, the judge emphatically stressed that he cared not for any pending action by the Supreme Court and tasked us, in the meantime, to provide him my most recent medical records so that he (and thus the prosecutors) could issue a directive that *when* I was incarcerated I would receive full and compassionate medical care for my life-threatening conditions.[9]

Compassionate? Like in the Gulag? A second chance for them at finishing me off through my plethora of debilitating physical ailments only barely controlled by prescription medications, notions, potions, and lotions? Our professional prison consultants (yes, a real thing), who had worked for decades directly for the Federal Bureau of Prisons, assured us *none* of my prescription medicines was available through the prison/industrial complex. They just weren't medicines that were *recognized* or *accepted* by the Feds. Kind of like equal treatment under the law: not recognized and not accepted by the Feds. Accordingly, I would be swallowed up in the necropolis.

The light of life and hope visibly drained from Sharon's face before my eyes as the federal judge spoke in a waggish way about my pending incarceration. My angelic wife lost her stoicism and her well-rehearsed poker face. The judge had the gall to chirp a wish for us to all have a "Merry Christmas" before ending the Zoom session.

The sum and substance of a later conversation with Dave Fischer that day is lost to my memory, so withdrawn was I now, steeped in my own tepid emptiness. I had been kicked in the scrotum by DOJ-directed scum on a lonely lane in rural Virginia nearly three years ago. Today I was kicked in a new way by a guy appropriately cloaked in black on a video screen. Only the latest in a succession of a different type of strikes, these could prove to be infinitely more destructive.

History tells us that people are capable of evil. And unless good people are willing to fight people capable of evil, evil will triumph."

— Joe Lieberman, Former U.S. Senator

The Shape of Things to Come

A return to prison and an extended stay in something akin to the thirteenth concentric circle of Dante's Inferno seemed inevitable now. Sharon and I tried as best we could to encourage each other but my fractured mind was ruled by images of renewed isolation confinement and torments to come.

My mind dredged up from a well of fear questions without answers. If the evil within our own government was off the leash as I had learned the hard way, what else were they capable of? Was my experience in solitary confinement merely scratching the surface of the depravity underway in prisons here and abroad?

A brilliant bioethicist named Caroline Thiriot paints a frightening image of what could soon be widespread. These types of horrors were not *my* imaginings. Ms. Thiriot shined the light on such unspeakable practices, some hidden under the guise of *research*, which are underway right now.[10]

There were mad doctors actually answering the question: what if you could give a prisoner, or anyone you dislike, whether convicted or not, a pill or an injection which changed their perception of time? What if you could make a 10-year sentence feel like a millennium? Or twist a person's brain with 15 years of perceived misery and suffering in only, say, 53 days of real time? The chance to torture to madness a political prisoner, or anyone for that matter, until they either died or had their personality and psyche permanently destroyed. What a deliciously diabolical way to neutralize the undesirables. You know: free thinkers, Constitutionalists, Christians, the disabled, senior citizens ...

There are numerous reported cases in which perceptual distortions such as "disorientation in time" certainly do occur and relate directly to the practice of solitary confinement. I had experienced some of these in the clutches of the DOJ. Way back on October 18, 2011, Special Rapporteur of the Human Rights Council on torture for the United Nations called on all countries "to ban the solitary confinement of prisoners." He stressed that "Solitary confinement is a harsh measure which is contrary to rehabilitation, the aim of the penitentiary system." I wonder if he is *still* under the misconception that the penitentiary system in the United States is interested in rehabilitation. Its actions argue against it.[11]

The DOJ and America's gulags demonstrate that the enemies of the leftists in our country are considered not deserving of humane treatment, so why would they give two shakes about the UN special what-not?

But my mind wanted to scream to a disinterested humanity that allowing the current use of ill treatment or *any* present or future use of psychotropic drugs to further warp a prisoner's perception of time may be the most sadistic of all tortures and serves no purpose other than to permanently injure. Such practices are at their root *criminal.* Torture and violence seemed to be the language of those arrayed against me and perhaps millions of others. This was not science fiction. These things are going on throughout the world.[12]

Would I be next?

It's curious to me how the mistreatment of others, whether technologically advanced or as basic as a kick to the crotch, appears to be so very *REgressive* rather than *PROgressive.*

***

Armed with our belief that the Lord had us in the palm of His hand as He had since the beginning of this miscarriage of justice, we remained steadfast in our belief in Him and in the promises of the Bible. We believed it and we told people so.

An early spring teased us a bit as we considered all of the work that should be done to get this farm back into shape. But we weren't really free to accomplish what farmers should at that time of year. I'm not a young guy anymore, and even if we still had the normal farm equipment, I wasn't sure how much energy I could muster as the accumulation of a neglected rehab from hip replacement and the effects of rapid aging provided a new kind of shackle to accompany the government one that snagged and sliced with each step.

At Casa de Caldwell, the pace some days was delightfully slow and borderline peaceful. The breeze through the window screens brought with it the wonder of how much longer before the trees would begin to leaf and drop a green veil between us and the little pond in front of our house. How long before the spring peepers and the turtles would rule the tarn and sing us into the season of early buds and early bugs?

It was a time mostly of prayer and introspection. In so many ways, our life was held in limbo by forces we could not influence, let alone control.

Our emotions went every which way because we could be sure of nothing and could imagine anything. How then to come to grips with the insider knowledge that justice, equal protection under the law, presumption of innocence, fairness, and even the Constitution itself were empty promises? I thought: You go through your whole life believing one thing. And then suddenly you look deep inside yourself to find something else. A truth you never knew ...

One day, our dear friends in Christ, Mavis and Dan, traveled here from New York to spend time with us in fellowship. The spiritual days with them on the farm were such a relief and a blessing. The stories they shared of their lives and how Faith pulled them through times of otherworldly turmoil and doubt were an inspiration to Sharon and me. This was such a touching example of how people can minister to one another.

To assist in this stage of my spiritual growth and in light of my need for protection, they brought along some anointing oil representative of the power of God to shield us. They not only anointed us during prayers but went with us throughout our beautiful fields and forest and blessed them while telling any demonic energy to get out and stay out. Mavis taught me how to do this, and with the oil she left I would later bless each room of this house to block and expel any non-Godly energy.

We had seen enough of the ungodly in Washington, DC.

***

The DOJ policy aimed at causing the most harm to J6 defendants and guaranteed to incarcerate them as long as possible called for attachment of a "terrorist enhancement" to the mandatory sentences for each person found guilty of certain felonies. This administrative action added time to defendant sentences of as many as twenty-one years! This was intended also to be applied to any sentence given to me.

Now came the decision from a three-judge panel in an Appeals Court in the District of Columbia ruling that these enhancements had been misapplied (no surprise) by the DOJ prosecution and that they could not be used. The result is that the multi-paged sentencing recommendation for so many of us must be recalculated, *removing* the terrorist enhancements and the demanded-for extra years of imprisonment.[13]

My particular sentencing recommendation was about as thick as the first draft of *War and Peace*. For the DOJ, fashioning a new document filled with malevolent make-believe would take a lot of effort. Allowing time for the prosecutors' gyrations, Dave Fischer's required responses, *and* the medical report still waiting in the wings, another delay in my sentencing would surely be required. What would the judge do?

Our next date certain for a pronouncement of return to torture in solitary confinement became April 4, 2024. That would be 1,172 days since this nightmare began for us. April 4. Isn't that the anniversary of the assassination of Dr. Martin Luther King? Another soul, just like me, who was accused by a corrupt DOJ of sedition against the United States. How about the irony in that?

***

Audrey began life as a mail-order member of the family—an amaryllis plant so scrawny, so raggedy looking, and, well, so irresistibly needy. Sharon and I thought what she needed was a chance, some basic support and sunshine. And a lot of love. As advertised, her strap-shaped long green leaves eventually sprouted from her base to produce clusters of funnel-shaped flowers each Christmas. But instead of cutting her away as instructed to save the bulb for replanting annually, we kept her with us as she and her root ball grew to over 100 pounds.

In the midst of all the joy she brought us, we didn't know that Audrey's assignment during these days was to encourage us.

She had blossomed quite out of season, welcoming me home from wretched prison detention in delicate sweet-smelling full flower on March 12, 2021. Audrey gave us the only homecoming gift she could. *This* year, as we made the run-up to an April 4 sentencing, she and her closely held offspring in a huge, wheeled planter began to bloom in early March. Sharon and I found her beautiful display very reassuring. We couldn't know that she would send up shoots in a continuous outpouring of lovely red flowers well into the month of June. Another fortifying sign of encouragement and an unheard-of four-month cycle of bloom! Isn't the Lord's creation something! He is the God of details. He is the God of comfort.

Audrey sits beside me every day.

***

Plans for my sentencing stopped when the Supreme Court announced they would hear oral arguments on April 15 about that foolish 1512(c)(2) charge. We had contended even before trial that it had been wrongly used to lock up J6ers. The judge in our case, not previously disposed to await arguments before the Court, much less their decision on any matter, now faced a dilemma. Maybe he considered that, at least in my case, would it not be more beneficial for *him* to await the decision by the Supremes? He had to wait for new sentencing documentation from the prosecutors anyway, due to the DC Appellate Court decision that "terrorist enhancements" in sentencing recommendations could no longer be used.

All of these delays and machinations made Sharon and me feel like we'd been jammed into a front-loading washer at the laundromat. Up and down, round and round, our emotions and worries were tossed, all the while knowing the entire prosecution was a farce. And now the word that our judge had postponed sentencing once again, this time until July 26, 2024! Surely the Supremes would issue their ruling on all cases they were deliberating by their July 4 recess. My intelligence analyst powers told me the last thing the presiding judge in our case wants is to be overturned by a Supreme Court decision only a few months out, so he changed the date of sentencing once again.

But the question remained as to whether the Supremes had the courage to properly interpret the law and say so in their ruling. Do they have the juice also to declare that all of the insane obstruction of Congress guilty verdicts tied to this statute must be thrown out? Or will they issue something that falls short and is totally wishy-washy? A victory could clear the path for perhaps a final appeal for *total acquittal* and my exoneration.

While we asked our nationwide family for their continued prayers, I was still haunted. Haunted by a vision of having to go back into the DC swamp in a few weeks for pronouncement of a prison sentence. Haunted by the prospect of the Supreme Court misinterpreting the law and thus handing me over to Satan. Haunted by the knowledge that the judge could simply ignore the Supremes, regardless of what they decided, and do whatever the heck he wanted to.

Lord, whenever I feel fear, draw me back into your promised Peace!

I think we'll just stay in Faith here on the farm and see what happens.

***

Substack: Declassified with Julie Kelly Jul 10, 202

After Fischer, What Next?

Every 1512(c)(2) indictment against J6ers is defective but that is not stopping the DOJ from attempting a workaround.

This is a guest post by David W. Fischer, a Maryland and DC-based criminal defense attorney and the senior partner at Fischer & Putzi,

P.A. Most recently, Mr. Fischer defended January 6 defendant Thomas Caldwell, who was acquitted on seditious and other conspiracy charges.

On June 28, the United States Supreme Court handed down its opinion in Fischer v. United States, a decision that affects hundreds of January 6 defendants (J6ers) who were charged with felony "obstruction of an official proceeding" for their actions on January 6.

Writing for the 6-3 majority Chief Justice John Roberts rejected the DOJ's reading, instead holding that the government must prove that a defendant's alleged obstruction must relate to the impairment of evidence, i.e., "records, documents, or objects."

Contrary to the DOJ's recent spin, the Fischer decision was a massive defeat for the government, as it had (mis) used Section 1512(c)(2)—a felony that entailed draconian sentencing guidelines and a presumption that charged defendants be held pre-trial without bail—against nearly 340 J6ers.

How will Fischer affect January 6 defendants?

The Fischer decision opens the door to the dismissal of every single Section 1512(c)(2) count that was charged against January 6 defendants, even those defendants who have already entered a guilty plea (mostly under prosecutorial threat) or were found guilty by a judge or jury.

***

Our prayers and the prayers of many had been answered, as the Supreme Court ruled in our favor. It turned out that Dave Fischer was right and the judge was wrong when he denied Dave's motion on this very question last year. The Supremes sided with the law and with us!

The federal level is the big leagues of individual, personal rights squashing. But Dave Fischer began to craft a reconsideration of the Motion for Judgement of Acquittal in earnest, armed with the Supreme Court's ruling and proof positive that my actions on and around January 6 were as harmless, nonviolent, and Constitutionally protected as we had always contended. Again, it was time for long hours on the computer and long days at his law offices in Glen Burnie,

Maryland, to strategize and put words to paper. Through the just action of the Supreme Court, we've gone from figuring that the best we could hope for was a sentence of no further jail time to the belief that the Lord would move the judge to follow the law and erase my guilty verdicts outright. That would make me a free man.

What fast ball would next be thrown at our heads by the prosecutorial/judicial coven? Over a period of the next couple of weeks, we would have our sentencing date moved first to October 7, then to October 22, and finally to November 15. The latter date represented day number 1,397 in our fight against the satanic forces resident in the principality of Washington, DC.

I and so many like me are being deliberately and irreparably injured. All of the prosecutors and all of the FBI special agents and others involved in my case have enriched themselves professionally and politically and continue to celebrate their misdeeds in a consequence-free environment.

Only in the light of truth and with the commitment of good people can these wrongs be set right.

I had one of the toughest short-term assignments ever. I must continue to fight for my life and remain in Faith whatever comes.

*Trans*formed. Not *con*formed.

Chapter 14

Facing the Dragon

"An unbelievable story or a story of unbelievable endurance? Sometimes the battle to be believed can be every bit as challenging as the battle to survive."

— Jeremy Wade, adventurer, explorer, archeologist

It happened on a Tuesday. There was no sudden blunt force trauma. I didn't hurt myself skateboarding or trying some dumb stunt for laughs while being filmed by a friend. I wasn't injured by lumbering cows or while repairing farm equipment. This injury was termed *spontaneous* and it mangled everything for Sharon and me.

The rupture of a cervical disc blasted me back into a swirl of unimaginable pain. The nerves under attack from the squeezing and crushing abnormality threw up the fearful yellow-orange wall again. My right arm, beginning at the shoulder and radiating to my hand rapidly degenerated from impaired to dangerously useless. Daily tasks were rendered impossible by an electric nerve assault I call the "I'm getting hit with a baseball bat again and again" kind of pain. After a round of X-rays, MRIs, and CT scans, I learned that I would need to undergo 4-level neck fusion surgery to stop my neck pain and regain the use of my right arm.

My sleep now was so near waking it's hardly worth calling it sleep at all. I was a prisoner of pain once again. The disc failure prevented me from lying down, and I struggled to sit upright in Sharon's aging recliner, fading periodically into a half-sleep hypnosis of exhaustion. If it were not so dire, it could have been mildly amusing for Sharon to be reading our scripture lessons only to see that I had drifted away for a few merciful moments of kaleidoscope unconsciousness with Jesus.

Dave submitted our second Motion for Judgement of Acquittal in early September 2024. There had been no weekends off for any of us, Sharon included. No Labor Day Holiday cookouts. No birthday celebration. No quiet sunsets. Just working with Dave Fischer, trying to help him in any way we could. We were all-in at this point in what was the *next* "final" pitched battle. After so many ups and downs. Now we three just collapsed.[1]

At the end of a *fourth* summer under wrongful attack from our government, it remained a waiting game. I could still type, but slowly and painfully. I laughingly considered the tired lament that "letter writing" is a lost art, but you can't prove it by us! Not so lost that we couldn't be moved by the loving words sent our way from angels in cities and towns all over. Not so lost as to keep us from exchanging hundreds of cards and letters with so many special people we longed to meet in person. As surely as a farmer plows the fields, I plowed our pain and our passion for every one. And they returned such love and understanding! We just *had* to win this thing.

Beginning during my interrogation by the FBI, and ever since, I had repeatedly said one thing: Show me a single picture or video clip of me entering the Capitol or committing any act of violence or moving a barrier or being in close proximity to a police officer. Show me the film! Despite the DOJ's claim they possess over forty thousand hours of CCTV and other video, none showing me breaking the law on January 6 has ever surfaced—because none exists. It never happened. Nearly four years on, the prosecutorial snow job continued. Lawfare is too cute a name for it. There *is* no name for it. Where is our justice?

A universal truth is that it's not paranoia if they truly *are* out to get you.

***

These were the anxious days of an inescapable convergence of forces in our lives for which there was no ready answer. The spectral freight trains of the government's despicable power from one side and the equally frightening spinal surgery and the surety of a long and very painful rehab from the other were speeding down the track. Both of these things were guaranteed to change our lives forever. Sharon and I could neither escape nor sidestep either one. Just as in the Navy, I felt this looming danger-close, described in nautical terms as constant bearing, decreasing range. They kept coming at us on the same track, the same angle of attack, and got closer and closer each hour of each day.

Lord, we ask Your Blessings always.

Sharon and I found comfort through knowledge that our neurosurgeon is a Believer placed on our path years ago. But the details of the surgery confronting me were staggering. He confidently described the operation, which would begin by slicing away at tissue through my throat, spreading collapsed vertebrae apart, and then coupling them forever like a cervical choo-choo train. Holes drilled and screws inserted, gummy disc material scraped away, an entire bone halved with the expert use of an electric saw, and presto-change-o! I didn't want to obsess over what he had told me to expect, but in the long days and nights leading up to the event, I couldn't help doing so.

I awakened in the hospital room with Sharon at my side. WOW, I hurt! Do I have what it takes in my battered and exhausted state to start at square one and rebuild *again*? To rehab without solid food, teetering on shaky legs, and relying upon my wife to help me dress? *Again*. One more time? I am so tired and the demons keep coming after us. The effects of filleting my body like a catfish are cumulative. How the heck can I do this again? Especially in prison.

In all these years bearing the yoke of government oppression, I never felt we would actually starve to death. We had lost our savings and possessions, that's true. We had fought as income and medical care were stripped away, and I fretted continually over the seemingly imminent loss of our precious homestead farm. Even so, the mighty *covered-dish legion* of our local community remained faithful. Between food banks and farmers, we continued to survive. While our neighbors and so many others supported us and fed us, now in the wake of this frightening operation, the loving support machinery never missed a beat.

Struggling to swallow after the surgery that accessed my spine by way of my throat, we received an outpouring of all manner of homemade soups, which were sweet as any birthday treat and fortifying as any manna. Donna, Angela, Charity, and Lorri joined MaryJane in the mothering throng that almost literally poured a manifestation of God's Grace upon Sharon and me. There was no question we could remain fortified and, through all the attacks of the enemy, be they legal or physical, continue to stand. I smile even now... remembering with deep gratitude.

***

One of the cruelest aspects of solitary confinement is that it creates people who are starved for companionship, and then these same people often become less fit for social interaction in a society that has gone forward without them. I'd call that a paradox. I had for too long existed in a world of torture with interpersonal contact being only an occasional phone call, a curse from a guard, or a snippet of speech shouted with another inmate in a cell far away. Now I tended to shy away from human interaction. This is not unique to me as a former detainee.

The post-surgery recovery cocoon of our little frame home would be my temporary shield. I avoided in-person visits, going out into "the world," or using a telephone. That, even after the mandatory bed rest. Because of the DOJ's psychological warfare against us, I sometimes saw myself as being "different" to the point where I was unwelcome in a larger culture that abhorred me. From what Sharon and I were experiencing, there was no denying their efforts to systematically dismantle us. Danger now seemed everywhere. The loneliest place in the world is where you are not wanted.

The narcotics prescribed after surgery fogged my brain more than blocked my pain. *Satan* when translated from the Hebrew is *adversary,* and I felt the adversary waited in the swamp of DC, anxious to devour me as he had so many others caught in this January 6 farce.

The chaos within me was something I could never have imagined. It was so difficult to sit and simply try to type one pitiful excuse for a letter to those so earnest in their desire to lift up both Sharon and me. I found the more I reached out and the more I shared, the more it seemed to help. As it had before. Our nationwide family that had risen up from near and far to whom I could pour out my turmoil, my thoughts, even my memories and dreams of freedom that seemed nothing more at times than a mirage—they heard and answered back.

Their hearts reached Sharon and me through cards and letters and precious phone calls. They pushed the darkness away and let us know that even mired in this demonic quicksand we were cared for and even loved. Loved by so many whom we had never met. Loved by those who might only have caught a glimpse of Sharon and me on a television screen. Loved by folks who were just like us in so many ways and for whom my feeble words had woven a picture of the peaceful Christian people we know we are and had ever been. When the waves meant to drown us splashed our faces, our loving family of support kept us afloat. One more kick. One more breath. Don't go under. Hang on ...

Week after week we kept the Faith on our windswept farm, waiting in vain for a judge's decision to set us free. Waiting for him to rule in our favor on Dave's revised Rule 29 motion to throw out my bogus convictions. But no word came from the court. No surprise, then, that we had lost all trust in the *ways of man*. A new date was assigned for my sentencing, and with it came a new raft of indignities and lies from Rakoczy and her accomplices. On the eve of the Presidential election of 2024, the DOJ's scathing new sentencing demand for me was published through a complicit press along with a new bag of propaganda to be spread far and wide.[2] The latest dump in a well-planned slander and misinformation campaign.

This is not mere mendacity for mendacity's sake. It was something much worse.

***

To accomplish some self-serving purpose, the monopoly of Google Limited Liability Corporation sent a terse email to my personal account, an account which by court order I was previously prohibited from using. The email was to inform me that Google had received and complied with a request from the DOJ for access to all of my email account history. Yep, endless government intrusion to the max built upon a foundation of false accusations.

The Google email went on to state that "a court order previously prohibited Google from notifying you of the legal process. We are now permitted to disclose the receipt of the legal process to you."

Was this a brand new inquiry by the DOJ still trying to find something, anything, to use against me in a legal proceeding? It looked like an effort to discover, through the use of a long-abandoned email account, some violation of the terms of my release. All the better to ensure my long-term commitment at sentencing. Was Google scrambling to cover themselves on the advice of their corporate counsel? They pointed a finger at a *federal judge* for specifically ordering that I not be told about this violation of my guaranteed right of privacy and my protections against wrongful prosecution. I understand the unbridled hatred of the prosecutors, but why would a federal judge do that? What were they up to?[3]

While America slept, I wondered if my fellow citizens knew this could happen to them under some cover story or suggested wide-ranging domestic terror investigation fantasy cooked up by a faceless, unelected wack-a-doodle. For the *greater good,* perhaps. But whose greater good would that be, exactly?

Big brother was indeed watching all of us.

With the expectation that the judge would dismiss one false verdict against me due to the Supreme Court decision, I would have only a single charge remaining. Found guilty of allegedly recalling, not deleting, 11 exculpatory J6 photos from one "private" text message. For this one charge, the DOJ was recommending that I be incarcerated for four years! *What*? By now we expected such things, but that didn't mean the nastiness failed to sting. How many times must I be found not-guilty for these people to release me?

As Dave Fischer said, their anger is fueled by the fact that we wouldn't back down.

It's too late to quit fighting now.

***

Roger and his wife Jean are precious members of our Christian family. I served with them in the Navy way back in the mid-80s. In those bygone days, Roger had received a Word from God which he shared with me. I credit this Message with jump-starting a stirring within me to know more about the Lord. Tonight, after dinner with them, they were bundling up to leave when Roger beckoned me down the hall. He shared with me that he had another crystal clear message provided by the Lord especially for me. He said he had never received such a Word since that one time decades ago. This night he told me that in a dream-state the Lord told him, "Roger, I'm glad you're a friend to Tom because I have need for him when this is over."

I was floored! What could I possibly do that is so important for *Him*? Look at this circumstance! I was overwhelmed and all I could do was thank Roger with what I am sure was a look of exhausted shock on my face. I couldn't even articulate my feelings when I considered it later. I replayed the message Roger had delivered over and over. I would focus upon it and draw strength from it in the many gloomy days ahead.

Today I woke as I usually do: shaky and disoriented from a lack of sufficient sleep. I stumbled to the kitchen and had a long, refreshing drink of cold water. I think most of the time, every day, I never even taste it, this cool and deep pleasure. So pressed am I with paperwork, an endless legal fight that confines and consumes both Sharon and me. Only with the hope pushed back into the subconscious that I might one day breathe the sweet taste of freedom again.

I mustn't think about that now. It will drag me into the thousand-yard stare again. For a moment I remembered when there was nothing as simple and comforting as this moment, this taste, in *Orangehabben,* my made-up place name for the concentration camp of my imprisonment in Orange, Virginia. The place where people's personalities and souls fracture. The touch of the refrigerator, the ability to look out an actual window and hear the muted daybreak sounds of the world through the glass; all of this simplicity had been taken from me. The door to the outside was right there. Even if I don't open it, at least I *could*. I could if I want, and right now, no one would try to stop me. Here in this moment with cold, clean water in my hand,

I see and hear and touch as for the very first time. Considering how our lives had been twisted around, it all seemed surreal and quite sad.

It might be true that some things are so tragic that they can't be seen clearly except through eyes that have cried.

We endured a *fourth* Christmas under the weight of a weaponized government. The date for my sentencing would be January 10, 2025, in the same federal courthouse where I had been prosecuted and where the evil things are. I thought of the symbol I had seen on the fourth floor, left there in a frantic attempt by someone, perhaps persecuted unjustly like me, to ward off ... something. Sharon and I would be summoned to hear the fate handed down by the judge: a judge besieged by prosecutors who continue to violate their oaths and who enjoy a thing called *absolute immunity*. This was nothing more than a legal stacking of the deck, such that no prosecutor could suffer consequences of any type for lying, suborning perjury, falsifying evidence, or any other chicanery. It's a real thing and it applies across the federal legal system in every state and the District. DOJ attorneys were free to do whatever voodoo they could do.

***

Joshua 6:2-5

Then the Lord said to Joshua... March around the city once with all the armed men. Do this for six days. Have priests carry trumpets of rams' horns in front of the ark. On the seventh day, march around the city seven times, with the priests blowing the trumpets. When you hear them sound a long blast on the trumpets, have all the people give a loud shout; then the wall of the city will collapse and the people will go up, every man straight in.

The Shofar horn is a reminder of the Day of the Final Judgment, calling upon all people to prepare for God's scrutiny of their deeds. The Lord's people blew the Shofar horns and followed His instructions. Sharon and I needed a miracle to bring the seemingly impenetrable walls of corruption and deceit in DC crashing down for our victory, too. Why not try what they did? We believed.

Seven days prior to our date with destiny, Sharon and I cleared the table in our sunny breakfast nook. We piled in the middle of the table all of the pre-sentencing reports, supplemental reports, charging documents, responses to motions, and other DOJ conjurings. Kathryn Rakoczy, she of the whole "fugitive from justice" nonsense that began our persecution, was the author or at least the signatory on most of the recent written prosecutorial schmutz.

Each day, Sharon and I, with Shofar music playing on the laptop computer she held, would slowly march around that table piled high with the papers from the DOJ. With Praise and entreaties, we circled the table as God had Joshua tell His people to do at Jericho to bring victory. We prayed God's power in Jesus' name to bring the dark forces and their lies crashing down and defeat at last what our country had come to know as lawfare. On the seventh day, like the people of Israel did, we shouted with all our might, calling upon the Most High God. The God of Justice and Freedom and of Rescue. Not corny. Biblical. We knew what and Who we believed.

We were ready like never before to oppose the darkness, with the Lord going before us.

This would be an Old Testament-style showdown.

***

There had been zero sleep for Sharon and me the night before my sentencing. We were both so very tired as once more we made the drive to the den of sorrows in Washington, the town of my birth and happy early childhood. It was a long, tiresome two-hour-plus drive from our sleepy home in the Virginia countryside to get there, a bundled walk through a biting wind for blocks to reach the place of my ten weeks of suffering more than two years before.

Through the X-ray scanners at the building's guard station and to a meeting with Dave Fischer down the hall, together we soon found our workspace upstairs in a lawyers lounge to await the pleasure of the judge.

There was time to talk and let Dave get his game face on. He sorted and ordered papers, and we chatted about this point and that point which he might make in my defense. Also we nervously wondered aloud what our chances of success were. Dave is a quiet but really smart guy who was so committed to us that he had let most of his other legal practice fall away for these four years of the most intense fight imaginable. We had prayed that this day he would once again have the "right stuff" in an adversarial courtroom.

Inside Judge Amit Mehta's court, there were only federal employees waiting. There were no friendly faces there until Roger and Jean showed up. They who were now more than ever the closest of family had made an arduous multi-hour pilgrimage to provide Sharon with desperately needed moral support as she sat on a hard bench. It's so horrible to be alone in that place.

The only thing we knew for certain was that the DOJ prosecutors were going to attempt to try the case over again in front of this judge by slandering me and accusing me of all the stuff of which I'd already been found innocent! They did not disappoint. They were as rotten as ever.

In terms of appearing before Judge Mehta, we had come full circle; back to where it all began. It was Judge Mehta who had seen my depleted state through videoconference and saved my life by ordering my release from prison. He learned that day back in 2021 that he had been lied to by the prosecutors. I wondered if he would admit he had been consistently lied to by the same legal hacks ever since.

Soon it was clear the judge was *not* going to approve our Motion for Judgement of Acquittal that had gathered dust somewhere since last September. He let the prosecution denigrate me for a while, then Dave was allowed a few minutes to speak. The judge summarily dismissed our request. Boom. Dave's well-researched arguments for my innocence and full acquittal, supported by mounds of *actual case law*, got brushed aside like so many crumbs from the tabletop.

One last hurrah for the Biden/Garland DOJ January 6 machine began. It was none other than Kathryn Rakoczy, for whom persecution of the wretched J6ers had become a family affair. Her husband, after all, had used many of the same scripted catch-phrases and dirty tricks she had spewed during the first Oath Keeper trial in his own prosecution of a January 6 captive.[4]

Rakoczy was all-in. She was determined and she was confident. And why not? No one in the web of J6 persecution had escaped the clutches of the DOJ before, and even with a new president taking office in only a few days, this could still be a personal triumph and an unmatched resume enhancement.

She tried with all her might to convince the judge to put me in jail for years. This for the crime of the century: allegedly removing a handful of *exculpatory* pictures (some just selfies of Sharon and me) from *one* Facebook text message string. The nonsensical and thoroughly baseless claim was that I *must* have been trying to hide "evidence" from a grand jury! *What*? Evidence of my *innocence*? Hide *that* from the grand jury? The argument *sounds* insane and it *is* insane.

In much the same way as the budding psychopath eventually tires of tearing the wings off butterflies, her play-pals had wandered away to find new people to torment. But Rakoczy remained. There was one last trophy to mount, one last pin to be driven through a peaceful creature from the countryside. She must complete the collection to have the chests of her patrons swell with pride and to ensure her next cushy assignment. First her part in the *Mueller Russia-gate* fraud, and now *this* hoax: how incredibly delicious! This was her moment and the glory and bragging rights would be hers alone at last.

When the villains in any story are simply wicked and nothing more, they don't really seem all that interesting. They could even seem a bit boring. Psychologists might urge us to examine the prosecutors' childhood issues born of insecurities and feelings of inadequacy in order to explain their offenses. I think the people involved in this small sliver of the National January six charade *would* make a very interesting psychological study. But I am of the school of thought that holds there's no underlying reason for their actions which should engender empathy from us whatsoever. That said, you don't have to be an empath to forgive. Forgiveness is hard when you're worn down from being attacked.

It's sad to see that some folks hurt others because they deeply enjoy it. And when the act of hurting people is rewarded by a system or a sicko, those who do it can become addicted to it for life.[5]

Well, it's easy to be a saint in paradise. The opposite is likewise true. The perverted system of injustice as exercised by the DOJ and the FBI might be able to twist and distort the morals and sensibility of virtually *anyone*, especially in the swamp of Washington, DC. Like no other place in the world, they grow scoundrels here and empower scoundrels here.

I noticed something different as I was slandered again and again by the prosecutor. It was something different *in me*. It was a serenity I had not felt since the madness of this tragedy began four years earlier. The lies no longer set my blood pressure climbing. Like a song overplayed from a dive-bar juke box, Rakoczy's effrontery was nothing more than an annoyance. Perhaps I had been living in her head rent-free for four years.

Insults did not have the same effect on me as in the past. Was this evidence of one of the changes the Lord was trying to lead me to on this Christian walk? Absolute trust and surrender? I had truly given it all to the Lord, and along with Sharon, I knew He had us in the palm of His hand. I was going to be okay with it, whatever *it* happened to be.

I never thought I'd be able to return to the days when I would be the most relaxed when things were the most intense.

I've heard that God seeks to calm his child before he calms the storm.

Sharon and I, separated by a distance of around 50 feet, might as well have been on opposite sides of the world. Who could know how the whole thing would turn out? We each prayed silently through most of the proceedings.

Finally, I guess Kathryn Rakoczy reached the end of her script. She yielded the podium and Dave was permitted to speak on my behalf.

Over these long years Sharon and I had often prayed for the Lord our God to give Dave the right words to say so that the judge would see the truth and have the courage to do the right thing. Here with hidden courtroom cameras positioned behind the smoked glass, Dave Fischer was magnificent. He did not simply go tit-for-tat in an effort to address each of the falsehoods of the DOJ lawyer. Those fabrications were so numerous that we could still be there watching him shred each one.

Dave Fischer told the judge how *disappointed* he was in the prosecution over several of the lies they kept pounding away on. He pointed out how they continued to waste the court's time with attacks on "Mr. Caldwell" like those they conducted during trial. He respectfully reminded the judge how very many times the lawyers of the DOJ argued with such passion and told the jury and the court things which were handily disproved in court. This went on for a while, but some things simply stood out as he demolished Rakoczy's tired deceptions.

While Rakoczy chatted absently with a colleague, Dave went on to oh-so-gently provide the judge one example of exculpatory *Brady* evidence not disclosed by the prosecution, while graciously letting her off the hook. This was what our paid forensic expert exposed as a glaring violation by the DOJ gang. Ah, the case of *Brady v. Maryland,* in which the Supreme Court ruled that suppression by the prosecution of evidence favorable to a defendant *violates due process.*[6]

Oops!

"Your Honor," Dave began, "we introduced an exhibit where Mr. Caldwell had messaged another defendant. This wasn't even in the government's discovery! We had a forensics expert that found this and dug it out. Fortunately, we found a message where Mr. Caldwell said to her, hey, I recommend you stay out—I forget where it was but it was somewhere out in Virginia—the battlefield. ..."[7]

The judge instantly connected to FBI Special Agent Hilgeman's sworn testimony supporting Dave's reminder of my harmless hotel recommendation to a place many miles from Washington and responded, "Manassas!"

"Manassas!" repeated Dave after the judge. "... out by Manassas and take the *metro* [subway] into DC! So he was not *organizing* a QRF hotel. I mean, this is just a myth."[8]

There was much more in this closing which became a tour de force for David Fischer, esquire. The judge had ordered me released from custody back in 2021 in part because he had been given only bogus information about me. Not until Dave came to our defense did the judge hear *any* truth. The lies first appearing in the media and spouted by the government lawyer appearing today had never stopped since the moment the FBI strike force led by Joshua Tidwell had nearly murdered sweet Sharon on the steps of our cottage.[9] Dave drove the point home.

Dave Fischer declared that Sharon and I had suffered enough, and so we had. I think every word he spoke made a difference. His recommendation before the court was a *commutation*: meaning a sentence of "time served." Then Dave sat down beside me.

We hoped the fact that I was the first person found innocent of *anything* during J6 jury trials, followed by the Supreme Court's ruling in our favor, would be foundational to judge Mehta's upcoming ruling. He spoke for a while and then, for the first time, the judge turned his attention directly to me.

Judge Mehta said with regard to proof of my guilt: "and in your case, Mr. Caldwell, the jury determined the government had NOT satisfied its burden."[10]

That was judge-speak recognizing I had been innocent all along.

The judge continued, now addressing Rakoczy and her office sidekick, "That is how the justice system is supposed to work and it worked for Mr. Caldwell. It may have taken longer than he would have liked, but sometimes our justice system doesn't move as quickly as we all might hope."

That's an understatement!

"Look, at the end of the day, there are also disparities to be cognizant of here, and that is, Mr. Caldwell stands convicted of a *single* count of 1512(c)(1)," Judge Mehta said.

He was referring to an administrative nothingburger false "conviction" after overcoming a fistful of bogus felony charges invented out of whole cloth by the DOJ.

"Mr. Caldwell has spent over 50 days in confinement," he continued. "They were, I dare say, torturous days for him personally. I do remember to this day the figure that you cut on the video screen in pain."

The courtroom was silent as Judge Mehta concluded, "The sentence of the court will be a period of time served. I am not going to impose a period of supervised release. Further restrictions on liberty are simply unwarranted at this point."[11]

There would be no prison sentence for the false charge of recalling selfie photos from a text message. There would be no monies demanded of our empty accounts since I had never broken anything nor hurt anyone. It had all been a raft of lies.

"All right. That'll be the sentence of the court," the judge concluded as our eyes met. "Mr. Caldwell, it's been a long road for you and me together. Take care of yourself and good luck. Thank you."

"ALL RISE!" someone called out. Everyone stood as his Honor left.

In the end, it was less like the Shootout at the O.K. Corral and more like Dave Fischer in a one-punch knockout of the neighborhood bully. Dave gave me a hearty handshake and a wide smile. In a few moments I was in Sharon's arms, then a hug from Jean and Roger and it was done.

It was in every way an exoneration. I was innocent and everyone here knew it. But the judge would not throw out the bogus "selfie" guilty verdict. We were too far down the road for that. Who can say what enormous pressure he was under to make one guilty verdict stand, however foolish and unfounded it was. Judge Mehta had "commuted" my sentence to time served, so the result was that there was no further *official* punishment to be borne. The 53 days of torture I had endured would be all the incarceration I would face. But I was still marked as a felon by the actions and the spoken falsehoods from what some might call the mouths of the wicked. Wrongfully branded and no longer truly a citizen. Felons are deprived of rights most people take for granted.

We were drained. But we were victorious.

1,453 days fighting for truth and justice. Could we really be *free*?

Our brilliant but unassuming lawyer Dave Fischer had been right about many things. Mine was a prosecution with no evidence whatsoever. It was an attack on our Constitutional rights and our privacy. As much as anything, it was an attack on my free speech, not on actions. This strong Kentuckian who had borne our standard had rightly stated, "This case was nothing more than the hypothesis of a group of millennial prosecutors and FBI agents."

As investigative journalist Joe Hanneman of *The Blaze* wrote in the aftermath:

> Fischer saw a strong message in Mehta's sentence that allowed his client to go free.
>
> "When a progressive D.C. jury, through its verdict, and a widely respected Obama-appointed Federal Judge, through his ultralight sentence, say the government got it wrong, the government *definitely* got it wrong," Fischer said. "Of the hundreds of J6ers who are worthy of Presidential pardons, Mr. Caldwell is arguably first among equals. [12]

The judge had used the word liberty. Could it ever have more meaning than it does right now? Who knows what tomorrow will bring? Just as in that dark parking lot outside a dank Virginia jail four years ago, I held Sharon tightly in my arms while silently giving thanks.

It had to happen just this way, here in an oppressive federal courtroom. *Before* the fast-approaching presidential inauguration. This way, so that we, all our nation of family and friends and everyone who will never hear about our persecution and pain until long after this moment, could wonder at this victory from The Lord. He heard every prayer and kept every promise.

I was grateful, and I was numb.

For Sharon and me, it had been a victory as powerful and life-affirming as any promised in the Holy Bible. The walls of deceit, corruption, and lies unending had been brought tumbling down as had the walls of the fortress city of Jericho in the Old Testament. The impregnable and all powerful had been brought low.

Brought low, even if not vanquished.

A Promise made and a Promise kept.

God had answered our prayers. We made the right choice to trust in God and not to rely on the institutions and the capriciousness of man. Even though a good man, one who many believed in ten short days would begin the rescue of an entire country, was on his way.

***

All these years removed from the Virginia prison, I sometimes hear a noise that flashes me to the soundtrack of the solitary blockhouse. I remember that in those locked-down days, I would close my eyes to wish myself to a peaceful place I never could touch. Soon even the image of my sweet wife was fading away and I couldn't really picture her anymore.

I remember trying hard to sleep in that tortuous time. With the maniacal sounds thrumming all the time, some days I could escape into a B-17 on a bombing run over Nazi Germany. The rumbling machine noises and the whooshing through the speaker and the vent on the wall made it easy to picture the right seat of that beauty. As we lurched through the clouds I even imagined getting out of the seat sometimes, undoing my oxygen mask and crouching my way through the fuselage. I could see and hear myself talking to the waist gunners, spying the navigator's station. I could smell the fuel and the oil and the metal skin of the aircraft. It was so darned cold in my icy cell, it was easy to identify with the terrible cold inside a metal tube hurtling along at altitude.

Long flights were sometimes just about reading instruments over and over, and looking out at the planes in formation. Looking for swooping fighters that heralded death. Seeing the Triangle-B on the vertical stabs of our squadron aircraft all around. And then the actual bomb run, flack and all. Kicking and slamming of steel doors in the SHU supplied the percussive explosions of doom. Praying for the darned bombs to drop already so we could pull away! We flew a lot of missions. My nameless, shivery companions and me.

Many did not make it back. Not on actual runs in the 1940s and not now in this tragic abomination of justice. Far fewer died as a result of our government recently, but so very many have been damaged as human beings to an existence beyond *lost*. Thank God I survived. I reached my number of missions even though they kept moving the targeted total, seemingly forever beyond reach. There would be no more flights for me.

***

Leading up to his inauguration, President Trump indicated he would consider pardoning many J6 defendants, particularly those who had committed no violence. As my only conviction had been for arguably the *most* non-violent of all J6 "crimes" (falsely charged with recalling *exculpatory* photos from a text message), we were hoping and praying for a pardon to come our way.

On the evening of January 20, 2025, nearly 1,600 people brutalized by the Biden administration were pardoned.

I was not.

On that same night, President Trump also commuted the sentences of a handful of J6ers, including mine. My already commuted sentence was once again commuted. Huh? As he signed this Executive Order, the President stated that some of these commutations would likely become pardons as his administration researched the cases.

In our disappointment we debated how we could have been left behind, when some who had been convicted of violent offenses were pardoned outright. The president is a man who knows full well the effects of wrongful prosecution and likely no one told him about *our* measly little situation. Heck, he had so many big, beautiful Executive Orders to sign on that day, we reasoned he could only sign what had been prepared for him, in a very tight timeframe, by government lawyers.

Something not open to debate was the urgency to get people out of prison who had been overcharged, over-sentenced, and over-confined, some held for years in pretrial custody. Theirs was the most burning need and President Trump had boldly and capably addressed it. Prisoners, many of whom did nothing more than participate in political protest, had lost all. And all had lost the comfort of the peaceful lives they once knew. Their long torment might soon begin to fade away. Praise the Lord!

Sharon and I would rejoice as we watched the limited news coverage of political prisoners being released from confinement across the country and being reunited with their families over the days that followed.

So, what now?

Four years plus of tyranny without end. The simple fact is that so many lawyers and staff members at "Main Justice" responsible for my malicious prosecution are still in power at the right hand of the attorney general. At the FBI, special agents and others who violated our rights and/or perjured themselves outright still lurk at the Bureau, perhaps poised to hurt other unsuspecting people on command. While there was some relief from the nightmare via a pardon for other families, for now there was none for us.

As was the case with most let-downs Sharon and I had endured 'till now, this one did not discolor our outlook for long. We were and are *still* victors against the Biden government's treachery! We have some freedom, albeit abridged from what it had been more than four years earlier. The specter of wrongful imprisonment has been exorcised. The struggle isn't over, but we are determined to shoulder the weight and fight on through the Court of Appeals for complete freedom and the return of my Constitutional rights.

On our precious little farm, it is a day-to-day thing, this adjustment to a life of peace and a lessening of fear. We absolutely reject the label of victim from the horrific onslaught we endured, just as we reject all labels invented by those of ill intent who seek to divide our country. Life has not yet slowed to the point where we can sit as though in an old-timey watercolor, rocking on our front porch in primitive wooden chairs. Oh, to just be able to linger in wonder at the lush greenery or marvel at the Glory of the Lord in every cloud that slips past on high. The sky really is beautiful, though I seldom stop to look either at clouds or evening stars anymore. I need to work on that.

We are so truly Blessed.

And what now for Sharon and me? We stand together in the rubble of our once idyllic lives facing an uncertain future.

Hand in hand.

Smiling.

Epilogue

"Some men say that things break even in this world of ours because the rich man gets his ice in the summer and the poor man gets his in the winter. Maybe so ... but I just don't see it that way."

— Bat Masterson, American lawman and writer

Sharon and I have lost four years of our lives fighting government gangsters. We've survived more than we thought we ever could, and we're learning to laugh again now that a commutation of my wrongful guilty verdict is ours. We stuck together and persevered against the full force of the perversion of what masqueraded as the government of the United States. The chains that held us have been broken.

The specter of inhumane incarceration has faded back into the edges of darkness as have the malevolent spirits within a dirty jail in Orange, Virginia. People will debate whether I am too harsh in my characterization of our victory over a group that had conducted malicious lawfare against me and whose intent was to imprison me, perhaps for life. Such people have that luxury to second-guess my words now that, in my opinion, our lives and the continuation of our Republic have been snatched from the brink.

It was confirmed by an act of Director of National Intelligence Tulsi Gabbard that the DOJ and all within it, in coordination with so many other warped branches of government had continued to attack me falsely because it was *National Policy* to do so!

The calendar year 2021 *Strategic Implementation Plan for Countering Domestic Terrorism,* which Ms. Gabbard declassified, designated many peaceful U.S. citizens, including January 6 protesters, believers in free speech, pro-lifers, and parents at schoolboard meetings as enemies of *The State*. This Biden Administration policy, activated across all agencies, called for arrest, pretrial imprisonment, and prosecution on the flimsiest of pretenses. The January 6 political protest was the catalyst for all phases of the Strategic (nationwide) plan. People such as Christians or those who questioned the government's coziness with Communist China were included in this imaginary community of *Domestic Violent Extremists* (DVE). For the first time ever, the deep state had prioritized the crushing of *Americans* over the countering of actual foreign-grown terrorism. This explains why the FBI, as far as I can tell, hasn't been tracking down genuine terrorists for over four years now.[1, 2, 3]

It's easy to deduce that I had been intended as J6 roadkill in the overarching attack against all of our citizens which by Divine Intervention Sharon and I had survived. Just being innocent alone couldn't have helped anyone.

In the Navy, we have a saying that goes, "It takes a long time to turn the Aircraft Carrier around." That's Officers' Club-speak for the notion that pivoting into radical and long-lasting change takes more time than you think. It might still be a while before many or most of the bad actors, cancerous though they are, within the Department of Justice and throughout the bloated federal bureaucracy can be shown the door, kicking and swearing all the way. It will be a battle waged by good people with much more energy than I have.

Hundreds of corrupt FBI agents and DOJ prosecutors actively involved in the wrongful conspiracy to target our citizens under the banner of J6 retain their status as overpaid government employees, though one or two might have been booted or demoted so far, if not de-fanged. If ever there were to be an inquiry, I wonder if they might adopt the trusty post-World War II Nuremberg trials tack, sailing toward the "*I was only following orders*" defense of their misdeeds.

In the grand scheme of things, our difficulties are but a blip on the radar screen. That's especially true when compared to all that I think needs to be changed so that this kind of horror can never again be repeated against American citizens. Pardon or no, for Sharon and me, our persecution and our legal woes are far from over. We are very tiny fish in a vast ocean of inconsequence, still swimming and trying to avoid the sharks.

Philippians 1:18-19 (NIV)
"...Yes, and I will continue to rejoice, for I know that through your prayers and God's provision of the Spirit of Jesus Christ what has happened to me will turn out"

The Christian life, like most lives, is a series of highs and lows. I believe I was privileged to see the Glory of God as well as the depths of despair in a hell on earth created through the tyranny of evil men and women. The tougher the situation, the more God revealed Himself and His love to Sharon and to me. I have seen the deepest part of God's love so far in my life in the darkest parts of my life. In those times and maybe only in those times, I was the most receptive.

I know for certain that it's the ordeals and hardships and, yes, evils, we face in life and how we respond to them that prove we are followers of Christ and actually have what it takes.

We've been asked if there is any high-level movement underway to help us or any victims of the J6 government conspiracy to be restored. If that means restoration the way so-called society understands the word as monies, health, property, or employment preference, then the answer I think is no. If, however, it means in Biblical terms, then the answer is a resounding *yes*!

For Sharon and me, our worship and prayer lives are stronger than ever and growing stronger still. The love that Sharon and I have for each other and for our Lord and Savior is stronger than ever and growing stronger still. Father God has always been stronger than the forces arrayed against us. Restoration comes from Him.

It never occurred to the fanatics in the DOJ that they wouldn't win.

It never occurred to *us* to stop fighting them. And we won't. Broke, but not broken, is our motto. Our task is to keep going, even with more than a bit of impatience, yearning to breathe truly free. We fight on in Faith. The Lord's Salvation is for everyone.

There is so much more to the story of how Sharon and I have come through the most difficult time we never imagined. It was our world turned upside down. We've passed through a storm of hate and now find ourselves on the other side of the worst of it, filled with gratitude, love, and hope for the future.

There are many more hurdles, and our lives will never be exactly the same as before.

Did I forget to mention that the Lord can do anything?

Prepare to be astonished at what happened next—and turn the page.

Executive Grant of Clemency

Donald J. Trump

President of the United States of America

To all to Whom These Presents Shall Come, Greeting:

Be it known, that This Day, I, Donald J. Trump, President of the United States, Pursuant to My Powers Under Article II, Section 2, Clause 1, of the Constitution, Have Granted Unto the Individual Named Below

A Full and Unconditional Pardon

For those offenses against the United States individually enumerated and set before me for my consideration:

United States v. Rhodes, III et al., 1:22-cr-15

Thomas Edward Caldwell

I Hereby Designate, direct, and empower the Attorney General, as my representative, to immediately sign the grant of clemency to the person named herein. The Attorney General shall declare that her action is the act of the President, being performed at my direction.

IN TESTIMONY WHEREOF, I have hereunto signed my name and caused the seal of the Department of Justice to be affixed.

Done at the City of Washington in the District of Columbia this 20th day of March in the year of our Lord Two Thousand Twenty-five and of the Independence of the United States the Two Hundred and Forty-ninth.

DONALD J. TRUMP
PRESIDENT

Thomas Edward Caldwell was pardoned by President Donald J. Trump on March 20, 2025. Tom was notified by email of this action by the United States Department of Justice on July 30, 2025.

About the Author

Thomas E. Caldwell is an author, humorist, artist, conservationist, farmer, aspiring screenwriter, former radio broadcast personality and a proud veteran of the United States Navy. A decorated retired Navy Lieutenant Commander, he honorably served our Nation around the world for nearly two decades, principally within the Navy's Intelligence Community. He is the author of countless strategic and tactical intelligence assessments and possesses a deep understanding and perspective of global and domestic threats to our Republic.

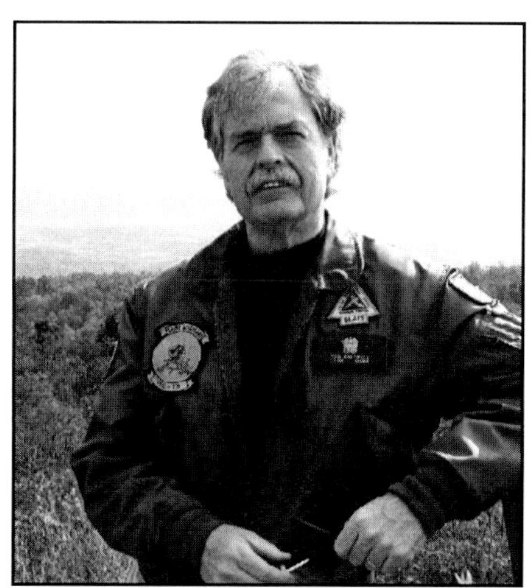

Born into humble circumstances in Washington, DC, Tom and his close-knit family moved to Virginia, where he adapted quickly to life on the farm and became an accomplished marksman and horseman. A child of the 1960s, this patriotic Boy Scout developed a love for the good earth and the rich history of his country and his adopted state.

After a successful military career, Tom returned to his youthful passion for broadcasting, this time as a radio personality and play-by-play sportscaster in Virginia. He and his wife Sharon next launched and operated a successful software systems development company serving multiple federal government agencies, including the U.S. Drug Enforcement Administration, the

Department of Housing and Urban Development, U.S. Army Personnel Command, and the Department of Justice. It was here that he was exposed to the machinery of the federal bureaucracy and observed questionable practices and motivations from an insider's point of view.

Tom first flexed his creative writing muscles by bringing to life the characters and events of his experiences around the world in screenplay and short story form. His home-spun writing style and mastery of imagery bring this first-person adventure narrative, his initial book offering, into gritty, near-cinematic focus.

Devout Christians, Tom and Sharon live on the small family farm of his youth in Virginia's Shenandoah Valley. On this hallowed and historic ground, they peacefully and responsibly nurture native plant and animal species while enjoying a quiet country lifestyle.

Acknowledgments

I am deeply grateful for the following dear brothers and sisters without whose help this uniquely American Victory story might never have been told.

My editors, teachers, and encouragers whose guidance and advice chiseled this work from the mounds of heartbreak and evidence, real and invented by our oppressors, that I compiled from my heart.

Mr. JP Watson
Ms. Diana West
CDR David G. Muller, Jr. USN (Retired)
Mrs. Stanley Reahard
Ms. Terry Lea
Ms. Linda Ensor

Our tiny but determined legal team who fought and won against a corrupt and weaponized government.

Mr. David W. Fischer, Esq.
Ms. Kim Bommersbach
Mrs. Sharon M. Caldwell
Mrs. Angie Weber

... and the many thousands of amazing, patriotic, and compassionate citizens, all of whom deserve to be recognized individually, who came to the aid of two beleaguered people on a tiny Virginia farm.

Endnotes

Chapter 1
The Defiling

1 FBI WFO Source File: CD: WF_WF-12345_WF-12345-BR_2021_01_19T07_05_54.mp4
Date: 01/19/21 VERBATIM TRANSCRIPTION (Transcript of Interrogation) File Number:176-WF-3366759-Caldwell Requesting Official SA Michael Palian, Jr., WFO Name and Office of Transcriber: OST Sara J. Van Roe

2 Ibid.

Chapter 2
Descent into Hell

1 FD-302 (Rev. 5-8-10) UNCLASSIFIED//FOUO FEDERAL BUREAU OF INVESTIGATION Date of entry 01/20/20210176-WF-3366759-CALDWELL_0000004.pdf

2 Case 5:21-mj-00004-JCH Document 10 *USA v. Thomas Edward Caldwell* - 1/19/2021
Rule 5 - Initial Appearance Zoom Videoconference Before: Honorable Joel C. Hoppe U.S. District Magistrate Judge Western District of Virginia

3 Ibid. p 20

4 Ibid. p 20

5 Ibid.

6 https://www.justice.gov/usao-wdva/pr/united-states-attorney-christopher-r-kavanaugh-steps-down https://en.wikipedia.org/wiki/Christopher_R._Kavanaugh

7 https://en.wikipedia.org/wiki/Jasmine_H._Yoon

8 "Eight on deck: General Assembly taps new judges for appeals court", Virginia Lawyers Weekly August 9, 2021;
https://scvahistory.org/courtofappeals/l/lisa-m-lorish/

9 Government's Omnibus Reply Sentencing Memorandum, Document 580, Filed 05/15/23. Ex. Sent-Caldwell-9 CVRJ Medical staff acknowledgement of receipt of meds and CPAP (Caldwell Jail Medical Records)

10 Ibid.

Chapter 3
Darkness and the Terror Tower

1 Government's Omnibus Reply Sentencing Memorandum, Document 580, Filed 05/15/23. Ex. Sent-Caldwell-9 Caldwell Jail Records

2 Government's Omnibus Reply Sentencing Memorandum, Document 580, Filed 05/15/23. Ex. Sent-Caldwell-9 DUSM D. Bender Transportation Authority Ltr

3 Tom and Sharon Caldwell January 6, 2021, Peace Monument selfie photo 20210106_131913.jpg copyright 2021 Thomas Caldwell all rights reserved

4 Tom and Sharon Caldwell January 6, 2021 plywood safety tunnel photo 20210106_144306.jpg copyright 2021 Thomas Caldwell all rights reserved

5 *USA vs. Elmer Stewart Rhodes III*, ET AL. CR No. 22-15 discovery provided Govt. CCTV 0944_USCS_RF_West_Roof_-_2021-01-06_19h42min20s.mp4

Govt. CCTV 0944_USCS_RF_West_R00f_-_2021-01-06_19h51min17s.mp4

6 *Government Exhibit 22.V.2 USA vs. Elmer Stewart Rhodes III*, ET AL. CR No. 22-15 Washington, D.C. October 20, 2022 Afternoon session 1:40 p.m. Day 15 P4826-4827) Cross examination of SA Whitney Drew re: Caldwell Exhibit 87- Sharon Caldwell balcony video Sharon Caldwell January 6, 2021 video 20210106_145156.mp4 copyright 2021 Sharon Caldwell all rights reserved

Chapter 4
Isolation and the SHU

1 Government's Omnibus Reply Sentencing Memorandum, Document 580, Filed 05/15/23. Ex. Sent-Caldwell-9

2 Ibid.

3 Central Virginia Regional Jail Institutional Classification Committee Recommendations Memo dtd 2/2/2021 prisoner copy

4 https://www.courthousenews.com/prison-phone-providers-deny-inflating-price-of-inmate-calls/"Prison phone providers deny inflating price of inmate calls Attorneys sparred before a three-judge panel over how much families of inmates must pay for taking their calls" by Joe Dodson / January 26, 2023

5 Government recorded telephone calls from Central Virginia Regional Jail (CVRJ) provided through discovery 10.61.0.21-xx.wav series through 10.89.0.21-xx.wav series SECURUS phone account Mrs. Sharon Caldwell dated January 23, 2021 through February 11, 2021

6 Government's Omnibus Reply Sentencing Memorandum, Document 580, Filed 05/15/23. Ex. Sent-Caldwell-9

7 Modern reference source: https://en.wikipedia.org/wiki/Duppy "Duppy" is a word of African origin commonly used in various Caribbean Islands, meaning ghost or malevolent spirit that brings misfortune and woe to those they set upon. (pl. "duppies") In many of the islands of the Lesser Antilles, duppy are known as jumbies.

8 Case 1:21-cr-00028-APM Document 25 *USA v. Thomas Edward Caldwell* - 2/12/2021

CR No. 21-28-1 Washington, DC Transcript of Initial Appearance Via Videoconference Proceedings Before The Honorable Amit P. Mehta U.S. District Judge

9 Ibid. P 67

Chapter 5
Last Chance

1 Government's Omnibus Reply Sentencing Memorandum, Document 580, Filed 05/15/23. Ex. Sent-Caldwell-9 (Caldwell Jail Medical Records)

2 *U.S.A. vs. Thomas E. Caldwell, et al* CR No. 21-28 Washington, DC March 12, 2021 3 p.m. Transcript of status Conference/Arraignment via videoconference proceedings before the Honorable Amit P. Mehta U.S. District Judge (P41)

3 Ibid. P 45-46

4 Ibid. P 47

5 Ibid. P 50

6 Ibid. P 53

7 Ibid. P53-54

8 Ibid. P 57

Chapter 6
Lazarus Man

1 Order Setting Conditions of Release Case 1:21-cr-00028-APM Document 75 Filed 03/12/21 USA vs Thomas Edward Caldwell signed 2021.03.12 by Amit P. Mehta, U.S. District Court Judge.

2 FBI WFO Source File: CD: WF_WF-12345_WF-12345-BR_2021_01_19T07_05_54.mp4
Date: 01/19/21 VERBATIM TRANSCRIPTION (Transcript of Interrogation) File Number:176-WF-3366759-Caldwell Name and Office of Transcriber: OST Sara J. Van Roe

3 Palian cellphone exchange w Rakoczy stills 1_19_21.docx Still frame images document file from FBI WFO Source File: CD: WF_WF-12345_WF-12345-BR_2021_01_19T07_05_54.mp4 Date: 01/19/21

4 Central Virginia Regional Jail Orange Virginia U.S. Postal Service Envelope tracking number 7019 0140 0001 0942 0864 contents medical records for former inmate Perm ID # PCP-041468

5 *USA v. Thomas Edward Caldwell et al.*, Criminal No. 21-28 (APM) Case 1:21-cr-00028-APM Document 145 Filed 04/07/21 Motion to Continue and to Exclude Time Under the Speedy Trial Act

6 POLITICO *"Feds agree to pay $6.1M to create database for Capitol riot prosecutions"* By Josh Gerstein and Kyle Cheney 07/09/2021 06:45 AM EDT https://www.politico.com/news/2021/07/09/doj-database-capitol-riot-prosecutions-498911

7 *USA v. THOMAS EDWARD CALDWELL et al.*, Criminal No. 21-cr-28 (APM) Case 1:21-cr-00028-APM Document 349 Filed 08/018/21 US Notice Regarding the Status of Discovery

8 *USA v. THOMAS EDWARD CALDWELL et al.*, Criminal No. 21-cr-28 (APM) Case 1:21-cr-00028-APM Document 417 Filed 09/15/21 US Notice Regarding the Status of Discovery in Advance of September16, 2021 hearing.

9 *USA v. THOMAS EDWARD CALDWELL et al.*, Criminal No. 21-cr-28 (APM) Case 1:21-cr-00028-APM Document 610 Filed 02/20/22 US Notice Regarding the Status of Discovery as of February 9. 2022.

10 FBI WFO Source File: CD: WF_WF-12345_WF-12345-BR_2021_01_19T07_05_54.mp4
Date: 01/19/21 VERBATIM TRANSCRIPTION (Transcript of Interrogation) File Number:176-WF-3366759-Caldwell Requesting Official SA Michael Palian, Jr., WFO Name and Office of Transcriber: OST Sara J. Van Roe

11 Discover US-OK-000004975.pdf Grand Jury Subpoena GJ2021013070791 USAO 2021R00494 signed by Kathryn Rakoczy for Michael Sherwin

12 FD-302 FBI Federal Grand Jury Information 266T-RH-3374021-GJ Serial 17 (doctored by Sara Karol of the FBI) report from Discover

13 DISCOVER, New Albany Ohio ltr Account number ending XX06 dtd April 15, 2021

14 USAA Customer Service email letter dtd Tuesday, March 22, 2022 regarding USAA Federal Savings Bank (Credit Card) signed by "Advocacy Advisor I" April L. Avila

15 FBI Grand Jury subpoena to Experian 01/24/2021 for accounts pertaining to Thomas and Sharon Caldwell 266T-RH-337402-GJ Serial 15 Credit Profile from Experian Inc. Thomas Caldwell TTX2 SDS 0999814 https://ea2.ec.experiannet.com/jAccess/inquiry 1/29/2021 2pgs

16 Social Security Administration Retirement, Survivors and Disability Insurance Notice of Planned Action Social Security 323 Hope Drive Winchester, Va letter dated April 08, 2021 BNC# 21d1805f93100-A CEL "Plan to stop Social Security Benefits"

17 FBI Section Chief Steven Jensen, Domestic Terrorism Operations Section ltr dtd May 13, 2021

Chapter 7
Outrage and Treachery

1 (NSO) Cellbrite USA website https://cellebrite.com/en/cellebrite-facts/ April 2021

2 Signal Blog by Moxie Marlinspike *"Exploiting vulnerabilities in Cellebrite UFED and Physical Analyzer from an app's perspective"* 21 Apr 2021 https://signal.org/blog/cellebrite-vulnerabilities/

3 FD-1057 FBI Electronic Communication 266T-RH-3374021 Serial 128 Title: Defense review of evidence on 04/28/2022 Drafted by: Michael M. Palian Jr. *"Thomas E. Caldwell; UNITED STATES CAPITOL BUILDING, WASHINGTON, DC.; MILITIA EXTREMISM"*

4 U.S. Department of Justice Website: https://www.justice.gov/archives/usao-dc/meet-us-attorney-sherwin

5 *Committee on Oversight and Reform of the U.S. House of Representatives v. William Barr, in his official capacity as Attorney General of the United States* USCA Case #16-5078 Document 1786986 Filed 05/08/2019.

6 Politico Article *"Contempt: House panel moves against Holder"* By John Bresnahan and Jake Sherman 06/20/2012 09:51 AM EDT https://www.politico.com/story/2012/06/holder-contempt-vote-still-on-077632

7 Acting US Attorney for the District of Columbia Michael Sherwin interview with Scott Pelley appearing on CBS Television program *60 Minutes* aired March 23, 2021 https://www.youtube.com/watch?v=FoAqWnD7NTI https://www.cbsnews.com/news/capitol-riot-investigation-sedition-charges-60-minutes-2021-03-21/ *"Inside the prosecution of the capitol rioters"*

8 Ibid.

9 Ibid.

10 Ibid

11 WSKG/PBS'NPR Online *"Judge Criticizes DOJ For Talking About Capitol Riot Conspiracy Case In The Press"* by Ryan Lucas March 23, 2021 https://wskg.org/npr-news/2021-03-23/judge-criticizes-doj-for-talking-about-capitol-riot-conspiracy-case-in-the-press

12 Ibid

13 Ibid

14 United States District Court for the District of Columbia Case 1:21-cr-00028-APM Document 18 Filed 02/11/21 GOVERNMENT'S OPPOSITION TO DEFENDANT'S MOTION FOR RELEASE

15 DOJ Reverse Proffer *USA v Thomas E. Caldwell* held remotely Tuesday, October 5, 2021 AUSA Kathryn Rakoczy, SA Michael Palian Jr, Mr. David W. Fischer, Esq., LCDR Thomas E. Caldwell USN (Retired)

16 Ibid.

17 *The Daily Beast "Inside Mueller's New Army"* Publ. Jul. 11 2018 5:01AM EDT "NATIONAL SECURITY"
https://www.thedailybeast.com/inside-muellers-new-army/

18 Ibid.

19 N.Y. Times article *"First Due Dilligence, then Romance"* by Vincent M. Mallozzi May 3, 2015
https://www.nytimes.com/2015/05/03/fashion/weddings/first-due-diligence-then-romance.html

20 From DOJ Official website transcript of United States Department of Justice Press Conference Friday, January 15, 2021, 1:00 p.m. Eastern Time

21 HeadlineUSA by Ken Silva*"Top FBI Official in Whitmer Kidnap Case Blames Assistants, Headquarters for Wrongdoing"'I wasn't involved in the inner workings of what was going on...'* (quote attributed to former special agent in charge, FBI Detroit field office, Steven D'Antuono).

22 POLITICO *"Lawyer concedes Jan. 6 defendant's partial guilt in closing arguments"* By Kyle Cheney and Josh Gerstein 03/07/2022 11:12 AM EST Updated: 03/07/2022 07:25 PM EST
https://www.politico.com/news/2022/03/07/capitol-police-officer-jan-6-confrontation-hearing-00014628

23 NPR Morning Edition *"Jan. 6 riot defendant was 'tip of this mob's spear,' prosecutor tells jury"* as reported by Tom Dreisbach March 2, 2022
https:// www.npr.org/ 2022/03/02/1083927209/jan-6-riot-defendant-was-tip-of-this-mobs-spear-prosecutor-tells-jury

24 Ibid

25 POLITICO *"Lawyer concedes Jan. 6 defendant's partial guilt in closing arguments"* By Kyle Cheney and Josh Gerstein 03/07/2022 11:12 AM EST Updated: 03/07/2022 07:25 PM EST
https://www.politico.com/news/2022/03/07/capitol-police-officer-jan-6-confrontation-hearing-00014628

26 NPR "In the first Jan. 6 trial, a jury found Capitol riot defendant Guy Reffitt guilty," March 8, 2022:10 PM ET Tom Dreisbach Updated at 4:45 p.m. ET
https://www.npr.org/2022/03/08/1085147532/in-the-first-jan-6-trial-a-jury-found-capitol-riot-defendant-guy-reffitt-guilty

27 Palian cellphone exchange w Rakoczy stills 1_19_21.docx Still frame images document file from FBI WFO Source File: CD: WF_WF-12345_WF-12345-BR_2021_01_19T07_05_54.mp4 Date: 01/19/21

28 Email string from Stripe Support < support@stripe.com > Sent Friday, March 5, 2021 9:28AM,
From Sharon Caldwell Email Monday, May 10, 6:55 PM, From Stripe Support < support@stripe.com > Sent Monday, May 10, 2021 7:03 PM

29 DOJ Reverse Proffer *USA v Thomas E. Caldwell* held remotely Tuesday, October 5, 2021 AUSA Kathryn Rakoczy, SA Michael Palian Jr, Mr. David W. Fischer, Esq., Thomas E. Caldwell

30 PBS News Hour broadcast report "*Unprecedented security in the nation's capital on the eve of the inauguration*" Jan 19, 2021 6:55 PM EST https://www.pbs.org/newshour/show/unprecedented-security-in-the-nations-capital-on-the-eve-of-the-inauguration

31 PBS News Hour broadcast report "*Biden repudiates white supremacy, calls for racial justice in inaugural speech*" Jan 20, 2021 6:49 PM EST https://www.pbs.org/newshour/politics/biden-repudiates-white-supremacy-calls-for-racial-justice-in-inaugural-speech

32 *USA vs. Elmer Stewart Rhodes III*, ET AL. CR No. 22-15 Washington, D.C. November 15, 2022 Morning session 9:00 a.m. Day 30 P 8773-8776)

33 *USA vs. Elmer Stewart Rhodes III*, ET AL. CR No. 22-15 Washington, D.C. October 6, 2022 Morning session 9:15 a.m. Day 6 P1941)

34 United States District Court for the District of Columbia *USA v CALDWELL, et al.* CASE NO. 2021-R-00494 21-cr-28 File: CE-WIL-20210823-CE_WM_Room_2.mp4 Interview of: GEORGE DOUGLAS SMITH Monday, August 23, 2021 (AUSA Kathryn Rakoczy Special Agent Sylvia Hilgeman, Special Agent Clint Morris (Wilmington, N.C.) Attorney Brett Wentz)

35 United States District Court for the District of Columbia CASE NO. 2021-R-00494 21-cr-28 *USA v CALDWELL, et al.* * *Unredacted* File: 0176-CE-3401049_0000064_1A0000022_0000001.mp3 0176-CE-3401049_0000064_1A0000022_0000002.mp3 File: 210909_0124.mp3 Interview of: PAUL STAMEY Thursday, September 9, 2021 (AUSA Kathryn Rakoczy, Special Agent Michael Palian, TFO Catherine Bowles. Appearing for the civilian sworn: Joseph Traficanti, Esq.)

36 Ibid.

37 Ibid.

38 FBI WFO Source File: CD: WF_WF-12345_WF-12345-BR_2021_01_19T07_05_54.mp4
Date: 01/19/21 VERBATIM TRANSCRIPTION (Transcript of Interrogation) File Number:176-WF-3366759-Caldwell Requesting Official SA Michael Palian, Jr., WFO Name and Office of Transcriber: OST Sara J. Van Roe

39 FD-302 (Rev. 5-8-10) UNCLASSIFIED//FOUO FEDERAL BUREAU OF INVESTIGATION Date of entry 01/24/2021 *Thomas Caldwell interview* Investigation on 01/19/2021 (In Person) File # 266T-RH-3374021 Date drafted 01/20/2021 by Michael M. Palian, Jr. 2 pages Includes statement "1025 hours: SA Palian noticed the battery on the cell phone video recorder was running low.....SA Palian did not ask any substantive or investigative questions. 1035 hours: SA Palian ended the interview."

40 United States District Court for the District of Columbia *USA v CALDWELL, et al.* CASE NO. 2021-R-00494 21-cr-28 File: CE-WIL-20210823-CE_WM_Room_2.mp4 Interview of: George Douglas Smith Monday, August 23, 2021 AUSA Kathryn Rakoczy, Special Agent Sylvia Hilgeman, Special Agent Clint Morris, Attorney Brett Wentz

41 In the United States District Court for the District of Columbia CASE NO. 2021-R-00494 21-cr-28 *USA v CALDWELL, et al.* * File: File: 0176-CE-3401049_0000064_1A0000022_0000001.mp3 0176-CE-3401049_0000064_1A0000022_0000002.mp3 File: 210909_0124.mp3 Interview of: PAUL STAMEY Thursday, September 9, 2021 (proffer of Paul Stamey in the presence of prosecutorial group AUSA Kathryn Rakoczy, Special Agent Michael Palian, TFO Catherine Bowles. Appearing for the civilian sworn: Joseph Traficanti, Esq.

42 United Nations press release GENEVA (28 February 2020) "United States: Prolonged solitary confinement amounts to psychological torture", by Nils Melzer, Special Rapporteur on torture and other cruel, inhuman or degrading treatment or punishment citing the Nelson Mandela Act updated 2015. https://www.ohchr.org/en/press-releases/2020/02/united-states-prolonged-solitary-confinement-amounts-psychological-torture

43 Shopkins® collectable toys manufactured by Moose Toys Vicki Vacuum.png photo taken with Samsung SM-G935A delivered through government discovery ic/w United States District Court for the District of Columbia CASE NO. 2021-R-00494 21-cr-28 *USA v CALDWELL, et al.*

44 Email string from Stripe Support < support@stripe.com > Sent Friday, March 5, 2021 9:28AM,
From Sharon Caldwell Email Monday, May 10, 6:55 PM, From Stripe Support < support@stripe.com > Sent Monday, May 10, 2021 7:03 PM

Chapter 8
We Are Not Alone

1 Tucker Carlson Tonight aired on the FOX Network October 4, 2021 "Interview with Thomas and Sharon Caldwell" https://rumble.com/vnbvyt-tucker-carlson-schools-liz-cheney-on-jan.-6-with-thomas-caldwell-and-wife-s.html

2 *U.S.A. vs. Thomas E. Caldwell, et al* CR No. 21-28 Washington, DC March 12, 2021 3 p.m. Transcript of status Conference/Arraignment via videoconference proceedings before the Honorable Amit P. Mehta U.S. District Judge P53-54

3 *U.S. District Court for the District of Columbia Grand Jury Indictment USA v. Elmer Stewart Rhodes III et.al* Received January 12, 2022 (first indictment with fictitious Count 1: 18 U.S.C. 2384 (Seditious Conspiracy)

4 https://lawandcrime.com/u-s-capitol-siege/federal-judge-to-probe-former-top-d-c-prosecutors-60-minutes-interview-in-oath-keepers-case-proud-boy-also-demands-review/ *"Federal Judge to Probe Former Top D.C. Prosecutor's '60 Minutes' Interview in Oath Keepers Case; Proud Boy Also Demands Review"* AARON KELLER Mar 23rd, 2021, 1:46 pm

5 Medsger, Betty *(2014). The Burglary: The Discovery of J. Edgar Hoover›s Secret FBI. Vintage.* ISBN 978-0804173667.

6 "COINTELPRO Revisited – Spying & Disruption – In Black & White: The F.B.I. Papers". *What Really Happened.* Archived *from the original on May 16, 2008. Retrieved June 23, 2008.*

7 *Blackstock, Nelson (1988). Cointelpro: The FBI's Secret War on Political Freedom. Pathfinder Press.* ISBN 978-0-87348-877-8.

8 *Cleaver, Kathleen (1998).* "Mobilizing for Mumia Abu-Jamal in Paris". *Yale Journal of Law & the Humanities.* ISSN 1041-6374. S2CID 141121370. Archived *from the original on April 6, 2019. Retrieved February 25, 2018.*

9 *On', Shaba (22 April 1996).* "25th Ann. of Panther 21 Acquittal: Program in NYC" *(Press release).* Archived *from the original on 28 December 2017. Retrieved 5 February 2018 – via Hartford Web Publishing.*

10 *Ogbar, Jeffrey O. G. (January 16, 2017).* "The FBI's War on Civil Rights Leaders". *The Daily Beast.* Archived *from the original on February 12, 2018. Retrieved February 25, 2018. Hoover explained the 'purpose of counterintelligence action is to disrupt ... and it is immaterial whether facts exist to substantiate the charge'.*

11 "The FBI'S Covert Action Program to Destroy the Black Panther Party". Archived *from the original on January 13, 2013. Retrieved April 20, 2005.*

12 "Assassination Archive and Research Center". Archived *from the original on September 18, 2014. Retrieved May 5, 2015.*

13 United States District Court for the District of Columbia Case no. 202-R-00494 United States of America v. Thomas Caldwell et al, Grand Jury 21-1, Wednesday January 27, 2021

14 FD-302 (Rev. 5-8-10) UNCLASSIFIED//FOUO FEDERAL BUREAU OF INVESTIGATION Date of entry 01/22/2021 Investigation on 01/22/2021 at Dayton, Ohio, United States (Review of Audio Recording)) File # 266T-CI-3371747 Date drafted 01/22/2021 by MORGAN JR PATRICK JAMES

15 United States District Court for the District of Columbia Case no. 202-R-00494 United States of America v. Thomas Caldwell et al, Grand Jury 21-1, Wednesday January 27, 2021 P15

16 Government recorded telephone calls from Central Virginia Regional Jail (CVRJ) provided through discovery 10.61.0.21-xx.wav series through 10.89.0.21-xx.wav series SECURUS phone account Mrs. Sharon Caldwell dated January 23, 2021 through February 11, 2021

17 US District Court for the District of Columbia case no. 2021-R-00494 21-cr-28 *USA v CALDWELL, et al.* Government provided discovery photographic image from defendant Jessica Watkins' personal cellphone with listing for "Commander Tom." (used to support Govt. Exhibit 9079 description 192.T.1615)

18 Form AO 442 In the United States District Court for the District of Columbia *USA v THOMAS EDWARD CALDWELL* ARREST WARRANT dated 01/17/2021 signed by Robin M. Meriwether, US Magistrate Judge

19 AFFIDAVIT IN SUPPORT OF AMENDED CRIMINAL COMPLAINT In the United States District Court for the District of Columbia Case No: 1:21-mj-0019 Assigned to: Faruqui, Zia M. Complaint w/Arrest Warrant *USA v Thomas Edward Caldwell*

Attested to by the applicant by telephone, this 19th day of January, 2021 12:54:09 – 05'00 (7:54 a.m. local time)

20 FD-1057 266T-RH-3374021 Serial 1 Federal Bureau of Investigation Electronic Communication dtd 01/18/2021 From: Richmond (VA) Special Agent Stephen Duke 540-678-3402 Approved by SSRA David Saul Matthew and A/CDC Jenelle D. Janabajal Case ID #: 266T-RH-3374021 (U) Thomas E. Caldwell; United States Capital Building, Washington, DC; Militia Extremism Sensitive Investigative Matter 176-WF-3366759-CALDWELL (U//FOUO) Thomas Edward Caldwell; Antiriot Laws Washington DC United States Capitol Building Synopsis: (U) To request that captioned full investigation be opened and assigned.

21 FBI WFO Source File: CD: WF_WF-12345_WF-12345-BR_2021_01_19T07_05_54.mp4

Date: 01/19/21 VERBATIM TRANSCRIPTION (Transcript of Interrogation) File Number:176-WF-3366759-Caldwell Requesting Official SA Michael Palian, Jr., WFO Name and Office of Transcriber: OST Sara J. Van Roe

22 In Lux Research ("ILR") community attitude survey ("CAS") of the DC Community and three additional Federal districts under engagement by Law Offices of Juli Haller and Fischer and Putzi, P.A. received April 2022 (P1-6)

23 Case 1:22-cr-00015-APM Document 654 Filed 04/15/22 *USA v. THOMAS CALDWELL* Criminal No. 1:22-cr-00015-APM And *USA v. CONNIE MEGGS* Criminal No. 1:21-cr-00028-APM Defendants' Joint Motion To Transfer Venue Memorandum Points and Authorities In Support.

24 Ibid. P 21-23

CHAPTER 9
A Secret Tribunal

1 www.linkedin.co/in/jeff-nestler-0583771a

2 *USA vs. Elmer Stewart Rhodes III*, ET AL. CR No. 22-15 Washington, D.C. October 3, 2022 Morning session 9:30 a.m. Day 4 p 1086- 1131

3 *USA vs. Elmer Stewart Rhodes III*, ET AL. CR No. 22-15 Washington, D.C. October 3, 2022 Afternoon session 1:33 p.m. Day 4 p 1191

4 Ibid. P 1199

5 Ibid. P 1199-2000

6 Ibid. P 1215-1216

7 Ibid. P 1217

8 *USA vs. Elmer Stewart Rhodes III*, ET AL. CR No. 22-15 Washington, D.C. November 3, 2022 1:26 p.m. Day 23 p 6951-6953

9 *USA vs. Elmer Stewart Rhodes III*, ET AL. CR No. 22-15 Washington, D.C. November 4, 2022 8:30 a.m. Morning session Day 24 p 7002

10 Ibid. P 7001

11 *USA vs. Elmer Stewart Rhodes III,* ET AL. CR No. 22-15 Washington, D.C. October 3, 2022 Afternoon session 1:33 p.m. Day 4 P 1209-1210

12 *USA vs. Elmer Stewart Rhodes III,* ET AL. CR No. 22-15 Washington, D.C. November 3, 2022 Afternoon session 9:30 a.m. Day 23 p 6712

13 *USA vs. Elmer Stewart Rhodes III,* ET AL. CR No. 22-15 Washington, D.C. October 4, 2022 Afternoon session 1:35 p.m. Day 5 p 1619

14 Ibid. P 1626

15 FD-26 0176-WF-3366759-CALDWELL_0000017_1A0000007_0000002 DOJ FBI Consent to Search dtd 1/19/2021 Signed by "SA" Stephen W. Duke

16 *USA vs. Elmer Stewart Rhodes III,* ET AL. CR No. 22-15 Washington, D.C. October 4, 2022 Afternoon session 1:35 p.m. Day 5 p 1638

17 Ibid. P 1646

18 Ibid. P 1649-1650

19 *USA v Thomas E. Caldwell* Case 1:21-cr-00028-APM Document 273 Filed 07/01/21 In the U.S. District Court for the District of Columbia Motion to Transfer Venue submitted by David W. Fischer, Esq.

20 *USA vs. Elmer Stewart Rhodes III,* ET AL. CR No. 22-15 Washington, D.C. November 3, 2022 Morning session 9:30 a.m. Day 23 p 6689-6694

21 *USA vs. Elmer Stewart Rhodes III,* ET AL. CR No. 22-15 Washington, D.C. October 4, 2022 Morning session 9:30 a.m. Day 5 Gov Exhibit 1530 P1461-1462

22 *USA vs. Elmer Stewart Rhodes III,* ET AL. CR No. 22-15 Washington, D.C. October 20, 2022 9:30 a.m. Day 15 Gov Exhibit 1530.1 P4535-4536

23 *USA vs. Elmer Stewart Rhodes III,* ET AL. CR No. 22-15 Washington, D.C. October 20, 2022 9:30 a.m. Day 15 Ibid. P4521-4522 Gov Exhibit 6740

24 *USA vs. Elmer Stewart Rhodes III,* ET AL. CR No. 22-15 Washington, D.C. November 16, 2022 8:00 a.m.. Day 31 Gov witness testimony regarding that Gov Exhibit 6740 is false P9262,9265

25 National Public Radio (NPR) "Members Of Right-Wing Militias, Extremist Groups Are Latest Charged In Capitol Siege" January 19, 20215:54 AM ET https://www.npr.org/sections/insurrection-at-the-capitol/2021/01/19/958240531/members-of-right-wing-militias-extremist-groups-are-latest-charged-in-capitol-si

26 Newsweek *"FBI Arresting Reporter Sparks MAGA Outrage"* by Rachel Dobkin Published Mar 01, 2024 at 12:47 PM EST Updated Mar 02, 2024 at 2:55 PM EST https://www.newsweek.com/fbi-arresting-reporter-sparks-maga-outrage-1875173

Chapter 10
Deception Most Foul

1 DC.gov Mayor Bowser Judicial Nominations Commission official website listing for *"Jeffrey S. Nestler"*
https://jnc.dc.gov/biography/jeffrey-s-nestler

2 Financial System Support Group (FSSG) Resource Management System 2A D & D under contract 6C-EOA02-0272 Task Order P142 Change order 5 "Allotments, attorney cash awards and special initiatives" Test while load of NFC data-files to RMS_DEVL and CONVERT_DB databases *"as individual attorney cash award limits within a specified period reach total funding limits for each USA "region" or "locale"....*

3 Federal Bureau of Investigation Evidence Collected Item Log FD-886 (Rev. 4-13-15) Date 1/19/2021 Case ID 266T-RH-33744021 Preparer Cameron Fricks

4 *USA vs. Elmer Stewart Rhodes III*, ET AL. CR No. 22-15 Washington, D.C. October 17, 2022 1:31 p.m. Day 12 P3687

5 Ibid.

6 Ibid. P 3688

7 Ibid.

8 Ibid. P 3689

9 Ibid. P 3701 line 21

10 *USA vs. Elmer Stewart Rhodes III*, ET AL. CR No. 22-15 Washington, D.C. October 3, 2022 Afternoon session 1:33 p.m. Day 4 P 1222-1223

11 *USA vs. Elmer Stewart Rhodes III*, ET AL. CR No. 22-15 Washington, D.C. October 17, 2022 Morning session 9:30 a.m. Day 12 p 3524 Government Exhibit 1510.8

12 *USA vs. Elmer Stewart Rhodes III*, ET AL. CR No. 22-15 Washington, D.C. November 14, 2022 Morning session 9:00 a.m. Day 29 p 8487-8490 Caldwell Exhibit 150

13 *USA vs. Elmer Stewart Rhodes III*, ET AL. CR No. 22-15 Washington, D.C. November 3, 2022 Morning session 9:30 a.m. Day 23 P6703-6704 Government Exhibit 1556, Caldwell 126

14 Ibid.

15 Ibid.

16 *USA vs. Elmer Stewart Rhodes III*, ET AL. CR No. 22-15 Washington, D.C. October 20, 2022 Morning session 9:30 a.m. Day 15 P6705 Government Exhibit 1500 animated video

17 *USA vs. Elmer Stewart Rhodes III*, ET AL. CR No. 22-15 Washington, D.C. Government exhibit 1533

18 *USA vs. Elmer Stewart Rhodes III*, ET AL. CR No. 22-15 Washington, D.C. November 1, 2022 Afternoon session 1:28 p.m. Day 21 P6261-6262 Not held in the presence of the jury.

19 Ibid. P 6262

20 Ibid.

21 *USA vs. Elmer Stewart Rhodes III*, ET AL. CR No. 22-15 Washington, D.C. November 1, 2022 Afternoon session 1:28 p.m. Day 21 P6263-6264 Not held in the presence of the jury.

22 *USA vs. Elmer Stewart Rhodes III*, ET AL. CR No. 22-15 Washington, D.C. October 3, 2022 Afternoon session 1:33 p.m. Day 21 P1285 Tainted Government Exhibit 22.V.2E

23 Ibid.

24 *USA vs. Elmer Stewart Rhodes III*, ET AL. CR No. 22-15 Washington, D.C. October 20, 2022 Afternoon session 1:40 p.m. Day 15 P4826-4827 Cross examination of SA Whitney Drew re: Caldwell Exhibit 87- Sharon Caldwell balcony video

25 *USA vs. Elmer Stewart Rhodes III*, ET AL. CR No. 22-15 Washington, D.C. October 20, 2022 Morning session 9:30 a.m. Day 15 P4620-4621 Caldwell selfie photo taken at the Peace Monument 2:19 p.m. and entered into evidence by the government during direct witness examination

26 *USA vs. Elmer Stewart Rhodes III*, ET AL. CR No. 22-15 Washington, D.C. October 20, 2022 Afternoon session 1:40 p.m. Day 15 P4819-4820 Cross examination of SA Whitney Drew

27 *USA vs. Elmer Stewart Rhodes III*, ET AL. CR No. 22-15 Washington, D.C. October 10, 2022 Afternoon session 1:40 p.m. Day 15 P4824-4825 Cross examination of SA Whitney Drew testimony location of Caldwell at the Peace Monument and no contact with Oath Keepers.

28 *USA vs. Elmer Stewart Rhodes III*, ET AL. CR No. 22-15 discovery provided Govt. CCTV 0944_USCS_RF_West_Roof_-_2021-01-06_19h42min20s.mp4

Govt. CCTV 0944_USCS_RF_West_R00f_-_2021-01-06_19h51min17s.mp4

29 U.S. Department of Justice Federal Bureau of Investigation 2012 Ronald Reagan Drive Cincinnati, Ohio 45236 (513) 421-4310 January 16,2021 Letter to: Facebook, Inc. Attn: Custodian of Records 1601 Willow Road Menlo Park, CA 94025 Re: Request for Voluntary Emergency Disclosure Information US Govt discovery document 0176-WF-3366759-CALDWELL_0000005_Import.pdf

30 FBI WFO Source File: CD: WF_WF-12345_WF-12345-BR_2021_01_19T07_05_54.mp4
Date: 01/19/21 VERBATIM TRANSCRIPTION (Transcript of Interrogation) File Number:176-WF-3366759-Caldwell Name and Office of Transcriber: OST Sara J. Van Roe

31 *USA vs. Elmer Stewart Rhodes III*, ET AL. CR No. 22-15 Washington, D.C. October 4, 2022 Afternoon session 1:35 p.m. Day 5 P1654-1658

32 Telephone interview on the record Thomas Caldwell and Joseph Traficante, esq. with review of notes, proffers and relevant records February 25, 2025 commencing 9:07 a.m. ET

33 *USA vs. Elmer Stewart Rhodes III*, ET AL. CR No. 22-15 Washington, D.C. November 8, 2022 Morning session 9:00 a.m. Day 26 P7585-7589 Discussion of possible testimony of Paul Stamey, including videotaped statement, with Judge Amit P. Mehta and as opposed by Rakoczy.

34 Ibid. P 7592-7693

Chapter 11
In Our Lord's Hands

1 *USA vs. Elmer Stewart Rhodes III*, ET AL. CR No. 22-15 November 14, 2022 Day 29 Afternoon Session 1:45 p.m. p8649

2 Ibid.

3 USA vs. Elmer Stewart Rhodes III, ET AL. CR No. 22-15 November 15, 2022 Day 30 Afternoon Session 2:00 p.m. p9042-9043

4 USA vs. Elmer Stewart Rhodes III, ET AL. CR No. 22-15 November 14, 2022 Day 29 Morning Session 9:00 a.m.p8442

5 Still Frame Extracts FBI File: 176-WF-3366759-Caldwell Transcription (U) Session: WF_WF-12345_WF-12345-BR_2021_01_19T07_05_54.mp4

6 FBI WFO Source File: CD: WF_WF-12345_WF-12345-BR_2021_01_19T07_05_54.mp4

Date: 01/19/21 VERBATIM TRANSCRIPTION (Transcript of Interrogation) File Number:176-WF-3366759-Caldwell Requesting Official SA Michael Palian, Jr., WFO Name and Office of Transcriber: OST Sara J. Van Roe

7 Ibid.

8 https://en.wikipedia.org/wiki/Absolute_immunity#Prosecutorial_immunity "In United States law, absolute immunity is a type of sovereign immunity for government officials that confers complete immunity from criminal prosecution and suits for damages, so long as officials are acting within the scope of their duties."

9 *USA vs. Elmer Stewart Rhodes III*, ET AL. CR No. 22-15 October 6, 2022 Day 6 Afternoon Session 2:00 p.m., P2019

10 Ibid. P 2035

11 Ibid. P 2039

12 Ibid. P 2040

Chapter 12
Manic Persecution

1 USA vs Elmer Stewart Rhodes et al. Case: 1:22-cr-00015-APM Document 432 Filed 12/23/22 Defendants Joint Motion for Judgement of Acquittal Pursuant to Rule 29

2 Ibid.

3 Department of Justice, Probation Department "Worksheet for Pre-Sentencing Report (PSR)" These forms are standard for individuals convicted in Federal Courts.

4 USA v Caldwell, Thomas PRESENTENCE INVESTIGATION REPORT : Docket No.: 0090 1:22CR00015-010 Case 1:22-cr-00015-APM Document 492 Filed 03/24/23 Prepared for: Amit P. Mehta United States District Judge

5 Ibid.

6 Webster's online Thesaurus (https://www.merriam-webster.com/thesaurus) defines "anosognosia" (ano·sog·no·sia ˌa-nō-ˌsäg-ˈnō-zh(ē-)ə) as a noun describing a person's inability or refusal to recognize a defect or disorder that is clinically evident. It is a prominent feature of schizophrenia and bipolar disorder where the sick person is unaware that he is sick at all. It is even more commonly found in people classified as psychopaths or sociopaths. In these cases a common manifestation is in an unwillingness to believe their ideation or conclusions could ever be wrong.

7 https://www.justice.gov/archives/opa/pr/attorney-general-merrick-b-garland-honors-justice-department-employees-and-partners-70th-and ; 71st Annual Attorney General's Awards – 2023

10th Distinguished Service Award recipients featuring Kathryn Rakoczy, Jeffrey Nestler, Michael Palian, Sylvia Hilgeman.

8 Ibid.

9 Financial System Support Group (FSSG) Resource Management System 2A D & D under contract 6C-EOA02-0272 Task Order P142 Change order 5 "Allotments, attorney cash awards and special initiatives" Test while load of NFC data-files to RMS_DEVL and CONVERT_DB databases "*as individual attorney cash award limits within a specified period reach total funding limits for each USA "region" or "locale" change numbers displayed in dollars to RED.*"

10 The Epoch Times "*Disputed Oath Keepers Trial Testimony Warrants Reversal of Convictions, Attorney Says*" by Joe Hanneman 10/5/2023 https://www.theepochtimes.com/us/disputed-oath-keepers-trial-testimony-warrants-reversal-of-convictions-attorney-says-5504232

11 The Epoch Times "*Disturbing': FBI's Alleged Altering of Evidence in Jan. 6 Proud Boys Case,Trial Paused: Defense Lawyer*" by Gary Bai March 9, 2023 https://www.theepochtimes.com/disturbing-fbis-alleged-altering-of-evidence-led-to-pause-of-jan-6-trial-for-proud-boys-member-defense-lawyer_51123...

12 Department of Veterans Affairs Health Eligibility Center Atlanta, GA *Cancellation of Benefits letter Thomas E. Caldwell dated March 2023*

13 Ibid.

14 USAA San Antonio Texas Ltr dated May 18, 2023 "*Reference: Your Auto Insurance Is Being Discontinued*", "*Dear Commander Caldwell*" signed by Jill Sharehart

15 FBI-302 UNCLASSIFIED//FOUO FEDERAL BUREAU OF INVESTIGATION File number 266T-RH-3374021 date of entry 4/11/23 Joanna Abrams

16 Ibid.

17 Audio Recording 9:34 a.m. Tuesday May 2, 2023 from the *Department of Veterans Affairs Health Eligibility Center in Atlanta, GA* "2023-05-02-13-11-08 HEALTH BENEFITS.WAV" Answer machine audio recording Tuesday 5/2/2023

18 FD-302 UNCLASSIFIED//FOUO FEDERAL BUREAU OF INVESTIGATION 266T-RH-3374021 Serial 154 dtd 04/20/23 signed by "Michael M. Palian Jr."

19 Government's Omnibus Reply Sentencing Memorandum, Document 580, Filed 05/15/23. Ex. Sent-Caldwell-9 Caldwell Jail Medical Records

20 *USA v CALDWELL, Defendant* CASE NO. 2021-R-00494 21-cr-28 *USA v CALDWELL, Defendant* May 22, 2023 10:30 a.m. Transcript of Rule 29 Hearing Proceedings Before the Honorable Amit P. Mehta

21 Ibid. P 76-77

22 Ibid. P 77-78

23 Ibid. P78

24 Ibid. P78

Chapter 13
The Long March

1 Deseret News *"He has a gun!' An eyewitness details what happened when the FBI came to a Provo neighborhood"* Published: Aug 9, 2023, 10:16 p.m. MDT By Kyle Dunphey
https://www.deseret.com/2023/8/9/23826780/witnesses-fbi-kill-utah-man-threats-biden-social-media/

2 Ibid.

3 U.S. Postal Service Express Mail Package Law Offices of Fischer and Putzi Glen Burnie, Maryland Oct. 10, 2023 w/partial response files from National Personnel Records Center 1 Archives Drive Saint Louis, MO 63138 received from offices of AUSA Kathryn Rakoczy.

4. USA vs. Thomas Edward Caldwell CR No. 22-15-10 September 19, 2023 8:30 a.m. Transcript of Oral Ruling via zoom proceedings before the Honorable Amit P. Mehta United States District Judge; AUSA Troy A. Edwards Jr

5 Ibid.

6 Government's Omnibus Reply Sentencing Memorandum, Document 580, Filed 05/15/23. Ex. Sent-Caldwell-9 Caldwell Jail Records

7 Ibid.

8 In the United States District Court for the District of Columbia *USA v Thomas E. Caldwell* Case No.: 22-15 APM Caldwell's Supplemental Sentencing Memo Case 1:22-cr-00015-APM Document 717 Filed 12/15/23 (Page 4)

9 Status Conference as to THOMAS EDWARD CALDWELL held via videoconference on 12/20/2023 before Judge Amit P. Mehta (Defendant's Submission due by 1/31/2024) Court Reporter: William Zaremba; Defense Attorney: David Fischer; US Attorneys: Kathryn Rakoczy and Troy Edwards

10 Kentlaw *"Altering Prisoners' Sense of Time: The Moral Regression of a Futuristic Technology"* by Caroline Thiriot Posted on February 8, 2017 by ISLAT Admin
https://blogs.kentlaw.iit.edu/islat/2017/02/08/753/

11 Kentlaw *"Altering Prisoners' Sense of Time: The Moral Regression of a Futuristic Technology"* by Caroline Thiriot Posted on February 8, 2017 by ISLAT Admin

https://blogs.kentlaw.iit.edu/islat/2017/02/08/753/
Special Rapporteur of the Human Rights Council on torture for the United Nations called on all countries "to ban the solitary confinement of prisoners." He stressed that "Solitary confinement is a harsh measure which is contrary to rehabilitation, the aim of the penitentiary system."

12 https://www.dailymail.co.uk/sciencetech/article-2580828/Could-soon-create-hell-EARTH-Biotechnology-let-extend-criminals-lives-makes-suffering-HUNDREDS-years.html *"Could we condemn criminals to suffer for hundreds of years?"* By Ellie Zolfagharifard 14 March 2014 | Updated: 15 March 2014 "Last year, a team of scientists led by Rebecca Roache began exploring technologies that could keep prisoners in an artificial hell."

13 *"Appeals Court Ruling Threatens 100+ Capitol Rioter Sentences: The "interference with the administration of justice" enhancement was wrongly applied."* by James Joyner Saturday, March 2, 2024
https://outsidethebeltway.com/appeals-court-ruling-threatens-100-capitol-rioter-sentences/ "must be recalculated, *removing* the terrorist enhancements."

Chapter 14
Facing the Dragon

1 In the United States District Court for the District of Columbia *USA vs. Thomas E. Caldwell* Case 1:22-cr-00015-APM Document 890 Filed 09/09/24 Case No.: 22-15-APM Motion For Reconsideration as to Caldwell's Motion for Judgement of Acquittal

2 https://x.com/julie_kelly2/status/1871612599810367562?s=42 Julie Kelly on "X" USA vs. Thomas E. Caldwell Government Supplemental Sentencing Memorandum CR No. 22-15-10 dated November 4, 2024 Ms Kelly: "As Biden spares the lives of child rapists and murderers, his DOJ continues to seek excessive prison time for J6 protesters. Tom Caldwell is a 70-year-old decorated and disabled Naval veteran. Assistant US Attorney Kathryn Rakoczy asked Judge Amit Mehta to put Tom Caldwell in a federal prison for 4 years."

3 Google LLC email <usernotice@google.com> Date: Fri, Nov 22, 2024 at 9:13 AM Subject: [9-6561000037321] Notification From Google Legal Investigations Support DOJ case number 21-sc-99

4 https://www.pbs.org/newshour/politics/man-pleads-guilty-to-seditious-conspiracy-for-the-jan-6-capitol-insurrection PBS News Oct 6, 2022 4:48 PM EDT "*Man pleads guilty to seditious conspiracy for the Jan. 6 Capitol insurrection*" By Michael Kunzelman, Associated Press "Prosecutor Erik Kenerson said estimated sentencing guidelines for Bertino's case recommend a prison sentence ranging from four years and three months to five years and three months."

5 https://www.justice.gov/archives/opa/pr/attorney-general-merrick-b-garland-honors-justice-department-employees-and-partners-70th-and ; 71st Annual Attorney General's Awards – 2023
10th Distinguished Service Award recipients featuring Kathryn Rakoczy, Jeffrey Nestler, Michael Palian, Sylvia Hilgeman.

6 From *Wikipedia, The Free Encyclopedia*: "Brady disclosure" Including excerpt "Following Brady, the prosecutor must disclose evidence or information that would prove the innocence of the defendant or would enable the defense to more effectively impeach the credibility of government witnesses." https://en.wikipedia.org/wiki/Brady_disclosure

7 *USA vs. Elmer Stewart Rhodes III*, ET AL. CR No. 22-15 Washington, D.C. October 17, 2022 Afternoon session 8:30 a.m. Day 12 P3629-3632 Caldwell exhibit 116 introduced during redirect of FBI Hilgeman

8 *USA vs. Thomas E. Caldwell* Sentencing Proceedings before Honorable Amit P. Mehta US District Court Judge CR No. 22-15-10 Washington, D.C. January 10, 2025 2:20 p.m. P78-79

9 Federal Bureau of Investigation Evidence Collected Item Log FD-886 (Rev. 4-13-15) Date 1/19/2021 Case ID 266T-RH-33744021 Preparer Cameron Fricks *"JAN 19, 2021 06:49 AM 266T-RH-33744021 Person in Charge on Arrival Joshua Tidwell (FBI SWAT) Control of Scene Obtained From FBI Date/Time of Control Acquisition Jan 19, 2021 07:05 AM"*

10 *USA vs. Thomas E. Caldwell* Sentencing Proceedings before Honorable Amit P. Mehta US District Court Judge CR No. 22-15-10 Washington, D.C. January 10, 2025 2:20 p.m. P93

11 Ibid. P 95

12 Blaze Media: *"Nightmare January 6 case delivers miracle outcome for Thomas Caldwell,"* by Joseph M. Hanneman January 14, 2025 https://www.theblaze.com/news/exclusive-nightmare-january-6-case-delivers-miracle-outcome-for-thomas-caldwell

Epilogue

1 American Thinker "*Biden's National Censorship Regime*" By Wendi Strauch Mahoney April 23, 2025 https://www.americanthinker.com/articles/2025/04/biden_s_national_censorship_regime.html

2 Office of the Director of National Intelligence (ODNI) Directors Initiatives Group (DIG) declassification of "Strategic Implementation Plan for Countering Domestic Terrorism" P1-15 https://www.odni.gov/files/ODNI/documents/DIG/DIG-Declassified-Strategic-Implementation-Plan-for-CT-April2025.pdf

3 American Thinker "*Tulsi Gabbard's latest Biden revelation*" By Mike McDaniel April 22, 2025 https://www.americanthinker.com/blog/2025/04/tulsi_gabbards latest_biden_revelation.html